Bloom's Modern Critical Interpretations

Bloom's Modern Critical Interpretations

Ernest Hemingway's
A Farewell to Arms
New Edition

Edited and with an introduction by
Harold Bloom
Sterling Professor of the Humanities
Yale University

BLOOM'S
LITERARY CRITICISM
An imprint of Infobase Publishing

Editorial Consultant, Matthew J. Bruccoli

Bloom's Modern Critical Interpretations:
Ernest Hemingway's *A Farewell to Arms*—New Edition

Bloom's Literary Criticism
An imprint of Infobase Publishing
132 West 31st Street
New York NY 10001

Library of Congress Cataloging-in-Publication Data

Ernest Hemingway's A farewell to arms / edited and with an introduction by Harold Bloom.—New ed.
    p. cm.—(Bloom's modern critical interpretations)
Includes bibliographical references and index.
ISBN 978-0-7910-9624-6 (hardcover : alk. paper) 1. Hemingway, Ernest, 1899-1961. Farewell to Arms. 2. World War, 1914-1918—United States—Literature and the war. I. Bloom, Harold.

PS3515.E37F3535 2008
813'.52—dc22

                              2008044409

Cover design by Ben Peterson

Printed in the United States of America
Bang BCL 10 9 8 7 6 5 4 3 2 1

This book is printed on acid-free paper.

Contents

Editor's Note

My Introduction briefly but poignantly describes the style of *A Farewell to Arms* as aesthetic impressionism in the tradition of Keats, Pater, Conrad, and Stephen Crane.

As the late Matthew J. Bruccoli gathered together a large bevy of reviews and essays, I will comment here upon only a few high points.

The reviews by Malcolm Cowley, John Dos Passos and H. L. Mencken are all of undoubted historical interest.

For critical perceptiveness, Robert Penn Warren comes first, while Carlos Baker and Millicent Bell investigate aspects of Hemingwayan self-mystification.

Bruccoli himself contributes a useful pedagogical intervention, after which the remaining essayists return to linguistic and psychological issues in the novel.

HAROLD BLOOM

Introduction

If *A Farewell to Arms* fails to sustain itself as a unified novel, it does remain Hemingway's strongest work after the frequent best of the short stories and *The Sun Also Rises*. It also participates in the aura of Hemingway's mode of myth, embodying as it does not only Hemingway's own romance with Europe but the permanent vestiges of our national romance with the Old World. The death of Catherine represents not the end of that affair, but its perpetual recurrence. I assign classic status in the interpretation of that death to Leslie Fiedler, with his precise knowledge of the limits of literary myth: "Only the dead woman becomes neither a bore nor a mother; and before Catherine can quite become either she must die, killed not by Hemingway, of course, but by childbirth!" Fiedler finds a touch of Poe in this, but Hemingway seems to me far healthier. Death, to Poe, is after all less a metaphor for sexual fulfillment than it is an improvement over mere coition, since Poe longs for a union in essence and not just in act.

Any feminist critic who resents that too-lovely Hemingwayesque ending, in which Frederic Henry gets to walk away in the rain while poor Catherine takes the death for both of them, has my sympathy, if only because this sentimentality that mars the aesthetic effect is certainly the mask for a male resentment and fear of women. Hemingway's symbolic rain is read by Louis L. Martz as the inevitable trope for pity, and by Malcolm Cowley as a conscious symbol for disaster. A darker interpretation might associate it with Whitman's very American confounding of night, death, the mother, and the sea, a fourfold mingling that Whitman bequeathed to Wallace Stevens, T.S. Eliot, and Hart Crane, among many others. The death of the beloved

1

woman in Hemingway is part of that tropological cosmos, in which the moist element dominates because death the mother is the true image of desire. For Hemingway, the rain replaces the sea, and is as much the image of longing as the sea is in Whitman or Hart Crane.

Robert Penn Warren, defending a higher estimate of *A Farewell to Arms* than I can achieve, interprets the death of Catherine as the discovery that "the attempt to find a substitute for universal meaning in the limited meaning of the personal relationship is doomed to failure." Such a reading, though distinguished, seems to me to belong more to the literary cosmos of T.S. Eliot than to that of Hemingway. Whatever nostalgia for transcendental verities Hemingway may have possessed, his best fiction invests its energies in the representation of personal relationships, and hardly with the tendentious design of exposing their inevitable inadequacies. If your personal religion quests for the matador as messiah, then you are likely to seek in personal relationships something of the same values enshrined in the ritual of bull and bullfighter: courage, dignity, the aesthetic exaltation of the moment, and an all but suicidal intensity of being—the sense of life gathered to a crowded perception and graciously open to the suddenness of extinction. That is a vivid but an unlikely scenario for an erotic association, at least for any that might endure beyond a few weeks.

Wyndham Lewis categorized Hemingway by citing Walter Pater on Prosper Mérimée: "There is the formula . . . the enthusiastic amateur of rude, crude, naked force in men and women. . . . Painfully distinct in outline, inevitable to sight, unrelieved, there they stand." Around them, Pater added, what Mérimée gave you was "neither more nor less than empty space." I believe that Pater would have found more than that in Hemingway's formula, more in the men and women, and something other than empty space in their ambiance. Perhaps by way of Joseph Conrad's influence upon him, Hemingway had absorbed part at least of what is most meaningful in Pater's aesthetic impressionism. Hemingway's women and men know, with Pater, that we have an interval, and then our place knows us no more. Our one chance is to pack that interval with the multiplied fruit of consciousness, with the solipsistic truths of perception and sensation. What survives time's ravages in *A Farewell to Arms* is precisely Hemingway's textually embodied knowledge that art alone apprehends the moments of perception and sensation, and so bestows upon them their privileged status. Consider the opening paragraph of chapter 16:

> That night a bat flew into the room through the open door that
> led onto the balcony and through which we watched the night over
> the roofs of the town. It was dark in our room except for the small
> light of the night over the town and the bat was not frightened but
> hunted in the room as though he had been outside. We lay and

watched him and I do not think he saw us because we lay so still. After he went out we saw a searchlight come on and watched the beam move across the sky and then go off and it was dark again. A breeze came in the night and we heard the men of the anti-aircraft gun on the next roof talking. It was cool and they were putting on their capes. I worried in the night about some one coming up but Catherine said they were all asleep. Once in the night we went to sleep and when I woke she was not there but I heard her coming along the hall and the door opened and she came back to the bed and said it was all right she had been downstairs and they were all asleep. She had been outside Miss Van Campen's door and heard her breathing in her sleep. She brought crackers and we ate them and drank some vermouth. We were very hungry but she said that would all have to be gotten out of me in the morning. I went to sleep again in the morning when it was light and when I was awake I found she was gone again. She came in looking fresh and lovely and sat on the bed and the sun rose while I had the thermometer in my mouth and we smelled the dew on the roofs and then the coffee of the men at the gun on the next roof.

The flight of the bat, the movement of the searchlight's beam and of the breeze, the overtones of the antiaircraft gunners blend into the light of the morning, to form a composite epiphany of what it is that Frederic Henry has lost when he finally walks back to the hotel in the rain. Can we define that loss? As befits the aesthetic impressionism of Pater, Conrad, Stephen Crane, and Hemingway, it is in the first place a loss of vividness and intensity in the world as experienced by the senses. In the aura of his love for Catherine, Frederic Henry knows the fullness of "It was dark" and "It was cool," and the smell of the dew on the roofs, and the aroma of the coffee being enjoyed by the anti-aircraft gunners. We are reminded that Pater's crucial literary ancestors were the unacknowledged Ruskin and the hedonistic visionary Keats, the Keats of the "Ode on Melancholy." Hemingway too, particularly in *A Farewell to Arms*, is an heir of Keats, with the poet's passion for sensuous immediacy, in all of its ultimate implications. Is not Catherine Barkley a belated and beautiful version of the goddess Melancholy, incarnating Keats's "Beauty that must die"? Hemingway too exalts that quester after the Melancholy,

> whose strenuous tongue
> Can burst Joy's grape against his palate fine;
> His soul shall taste the sadness of her might,
> And be among her cloudy trophies hung.

JAMES ASWELL

Critic Lavishes Praise
On New Hemingway Novel

I have finished "A Farewell to Arms," and am still a little breathless, as people often are after a major event in their lives. If before I die I have three more literary experiences as sharp and exciting and terrible as the one I have just been through, I shall know it has been a good world.

That, I am aware, is extravagant praise. Perhaps I should have begun more cautiously. Because I do not know whether "A Farewell to Arms" is a "great" book or not, or whether it will "live." I do not know and I do not give a damn; those are considerations for The New York Times and the sages in the great institution ninety miles to Richmond's northwest. I only know that there are many people who will be deeply stirred by this tender, brutal, devastatingly simple love story; stirred as they have never been by Dreiser's clumsy magnificence, or Anderson's naively cynical rusticism, or Cabell's ana-grams. These people may well stand before some imposing fifty-foot shelf and wonder, frightened, "Where is there another to go, candidly, by his side? Where can I match that hot, four-dimensional life or that prose stripped of a thousand years of prolixities? With all the great names it's unnerving that I should have to think at all!"

"A Farewell to Arms" is not a war story primarily, despite the publisher's blurbs and the assumption of the two or three reviews I have read. The war is always there, a background, "in the mountains," but it can no more be

Richmond Times-Dispatch (October 6, 1929): p. 3. Copyright © *Richmond Times-Dispatch.*

considered the theme than hospitals can be considered the theme because the last few thousand words have their setting in one. What Hemingway wants to do, and does do, is to tell the story of Frederick [*sic*] Henry and Catherine Barkley. It is the story of two young people and what they said to each other and the loving they had together. And secondarily it is a story of the sentient natural world enjoyed not through the head but through the senses properly, of cold mornings and rain and good food; of wine and pain and fear and deep sleep; of the rank, healthy talk of men together and fine, blasphemous laughter.

More than any other writer I know Hemingway has eliminated the odor of the lamp from his prose. Years ago in Paris he told Sisley Huddleston that he wanted to divorce language "from its superfluities." No wonder poor, old, grandiloquent Sisley didn't like him at all! I cannot imagine Hemingway in his first literary company, under the pale, effete, pseudo-cerebral auspices of This Quarter and The Dial and The Little Review. But it is certain he could not have gotten his stuff into print anywhere else, and I suppose they saw only that he was "different," without recognizing his, to them, treacherous masculinity.

* * *

Perhaps the thing that sets Hemingway head and shoulders above the "sophisticates" with whom he has often been libelously grouped, is his not being afraid of tenderness. But the tenderness is always removed a little, in space, as it were, from the passage. He seeks no euphemisms: he is never whimsical in the revolting Milne-Barrie sense. But he is sensitive to sorrowful beauty without feeling pity about it. He seems to say, "These people are headed for a bad time, but it is good that they are living fully now." Once Catherine asks Frederick whether they shoot larks in America. "Not especially," he replies. It may be that I am sinking into obscurantism, but I believe that interchange conveys the sort of tenderness, humorous, warm[th], that Hemingway has. Its absence is what frequently betrays imitators of the Hemingway manner such as Morley Callaghan.

"A Farewell to Arms" is a rhythmic, plethoric, bitterly lovely story. If anything better has been produced by a native of the New World I do not know what it is. And as for me, I have never gotten a greater kick out of any book.

MALCOLM COWLEY

Not Yet Demobilized

Ernest Hemingway during the last five years has won an extraordinary place in American letters. He has thousands of adherents among the readers of his own age; there are younger writers of talent who accept his leadership; he is imitated by writers much older than himself—a rare phenomenon—and one finds traces of his influence almost everywhere. His name is generally mentioned with the respect that one accords to a legendary figure. From critics he has received a quite special treatment—many of them have praised him equally for his own qualities and for others he never possessed, and a few did not wait for his second novel before comparing him with James Joyce, with Smollett and Defoe, almost with Homer.

Doubtless some of the reasons for this sudden fame are extraliterary: it may partly be attributed to his living away from New York and its literary jealousies, to his ability to surround himself with a legend, to the pride which has kept him from commercializing his work, and also in some degree to his use of rather sensational material; but nevertheless one is forced to conclude that the principal explanation lies in his having expressed better than any other writer, the limited viewpoint of his contemporaries, of the generation which was formed by the war and which is still incompletely demobilized.

Even today, eleven years after the armistice, there are many who retain the attitude of soldiers on an extended but uncertain furlough; at any moment

New York Herald Tribune Books, XII (October 6, 1929): pp. 1, 16.

they are liable to be summoned back to the guns which, for them, still thunder along the Aisne and the Isonzo. They attach very little importance to the laborious ambitions of a world at peace with itself. They have the wartime state of mind, with its dislike for responsibility, its sense of impermanence, its thirst for novelty and danger.

Most of the characters in Hemingway's stories belong to this category of the undemobilized. Their standards are the very simple standards of men at war. The virtues they admire are generosity, courage, a certain resignation and also the ability to hold one's liquor. The vices they ridicule are vices only to men who have been soldiers: I mean thrift, caution and sobriety. Their simple enjoyments are food, drink, love and perhaps fishing; their tragedies are love, parting, death; and they discuss these topics with the frankness of the barracks—beneath which is not too carefully hidden a martial sentimentality.

To describe these characters, Hemingway has adopted a simple and very appropriate method: we might agree on calling it subtractive. From the novel as conceived by older writers, he has subtracted the embellishments; he has subtracted all the descriptions, the meditations, the statements of theory and he has reserved only the characters and their behavior, their acts, their sensual perceptions, their words. The last he sets down almost stenographically. As for the acts and perceptions, he redates them in very great detail, almost redundantly, in brief sentences that preserve, in spite of certain mannerisms, the locutions, the rhythms and the loose syntax of common American speech. The general effect is one of deliberate unsophistication.

This method, which he developed in his first four books, has been somewhat modified in his new novel. The style has changed first of all: the rhythm is more definite, the sentences are often longer, and the paragraphs are more carefully constructed. In treatment Hemingway has departed to a certain extent from his former strict behaviorism: he has added landscapes and interior monologues to his range of effects, and he has even begun to discuss ideas. In mood he reveals a new tenderness, and it is interesting to observe that the present volume is his first love story, properly speaking. It is also his first long story about the war, his first novel in the strict sense—"The Sun Also Rises" was an extended episode—and undoubtedly the most important book he has written.

*　*　*

"A Farewell to Arms" is perhaps the only American war novel in which the hero drives an ambulance. I find this somewhat remarkable, and for a very simple reason. Just as the typical British war novels are written by former captains of infantry, and German novels of the same class by privates with a just grievance, so the typical American war novels, beginning with "Three

Soldiers" and perhaps not ending with the present volume, have been written by former ambulance drivers.

It is hard to say why this one branch of the army should have been so literary. Perhaps it is because young writers were patriotic in 1917, and because enlisting in the ambulance service was the quickest means of reaching the front. Perhaps it is because the idea of transporting the wounded, even in reconditioned Fords over bad roads, appealed to the romantic side of their natures. I doubt it. All I know for certain is that in one typical section of thirty men, there were three who later became professional writers, in addition to a painter, an architect, a philologist, and almost the whole football squad of a large preparatory school. The conditions were similar in other sections I visited; and, in fact, after reading a roster of the American Ambulance, one begins to regard it as a sort of college extension course for the present generation of writers.

But what did it teach? How did it color the minds of the young men who drove at the front? . . . The question is much too general. However, one important effect of the ambulance service on some of its members was to develop what might be called a *spectatorial* attitude toward the war.

* * *

Meanwhile let us return to the novel, and to Frederic Henry, American volunteer with the Italian army and lieutenant in charge of an ambulance section on the Isonzo front. His associates were less intellectual than those he might have met on the Chemin des Dames: most of them were tired and very middle-class Italian officers. However, his own attitude was the one I have tried to describe: that of a spectator who was beginning to lose his interest.

This attitude is especially evident in the first part of the novel. Everything—the war, the weather, the epidemic of cholera, the conversation at the mess table—is repeated impartially, as from a great distance or by the military observer of a neutral power. Even when the hero is wounded by a trench mortar he is only the spectator of his own disaster. "I sat up straight," he says, "and as I did so something inside my head moved like the weights on a doll's eyes and it hit me inside in back of my eyeballs. My legs felt warm and wet and my shoes were wet and warm inside. I knew that I was hit and leaned over and put my hand on my knee. My knee wasn't there. My hand went in and my knee was down on my shin. I wiped my hand on my shirt and another floating light came very slowly down and I looked at my leg and was very afraid."

He was carried off to the dressing station, still observing the war and his own wounds dispassionately. However, he was destined to be carried out of himself by two events which together form the plot of the novel. The first was his falling in love. The second was the Italian retreat from the Isonzo.

In Gorizia, before being wounded, he had met an English nurse and had desired her merely because "this was better than going every evening to the house for officers where the girls climbed all over you and put your cap on backward as a sign of affection between their trips upstairs." He met her again in Milan while in the hospital and fell completely and suddenly in love. She went on night duty to be alone with him. They would be married soon, very soon, the moment they could obtain the necessary papers. Catherine was going to have a child.

He was ordered back to the front before anything had really been arranged. Three days after his return the Germans broke through at Caporetto. The description of the Italian retreat, with its sleeplessness, its hunger, its growing disorganization, its lines of tired men marching in the rain, is perhaps the finest single passage that Hemingway has written. It calls to mind a great description by another writer: I mean Stendhal's account of the retreat from Waterloo. The two are by no means equal, but it is enough that they can be mentioned in the same breath.

At the end of the long wooden bridge over the Tagliamento Henry was halted by the battle police. They had been executing every officer above the rank of captain for abandoning his troops; now they were about to execute this American because he spoke Italian with an accent and might possibly be a spy. He escaped from them by diving into the flooded river; he made his way to Milan; he followed Catherine to Lake Maggiore, and the two of them, now both deserters, crossed the Swiss frontier at night. The passage that follows is a long winter idyll; the life of two lovers, alone in the mountains, a tender contrast to the retreat through the Venetian plain. The novel ends, however, in another hospital: it ends with Catherine dying in childbirth and with her lover standing beside her body after having ordered the nurses to leave the room. The final paragraph is entirely typical of Hemingway's method: it implies all the emotion of the scene by a simple statement of the acts performed:

> "But after I had got them out and shut the door and turned off the light it wasn't any good. It was like saying good-bye to a statue. After a while I went out and left the hospital and walked back to the hotel in the rain."

One cannot help thinking that "A Farewell to Arms" is a symbolic title; that it is Hemingway's farewell to a period, an attitude, and perhaps to a method also. As the process of demobilization draws slowly to its end the simple standards of wartime are being forgotten. Pity, love, adventurousness, anger, the emotions on which his earlier books were based, almost to the entire exclusion of ideas, are less violently stimulated in a world at peace. The emotions as a whole are more colored by thought; perhaps they are weaker and certainly they are becoming more complicated. They seem to demand expression in a subtler and richer prose. The present novel shows a change in this direction, and perhaps the change may extend still farther—who knows. Perhaps even Hemingway may decide in the end that being deliberately un-sophisticated is not the height of sophistication.

T. S. MATTHEWS

Nothing Ever Happens to the Brave

The writings of Ernest Hemingway have very quickly put him in a prominent place among American writers, and his numerous admirers have looked forward with impatience and great expectations to his second novel. They should not be disappointed: "A Farewell to Arms" is worthy of their hopes and of its author's promise.

The book is cast in the form which Hemingway has apparently delimited for himself in the novel—diary form. It is written in the first person, in that bare and unliterary style (unliterary except for echoes of Sherwood Anderson and Gertrude Stein), in that tone which suggests a roughly educated but sensitive poet who is prouder of his muscles than of his vocabulary, which we are now accustomed to associate with Hemingway's name. The conversation of the characters is as distinctly Hemingway conversation as the conversation in one of Shaw's plays is Shavian. But there are some marked differences between "A Farewell to Arms" and Hemingway's previous work.

For one thing, the design is more apparent, the material more solidly arranged. Perhaps the strongest criticism that could be levelled against "The Sun Also Rises" was that its action was concerned with flotsam in the eddy of a backwater. It was apparently possible for some readers to appreciate the masculinity of Hemingway's "anti-literary" style, to admit the authenticity of his characters, and still to say, "What of it?" This criticism I do not consider

The New Republic, "Fall Literary Section" (October 9, 1929): pp. 208–210.

valid—there has always been, it seems to me, in the implications of Hemingway's prose, and in his characters themselves, a kind of symbolic content that gives the least of his stories a wider range than it seems to cover—but such a criticism was certainly possible. It is not, however, a criticism that can possibly be directed against "A Farewell to Arms." Fishing, drinking, and watching bullfights might be considered too superficial to be the stuff of tragedy, but love and death are not parochial themes.

The story begins in the summer of one of the middle years of the War. The hero is an American, Frederick Henry, in the Italian army on the Isonzo, in charge of a section of ambulances. It is before America has declared war, and he is the only American in Gorizia. But an English hospital unit has been sent down: he meets one of the nurses, Catherine Barkley, and falls in love with her. In the Italian offensive, he is wounded, and taken back to the base hospital in Milan where she too manages to be transferred. He is ordered to the front again just in time to be caught in the Caporetto retreat. In the mad scramble across the plains he loses the main column, is almost cut off by the Germans, and then almost shot by the Italians for not being with his section. He escapes, makes up his mind to desert from the army, and gets to Milan, where he eventually finds Catherine again. He is in mufti, the police are suspicious, and with the connivance of a friendly barman they row across the border into Switzerland. Their passports are in order, so they escape being interned. Catherine is going to have a baby. They spend the winter in a little cottage in the mountains, and in the spring go down to Lausanne, where the baby is to be born. Everything goes well for a time; then the doctor advises a Caesarean operation; the baby is born dead, and Catherine has an unexpected hemorrhage and dies. Here the story ends. Or not quite here. Hemingway's characteristic last sentence is: "After a while I went out and left the hospital and walked back to the hotel in the rain."

The book has more in it than "The Sun Also Rises"; it is more of a story; and it is more carefully written. Sometimes this care is too evident.

> I had gone to no such place but to the smoke of cafes and nights when the room whirled and you needed to look at the wall to make it stop, nights in bed, drunk, when you knew that that was all there was, and the strange excitement of waking and not knowing who it was with you, and the world all unreal in the dark and so exciting that you must resume again unknowing and not caring in the night, sure that this was all and all and all and not caring. Suddenly to care very much and to sleep to wake with it sometimes morning and all that had been there gone and everything sharp and hard and clear and sometimes a dispute about the cost.

This is a good description, but it is Hemingway gone temporarily Gertrude Stein. There is one other striking example of this manner, not new to Hemingway, but new to his serious vein:

"I love your beard," Catherine said. "It's a great success. It looks so stiff and fierce and it's very soft and a great pleasure."

This speech of Catherine's occurs toward the end of the book. When she is first introduced, she talks, plausibly enough, in a manner which, though distinctly Hemingway, might also pass as British. In the last half of the book, (except for the Gertrude Stein lapse quoted above), she is pure Hemingway. The change that comes over her, the change that comes over both the main characters, is not, I think, due to the author's carelessness. Whether he deliberately planned this metamorphosis or half-consciously allowed it to take place is of minor interest. The interesting and the significant thing is the nature of the change. A typical Hemingway hero and a not-quite-so-typical Hemingway heroine are transformed, long before the end, into the figures of two ideal lovers.

Hemingway has been generally regarded as one of the most representative spokesmen of a lost generation—a generation remarkable chiefly for its cynicism, its godlessness, and its complete lack of faith. He can still, I think, be regarded as a representative spokesman, but the strictures generally implied against his generation will soon, perhaps, have to be modified or further refined. As far as Hemingway himself is concerned, it can certainly no longer be said that his characters do not embody a very definite faith.

"They won't get us," I said. "Because you're too brave. Nothing ever happens to the brave."

Rinaldi, the Italian surgeon who is the hero's room-mate in the first part of the book, has what almost amounts to a breakdown because he can discover nothing in life outside is three anodynes of women, wine and work. The note of hopelessness that dominated the whole of "The Sun Also Rises" is not absent in "A Farewell to Arms," nor is it weaker, but it has been subtly modified, so that it is not the note of hopelessness we hear so much as the undertone of courage. Hemingway is now definitely on the side of the angels, fallen angels though they are. The principal instrument of this change is Catherine. Brett, the heroine of "The Sun Also Rises," was really in a constant fever of despair; the selfless faith which Catherine gives her lover may seem to come from a knowledge very like despair, but it is not a fever. When we look back on the two women, it is much easier to believe in Brett's actual existence than in Catherine's—Brett was so imperfect, so unsatisfactory. And, like an old soldier, it would have been wrong for Brett to die. The Lady in the Green Hat died, but Brett must live. But Catherine is Brett—an ennobled, a purified Brett, who can show us how to live, who must die before she forgets how to show us—deified into the brave and lovely creature whom men, if they have never found her, will always invent. This apotheosis of bravery in the person of a woman is the more striking because Hemingway is still the same apparently blunt-minded writer of two-fisted words. He still has a horror of expressing delicate or noble sentiments, except obliquely.

> I did not say anything. I was always embarrassed by the words sacred, glorious, and sacrifice and the expression in vain. We had heard them . . . and had read them, on proclamations that were slapped up by billposters over other proclamations, now for a long time, and I had seen nothing sacred, and the things that were glorious had no glory and the sacrifices were like the stockyards at Chicago if nothing was done with the meat except to bury it. There were many words that you could not stand to hear and finally only the names of places had dignity.

And his prophecy of individual fate is, if anything, more brutally pessimistic than ever:

> The world breaks every one and afterward many are strong at the broken places. But those that will not break it kills. It kills the very good and the very gentle and the very brave impartially. If you are none of these you can be sure it will kill you too but there will be no special hurry.

He will not even call Catherine brave, except through the lips of her lover. Here he is describing how she acted in the first stages of labor:

> The pains came quite regularly, then slackened off. Catherine was very excited. When the pains were bad she called them good ones. When they started to fall off she was disappointed and ashamed.

Hemingway is not a realist. The billboards of the world, even as he writes about them, fade into something else: in place of the world to which we are accustomed, we see a land and a people of strong outlines, of conventionalized shadow; the people speak in a clipped and tacit language as stylized as their appearance. But Hemingway's report of reality is quite as valid as a realist's. The description of the War, in the first part of "A Farewell to Arms," is perhaps as good a description of war just behind the front as has been written; and a fresh report from a point of view as original as Hemingway's is an addition to experience. But this book is not essentially a war-story: it is a love-story. If love-stories mean nothing to you, gentle or hard-boiled reader, this is not your book.

The transition, indeed, from the comparative realism of the war scenes to the ideal reality of the idyll is not as effective as it might be. The meeting of the lovers after Henry's desertion from the army, and their escape into Switzerland, have not that ring of authenticity about them which from Hemingway we demand. We are accustomed to his apparent irrelevancies, which he knows how to use with such a strong and ironic effect, but the scene, for instance, between the lovers and Ferguson in the hotel at Stresa seems altogether too irrelevant, and has no ironic or dramatic value, but is merely an unwanted complication of the story. From this point until the time when the lovers are safely established in Switzerland, we feel a kind of uncertainty about everything that happens; we cannot quite believe in it. Why is it, then, that when our belief is reawakened, it grows with every page, until once more we are convinced, and passionately convinced, that we are hearing the truth?

I think it is because Hemingway, like every writer who has discovered in himself the secret of literature, has now invented the kind of ideal against which no man's heart is proof. In the conclusion of "A Farewell to Arms," he has transferred his action to a stage very far from realism, and to a plane which may be criticized as the dramatics of a sentimental dream. And it is a dream. Catherine Barkley is one of the impossibly beautiful characters of modern tragedy—the Tesses, the Alyoshas, the Myshkins[1]—who could never have existed, who could not live even in our minds if it were not for our hearts. In that sentimentalism, that intimation of impossible immortality, poets and those who hear them are alike guilty.

Hemingway himself is doubtless a very different sort of man from the people pictured in his books: he may well have very different ideas about the real nature of life; but as long as books remain a communication between us, we must take them as we understand them and feel them to be. "Nothing ever happens to the brave." It is an ambiguous statement of belief, and its implications are sufficiently sinister, but its meaning is as clear and as simple as the faith it voices. It is a man's faith; and men have lived and died by much worse.

NOTE

1. The protagonists of Hardy's *Tess of the D'Urbervilles* (1891), Dostoyevsky's *The Brothers Karamazov* (1880), and *The Idiot* (1868).

JOHN DOS PASSOS

Books

Hemingway's *A Farewell to Arms* is the best written book that has seen
the light in America for many a long day. By well-written I don't mean the
tasty college composition course sort of thing that our critics seem to consider good writing. I mean writing that is terse and economical, in which
each sentence and each phrase bears its maximum load of meaning, sense
impressions, emotions. The book is a first-rate piece of craftsmanship by a
man who knows his job. It gives you the sort of pleasure line by line that
you get from handling a piece of well-finished carpenter's work. Read the
first chapter, the talk at the officer's mess in Gorizia, the scene in the dressing station when the narrator is wounded, the paragraph describing the
ride to Milan in the hospital train, the talk with the British major about
how everybody's cooked in the war, the whole description of the disaster at
Caporetto to the end of the chapter where the battlepolice are shooting the
officers as they cross the bridge, the caesarian operation in which the girl
dies. The stuff will match up as narrative prose with anything that's been
written since there was any English language.

It's a darn good document too. It describes with reserve and exactness
the complex of events back of the Italian front in the winter of 1916 and the
summer and fall of 1917 when people had more or less settled down to the
thought of war as the natural form of human existence, when every individual

New Masses, Volume 5 (December 1, 1929): p. 16.

in the armies was struggling for survival with bitter hopelessness. In the absolute degradation of the average soldier's life in the Italian army there were two hopes, that the revolution would end the war or that Meester Weelson would end the war on the terms of the Seventeen Points. In Italy the revolution lost its nerve at the moment of its victory and Meester Weelson's points paved the way for D'Annunzio's bloody farce at Fiume and the tyranny of Mussolini and the banks. If a man wanted to learn the history of that period in that sector of the European War I don't know where he'd find a better account than in the first half of *A Farewell to Arms*.

This is a big time for the book business in America. The writing, publishing and marketing of books is getting to be a major industry along with beauty shops and advertising. Ten years ago it was generally thought that all writers were either drunks or fairies. Now they have a halo of possible money around them and are respected on a par with brokers or realtors. The American people seem to be genuinely hungry for books. Even good books sell.

It's not surprising that *A Farewell to Arms*, that accidentally combines the selling points of having a love story and being about the war, should be going like hotcakes. It would be difficult to dope out just why there should be such a tremendous vogue for books about the war just now. Maybe it's that the boys and girls who were too young to know anything about the last war are just reaching the bookbuying age. Maybe it's the result of the intense military propaganda going on in schools and colleges. Anyhow if they read things like *A Farewell to Arms* and *All Quiet on the Western Front*, they are certainly getting the dope straight and it's hard to see how the militarist could profit much. Certainly a writer can't help but feel good about the success of such an honest and competent piece of work as *A Farewell to Arms*.

After all craftsmanship is a damn fine thing, one of the few human functions a man can unstintedly admire. The drift of the Fordized world seems all against it. Rationalization and subdivision of labor in industry tend more and more to wipe it out. It's getting to be almost unthinkable that you should take pleasure in your work, that a man should enjoy doing a piece of work for the sake of doing it as well as he damn well can. What we still have is the mechanic's or motorman's pleasure in a smoothrunning machine. As the operator gets more mechanized even that disappears; what you get is a division of life into drudgery and leisure instead of into work and play. As industrial society evolves and the workers get control of the machines a new type of craftsmanship may work out. For the present you only get opportunity for craftsmanship, which ought to be the privilege of any workman, in novelwriting and the painting of easelpictures and in a few of the machinebuilding trades that are hangovers from the period of individual manufacture that is just closing. Most of the attempts to salvage craftsmanship in industry have been faddy movements like East Aurora and Morris furniture and have come to nothing. *A Farewell to Arms* is no worse a novel because it was written with a typewriter. But it's a magnificent novel because the writer felt every minute the satisfaction of working ably with his material and his tools and continually pushing the work to the limit of effort.

H. L. MENCKEN

Fiction by Adept Hands

Mr. Hemingway's "Farewell to Arms" is a study of the disintegration of two youngsters under the impact of war. The man, Frederic Henry, is a young American architect, turned into a lieutenant of the Italian Ambulance; the woman is Catherine Barkley, a Scotch nurse. They meet just after Catherine has lost her fiancé, blown to pieces on the Western front, and fall into each other's arms at once. For six months they dodge about between Milan and the Italian front, carrying on their affair under vast technical difficulties. Henry is badly wounded; the Italians, broken, retreat in a panic; earth and sky are full of blood and flames. Finally a baby is on its way, and the pair escape to Switzerland. There Catherine dies in childbirth, and Henry wanders into space. "It was like saying good-bye to a statue. After a while I went out and left the hospital and walked back to the hotel in the rain."

The virtue of the story lies in its brilliant evocation of the horrible squalor and confusion of war—specifically of war à la Italienne. The thing has all the blinding color of a Kiralfy spectacle.[1] And the people who move through it, seen fleetingly in the glare, are often almost appallingly real. But Henry and Catherine, it seems to me, are always a shade less real than the rest. The more they are accounted for, the less accountable they become. In the end they fade into mere wraiths, and in the last scenes they scarcely seem human

The American Mercury (January 1930): p. 127.

at all. Mr. Hemingway's dialogue, as always, is fresh and vivid. Otherwise, his tricks begin to wear thin. The mounting incoherence of a drunken scene is effective once, but not three or four times. And there is surely no need to write such vile English as this: "The last mile or two of the new road, where it started to level out, *would be able* to be shelled steadily by the Austrians."

NOTE

1. Imre Kiralfy (1845–1919), author and organizer of international exhibitions.

FORD MADOX FORD

Ford Madox Ford on the Opening

This excerpt is from the introduction to the Modern Library edition of A Farewell to Arms *by British novelist Ford Madox Ford, the author of* The Good Soldier *(1927).*

I experienced a singular sensation on reading the first sentence of "A Farewell to Arms." There are sensations you cannot describe. You may know what causes them but you cannot tell what portions of your mind they affect nor yet, possibly, what parts of your physical entity. I can only say that it was as if I had found at last again something shining after a long delving amongst dust. I daresay prospectors after gold or diamonds feel something like that. But theirs can hardly be so coldly clear an emotion, or one so impersonal. The three impeccable writers of English prose that I have come across in fifty years or so of reading in search of English prose have been Joseph Conrad, W. H. Hudson . . . and Ernest Hemingway. . . . Impeccable each after his kind! I remember with equal clarity and equal indefinableness my sensation on first reading a sentence of each. With the Conrad it was like being overwhelmed by a great, unhastening wave. With the Hudson it was like lying on one's back and looking up into a clear, still sky. With the Hemingway it was just excitement. Like waiting at the side of a coppice, when foxhunting, for the hounds to break cover. One was going on a long chase in dry clear weather, one did not know in what direction or over what country.

"Introduction," in *A Farewell to Arms* (New York: Random House, 1932): pp. ix, xviii–xx. Copyright © Random House.

25

In the last paragraph I have explained the nature of my emotion when I read a year or so ago that first sentence of *Farewell to Arms*. It was more than excitement. It was excitement plus re-assurance. The sentence was exactly the right opening for a long piece of work. To read it was like looking at an athlete setting out on a difficult and prolonged effort. You say, at the first movement of the limbs: "It's all right. He's in form. . . . He'll do today what he has never quite done before." And you settle luxuriantly into your seat.

So I read on after the first sentence:

In the bed of the river there were pebbles and boulders dry and white in the sun, and the water was clear and swiftly moving and blue in the channels. Troops went by the house and down the road and the dust they raised powdered the leaves of the trees. The trunks of the trees were dusty and the leaves fell early that year and we saw the troops marching along the road and the dust rising and the leaves, stirred by the breeze falling and the soldiers marching and afterwards the road bare and white except for the leaves.

I wish I could quote more, it is such pleasure to see words like that come from one's pen. But you can read it for yourself.

A Farewell to Arms is a book important in the annals of the art of writing because it proves that Hemingway, the writer of short, perfect episodes, can keep up the pace through a volume. There have been other writers of impeccable—of matchless—prose but as a rule their sustained efforts have palled because precisely of the remarkableness of the prose itself. You can hardly read *Marius the Epicurean*. You may applaud its author, Walter Pater. But *Farewell to Arms* is without purple patches or even verbal "felicities." Whilst you are reading it you forget to applaud its author. You do not know that you are having to do with an author. You are living.

A Farewell to Arms is a book that unites the critic to the simple. You could read it and be thrilled if you had never read a book—or if you had read and measured all the good books in the world. That is the real province of the art of writing.

Hemingway has other fields to conquer. That is no censure on *A Farewell to Arms*. It is not blaming the United States to say that she has not yet annexed Nicaragua. But whatever he does can never take away from the fresh radiance of this work. It may close with tears but it is like a spring morning.

ROBERT PENN WARREN

The Story Behind the Love Story

Early in his essay, Warren notes the importance of Hemingway's "notion of a code."

We have said that the shadow of ruin is behind the typical Hemingway situation. The typical character faces defeat or death. But out of defeat or death the character usually manages to salvage something. And here we discover Hemingway's special interest in such situations and such characters. His heroes are not defeated except upon their own terms. They are not squealers, welchers, compromisers, or cowards, and when they confront defeat they realize that the stance they take, the stoic endurance, the stiff upper lip mean a kind of victory. Defeated upon their own terms, some of them have even courted their defeat; and certainly they have maintained, even in the practical defeat, an ideal of themselves, some definition of how a man should behave, formulated or unformulated, by which they have lived. They represent some notion of a code, some notion of honor, which makes a man a man, and which distinguishes him from people who merely follow their random impulses and who are, by consequence, "messy."

* * *

"Hemingway," *The Kenyon Review*, Volume 9 (Winter 1947): pp. 2–3, 4, 18–24. Copyright © 1947 The Kenyon Review.

For Hemingway, it "is the discipline of the code which makes man human, a sense of style or good form"; it "can give meaning, partially at least, to the confusions of living":

> . . . the code and the discipline are important because they can give meaning to life which otherwise seems to have no meaning or justification. In other words, in a world without supernatural sanctions, in the God-abandoned world of modernity, man can realize an ideal meaning only in so far as he can define and maintain the code. The effort to define and maintain the code, however limited and imperfect it may be, is the characteristically human effort and provides the tragic or pitiful human story.

* * *

In A Farewell to Arms *"there is an attempt to make the relationship of love take on a religious significance in so far as it can give meaning to life."*

A Farewell to Arms is a love story. It is a compelling story at the merely personal level, but is much more compelling and significant when we see the figures of the lovers silhouetted against the flame-streaked blackness of war, of a collapsing world, of nada. For there is a story behind the love story. That story is the quest for meaning and certitude in a world which seems to offer nothing of the sort. It is, in a sense, a religious book; if it does not offer a religious solution it is nevertheless conditioned by the religious problem.

The very first scene of the book, though seemingly casual, is important if we are to understand the deeper motivations of the story. It is the scene at the officers' mess where the captain baits the priest. "Priest every night five against one," the captain explains to Frederick. But Frederick, we see in this and later scenes, takes no part in the baiting. There is a bond between him and the priest, a bond which they both recognize. This becomes clear when, after the officers have advised Frederick where he should go on his leave to find the best girls, the priest turns to him and says that he would like for him to go to Abruzzi, his own province:

> "There is good hunting. You would like the people and though it is cold it is clear and dry. You could stay with my family. My father is a famous hunter."
>
> "Come on," said the captain. "We go whorehouse before it shuts."
>
> "Goodnight," I said to the priest.
>
> "Goodnight," he said.

In the preliminary contrast between the officers, who invite the hero to go to the brothels, and the priest, who invites him to go to the cold, clear, dry country, we have in its simplest form the issue of the novel.

Frederick does go with the officers that night, and on his leave he does go to the cities, "to the smoke of cafes and nights when the room whirled and you needed to look at the wall to make it stop, nights in bed, drunk, when you knew that that was all there was, and the strange excitement of waking and not knowing who it was with you, and the world all unreal in the dark and so exciting that you must resume again unknowing and not caring in the night, sure that this was all and all and all and not caring." Frederick at the opening of the novel lives in the world of random and meaningless appetite, knowing that it is all and all and all, or thinking that he knows that. But behind that there is a dissatisfaction and disgust. Upon his return from his leave, sitting in the officers' mess, he tries to tell the priest how he is sorry that he had not gone to the clear, cold, dry country—the priest's home, which takes on the shadowy symbolic significance of another kind of life, another view of the world. The priest had always known that other country.

> He had always known what I did not know and what, when I learned it, I was always able to forget. But I did not know that then, although I learned it later.

What Frederick learns later is the story behind the love story of the book.

But this theme is not merely stated at the opening of the novel and then absorbed into the action. It appears later, at crucial points, to define the line of meaning in the action. When, for example, Frederick is wounded, the priest visits him in the hospital. Their conversation makes even plainer the religious background of the novel. The priest has said that he would like to go back after the war to the Abruzzi. He continues:

> "It does not matter. But there in my country it is understood that a man may love God. It is not a dirty joke."
> "I understand."
> He looked at me and smiled.
> "You understand but you do not love God."
> "No."
> "You do not love him at all?" he asked.
> "I am afraid of him in the night sometimes."
> "You should love Him."
> "I don't love much."
> "Yes," he said. "You do. What you tell me about in the nights. That is not love. That is only passion and lust. When you love

you wish to do things for. You wish to sacrifice for. You wish to
serve."

"I don't love."

"You will. I know you will. Then you will be happy."

We have here two items of importance. First, there is the definition of
Frederick as the sleepless man, the man haunted by nada. Second, at this stage
in the novel, the end of Book I, the true meaning of the love story with Catherine has not yet been defined. It is still at the level of appetite. The priest's
role is to indicate the next stage of the story, the discovery of the true nature
of love, the "wish to do things for." And he accomplishes this by indicating a parallel between secular love and Divine love, a parallel which implies
Frederick's quest for meaning and certitude. And to emphasize further this
idea, Frederick, after the priest leaves, muses on the high, clean country of the
Abruzzi, the priest's home which has already been endowed with the symbolic significance of the religious view of the world.

In the middle of Book II (Chapter xviii), in which the love story begins
to take on the significance which the priest had predicted, the point is indicated by a bit of dialogue between the lovers.

"Couldn't we be married privately some way? Then if anything
happened to me or if you had a child."

"There's no way to be married except by church or state. We
are married privately. You see, darling, it would mean everything
to me if I had any religion. But I haven't any religion."

"You gave me the Saint Anthony."

"That was for luck. Some one gave it to me."

"Then nothing worries you?"

"Only being sent away from you. You're my religion. You're all
I've got."

Again, toward the end of Book IV (Chapter xxxv), just before Frederick
and Catherine make their escape into Switzerland, Frederick is talking with a
friend, the old Count Greffi, who has just said that he thought H. G. Wells's
novel *Mr. Britling Sees It Through* a very good study of the English middle-
class soul. But Frederick twists the word soul into another meaning.

"I don't know about the soul."

"Poor boy. We none of us know about the soul. Are you
Croyant?"

"At night."

Later in the same conversation the Count returns to the topic:

"And if you ever become devout pray for me if I am dead. I am asking several of my friends to do that. I had expected to become devout myself but it has not come." I thought he smiled sadly but I could not tell. He was so old and his face was very wrinkled, so that a smile used so many lines that all graduations were lost.

"I might become very devout," I said. "Anyway, I will pray for you."

"I had always expected to become devout. All my family died very devout. But somehow it does not come."

"It's too early."

"Maybe it is too late. Perhaps I have outlived my religious feeling."

"My own comes only at night."

"Then too you are in love. Do not forget that is a religious feeling."

So here, again, we find Frederick defined as the sleepless man, and the relation established between secular love and Divine love.

In the end, with the death of Catherine, Frederick discovers that the attempt to find a substitute for universal meaning in the limited meaning of the personal relationship is doomed to failure. It is doomed because it is liable to all the accidents of a world in which human beings are like the ants running back and forth on a log burning in a campfire and in which death is, as Catherine says immediately before her own death, "just a dirty trick." But this is not to deny the value of the effort, or to deny the value of the discipline, the code, the stoic endurance, the things which make it true—or half true—that "nothing ever happens to the brave."

This question of the characteristic discipline takes us back to the beginning of the book, and to the context from which Frederick's effort arises. We have already mentioned the contrast between the officers of the mess and the priest. It is a contrast based on the man who is aware of the issue of meaning in life and those who are unaware of it, who give themselves over to the mere flow of accident, the contrast between the disciplined and the undisciplined. But the contrast is not merely between the priest and the officers. Frederick's friend, the surgeon Rinaldi, is another who is on the same "side" of the contrast as the priest. He may go to the brothel with his brother officers, he may even bait the priest a little, but his personal relationship with Frederick indicates his affiliations; he is one of the initiate. Furthermore, he has the discipline of his profession, and as we have seen, in the Hemingway world, the discipline which seems to be merely technical, the style of the artist or the form of the athlete or bull fighter, may be an index to a moral value. "Already," he says, "I am only happy when I am working." (Already because the seeking of pleasure in sensation is inadequate for Rinaldi.) This point appears more sharply in the remarks about the doctor who first attends to Frederick's wounded leg. He is incompetent and does not wish to take the responsibility for a decision.

> Before he came back three doctors came into the room. I have noticed that doctors who fail in the practice of medicine have a tendency to seek one another's company and aid in consultation. A doctor who cannot take out your appendix properly will recommend to you a doctor who will be unable to remove your tonsils with success. These were three such doctors.

In contrast with them there is Dr. Valentini, who is competent, who is willing to take responsibility, and who, as a kind of mark of his role, speaks the same lingo, with the same bantering, ironical tone, as Rinaldi—the tone which is the mark of the initiate.

So we have the world of the novel divided into two groups, the initiate and the uninitiate, the aware and the unaware, the disciplined and the undisciplined. In the first group are Frederick, Catherine, Rinaldi, Valentini, Count Greffi, the old man who cut the paper silhouettes "for pleasure," and Passini, Manera, and the other ambulance men in Frederick's command. In the second group are the officers of the mess, the incompetent doctors, the "legitimate hero" Ettore, and the "patriots"—all the people who do not know what is really at stake, who are decided by the big words, who do not have the discipline. They are the messy people, the people who surrender to the flow and illusion of things. It is this second group who provide the context of the novel, and more especially the context from which Frederick moves toward his final complete awareness.

The final awareness means, as we have said, that the individual is thrown back upon his private discipline and his private capacity to endure. The hero cuts himself off from the herd, the confused world, which symbolically appears as the routed army at Caporetto. And, as Malcolm Cowley has pointed out, the plunge into the flooded Tagliamento, when Frederick escapes from the battle police, has the significance of a rite. By this "baptism" Frederick is reborn into another world; he comes out into the world of the man alone, no longer supported by and involved in society.

> Anger was washed away in the river along with my obligation. Although that ceased when the carabiniere put his hands on my collar. I would like to have had the uniform off although I did not care much about the outward forms. I had taken off the stars,

but that was for convenience. It was no point of honor. I was not against them. I was through. I wished them all the luck. There were the good ones, and the brave ones, and the calm ones and the sensible ones, and they deserved it. But it was not my show any more and I wished this bloody train would get to Maestre and I would eat and stop thinking.

So Frederick, by a decision, does what the boy Nick, in *In Our Time*, does as the result of the accident of a wound. He makes a "separate peace." And from the waters of the flooded Tagliamento arises the Hemingway hero in his purest form, with human history and obligation washed away, ready to enact the last phase of his appropriate drama, and learn from his inevitable defeat the lesson of lonely fortitude.

CARLOS BAKER

The Mountain and the Plain

"Learn about the human heart and the human mind in war from this book."

—Hemingway, in another connection [1]

I. Landscape in Gorizia

The opening chapter of Hemingway's second novel, *A Farewell to Arms*, is a generically rendered landscape with thousands of moving figures. It does much more than start the book. It helps to establish the dominant mood (which is one of doom), plants a series of important images for future symbolic cultivation, and subtly compels the reader into the position of detached observer.

In the late summer of that year we lived in a house in a village that looked across the river and the plain to the mountains. In the bed of the river there were pebbles and boulders, dry and white in the sun, and the water was clear and swiftly moving and blue in the channels. Troops went by the house and down the road and the dust they raised powdered the leaves of the trees. The trunks of the trees too were dusty and the leaves fell early that year and we saw the troops marching along the road

In *Hemingway: The Writer as Artist* (Princeton, N.J.: Princeton University Press, 1956): pp. 94-116. Copyright © 1956 Princeton University Press.

and the dust rising and leaves, stirred by the breeze, falling and
the soldiers marching and afterward the road bare and white,
except for the leaves.

The first sentence here fixes the reader in a house in the village where he
can take a long view across the river and the plain to the distant mountains.
Although he does not realize it yet, the plain and the mountains (not to mention the river and the trees, the dust and the leaves) have a fundamental value
as symbols. The autumnal tone of the language is important in establishing
the autumnal mood of the chapter. The landscape itself has the further importance of serving as a general setting for the whole first part of the novel.
Under these values, and of basic structural importance, are the elemental images which compose this remarkable introductory chapter.
       The second sentence, which draws attention from the mountainous
background to the bed of the river in the middle distance, produces a sense
of clearness, dryness, whiteness, and sunniness which is to grow very subtly
under the artist's hands until it merges with one of the novel's two dominant
symbols, the mountain-image. The other major symbol is the plain. Throughout the substructure of the book it is opposed to the mountain image. Down
this plain the river flows. Across it, on the dusty road among the trees, pass the
men-at-war, faceless and voiceless and unidentified against the background
of the spreading plain.
       In the third and fourth sentences of this beautifully managed paragraph
the march-past of troops and vehicles begins. From the reader's elevated
vantage-point, looking down on the plain, the river, and the road, the con-
tinuously parading men are reduced in size and scale—made to seem smaller,
more pitiful, more pathetic, more like wraiths blown down the wind, than
would be true if the reader were brought close enough to overhear their conversation or see them as individualized personalities.
       Between the first and fourth sentences, moreover, Hemingway accom-
plishes the transition from late summer to autumn—an inexorability of sea-
sonal change which prepares the way for the study in doom on which he is
embarked. Here again the natural elements take on symbolic function. In the
late summer we have the dust, in the early autumn the dust and the leaves
falling; and through them both the marching troops impersonally seen. The
reminder, through the dust, of the words of the funeral service in the prayer-
book is fortified by the second natural symbol, the falling leaves. They dry out,
fall, decay, and become part of the dust. Into the dust is where the troops are
going—some of them soon, all of them eventually.
       The short first chapter closes with winter, and the establishment of rain
as a symbol of disaster. "At the start of the winter came the permanent rain
and with the rain came the cholera. But it was checked and in the end only

seven thousand died of it in the army." Already, now in the winter, seven thousand of the wraiths have vanished underground. The permanent rain lays the dust and rots the leaves as if they had never existed. There is no excellent beauty, even in the country around Gorizia, that has not some sadness to it. And there is hardly a natural beauty in the whole first chapter of *A Farewell to Arms* which has not some symbolic function in Hemingway's first study in doom.

II. Not in Our Stars

To call *A Farewell to Arms* a "first" study in doom might seem unfair to *The Sun Also Rises*. But the total effect of the first novel, whatever its author's intention, is closer to that of tragicomedy than of tragedy. The tragic sense of life exists in the undertones of *The Sun Also Rises*. Its surface tone is, however, somewhere within the broad range of the comic. Reading it, one is oftener reminded of the tragi-comic irony of a work like Chaucer's *Troilus and Criseyde* than, say, the tragic irony of the Greeks and the Elizabethans. The operation of pity—again as in Chaucer—is carefully equivocal, somehow in itself a phase of irony, and under a restraint so nearly complete that it can scarcely move. Possibly because of the nature of the material, possibly because of the cultivated habit of understatement, one does not find in *The Sun Also Rises* the degree of emotional commitment which becomes visible in *A Farewell to Arms*.

After the experience of writing and revising his first novel, Hemingway worked more wisely and more slowly on his second. The preparation of the first draft took six months instead of six weeks. It was begun in Paris about the first of March, 1928. Through the spring and summer the work went on in Key West, where Hemingway made himself relax by deep-sea fishing while writing some 40,000 words. He continued the draft in Piggott, Arkansas, and Kansas City, Missouri, where he ran the total number of words to something like 87,000. The book was completed in preliminary form near Big Horn, in Sheridan County, Wyoming, about the end of August, 1928.

Following a brief interlude, he began revision, an extremely painstaking job of cutting and rewriting which filled another five months. On January 22, 1929, he wrote Perkins that the final draft stood complete in typescript, and by mid-February it had been decided to serialize the book in *Scribner's Magazine*, beginning with the number of May, 1929. Still Hemingway was dissatisfied. In Paris during the spring he continued to labor over the galley-proofs of the magazine version, rewriting some portions and keeping them by him until the last possible moment. Book-proof reached him in Paris on June 5, 1929.[2] By the twenty-fourth, when he had finally satisfied himself that everything possible had been done, he was able to report to Perkins that he had at last achieved a "new and much better ending" for his novel. There is a persistent tradition that the present ending was rewritten seventeen times before Hemingway got the corrected galley-proof aboard the boat-train.

In the midst of life, runs the Book of Common Prayer, we are in death. "During the time I was writing the first draft" said Hemingway in 1948, "my second son Patrick was delivered in Kansas City by Caesarean section, and while I was re-writing my father killed himself in Oak Park, Illinois. . . . I remember all these things happening and all the places we lived in and the fine times and the bad times we had in that year. But much more vividly I remember living in the book and making up what happened in it every day. Making the country and the people and the things that happened I was happier than I had ever been. Each day I read the book through from the beginning to the point where I went on writing and each day I stopped when I was still going good and when I knew what would happen next. The fact that the book was a tragic one did not make me unhappy since I believed that life was a tragedy and knew it could only have one end. But finding you were able to make something up; to create truly enough so that it made you happy to read it; and to do this every day you worked was something that gave a greater pleasure . . . than any I had ever known. Beside it nothing else mattered."[3]

The appearance of *A Farewell to Arms* in book form on September 27, 1929, marked the inception of Hemingway's still lengthening career as one of the very few great tragic writers in twentieth-century fiction. His next book, *Death in the Afternoon*, furthered his exploration into the esthetics of tragedy. Through the 1930's he continued at intervals to wrestle with the problem. *To Have and Have Not* (though with limited success) examined the tragic implications of social and political decay. *For Whom the Bell Tolls* attacked a similar problem on an epic and international scale. Ten years after that, at the age of fifty, Hemingway rounded out a full twenty years of work in tragedy with his character-study of Colonel Richard Cantwell.

The position occupied by *A Farewell to Arms* among Hemingway's tragic writings may be suggested by the fact that he once referred to the story of Lieutenant Frederick [*sic*] Henry and Catherine Barkley as his *Romeo and Juliet*.[4] The most obvious parallel is that Henry and Catherine, like their Elizabethan prototypes, might be seen as star-crossed lovers. Hemingway might also have been thinking of how rapidly Romeo and Juliet, whose affair has begun as a mere flirtation, pass over into the status of relatively mature lovers. In the third place, he may have meant to imply that his own lovers, caught in the tragic pattern of the war on the Austrian-Italian front, are not far different from the young victims of the Montague-Capulet family feud.

Neither in *Romeo and Juliet* nor in *A Farewell to Arms* is the catastrophe a direct and logical result of the immoral social situation. Catherine's bodily structure, which precludes a normal delivery for her baby, is an unfortunate biological accident. The death of Shakespeare's lovers is also precipitated by

an accident—the detention of the message-bearing friar. The student of esthetics, recognizing another kind of logic in art than that of mathematical
cause-and-effect, may however conclude that Catherine's death, like that of
Juliet, shows a kind of artistic inevitability. Except by a large indirection, the
war does not kill Catherine any more than the Veronese feud kills Juliet. But
in the emotional experience of the novel, Catherine's dying is directly associated and interwoven with the whole tragic pattern of fatigue and suffering,
loneliness, defeat and doom, of which the war is itself the broad social manifestation. And one might make a similar argument about *Romeo and Juliet*.

In application to Frederick and Catherine, the phrase "star-crossed lovers" needs some qualification. It does not mean that they are the victims of
an actual malevolent metaphysical power. All their crises are caused by forces
which human human beings have set in motion. During Frederick's under-
standably bitter ruminations while Catherine lies dying in the Lausanne hospital, fatalistic thoughts do, quite naturally, cross his mind. But he does not, in
the end, blame anything called "Fate" for Catherine's death. The pain of her
labor reminds him that her pregnancy has been comfortable and apparently
normal; the present biological struggle is perhaps a way of evening things up.
"So now they got her in the end. You never got away with anything." But he
immediately rejects his own inference: that is, that her sufferings in labor are a
punishment for sinful pleasures. Scientifically considered, the child is simply
a by-product of good nights in Milan—and there is never a pretence that they
were not good. The parents do not happen to be formally married; still, the
pain of the child-bearing would have been just as it is even if they had been
married fifty times. In short, the pain is natural, inevitable, and without either
moral or metaphysical significance. The anonymous "they" is nothing but a
name for the way things are.

A little later Frederick Henry bitterly compares the human predicament
first to a game and then to a swarm of ants on a log in a campfire. Both are
homely and unbookish metaphors such as would naturally occur to any young
American male at a comparable time. Living now seems to be a war-like
game, played "for keeps," where to be tagged out is to die. Here again, there
is a moral implication in the idea of being caught off base—trying to steal
third, say, when the infield situation and the number of outs make it wiser to
stay on second. "They threw you in and told you the rules and the first time
they caught you off base they killed you." One trouble, of course, is that the
player rarely has time enough to learn by long experience; his fatal error may
come in the second half of the first inning, which is about as far as Catherine
seems likely to go. Even those who survive long enough to learn the rules
may be killed through the operation of chance or the accidents of the game.
Death may, in short, come "gratuitously" without the slightest reference to
"the rules."

It is plainly a gratuitous death which comes to the ants on the burning log in Frederick's remembered campfire. Some immediately die in flame, as Catherine is now dying. Others, like Lieutenant Henry, who has survived a trench-mortar explosion, will manage to get away, their bodies permanently scarred, their future course uncertain—except that they will die in the end. Still others, unharmed, will swarm on the still cool end of the log until the fire at last reaches them. If a Hardyan President of the Immortals takes any notice of them, He does little enough for their relief. He is like Frederick Henry pouring water on the burning campfire log—not to save the ants but only to empty a cup.

Catherine's suffering and death prove nothing except that she should not have become pregnant. But she had to become pregnant in order to find out that becoming pregnant was unwise. Death is a penalty for ignorance of "the rules": it is also a fact which has nothing to do with rule or reason. Death is the fire which, in conclusion, burns us all, and it may singe us along the way. Frederick Henry's ruminations simply go to show that if he and Catherine seem star-crossed, it is only because Catherine is biologically double-crossed, Europe is is war-crossed, and life is death-crossed. [5]

III. Home and Not-Home

As its first chapter suggests, the natural-mythological structure which informs *A Farewell to Arms* is in some ways comparable to the Burguete-Montparnasse, Catholic-Pagan, and Romero-Cohn contrasts of *The Sun Also Rises*. One has the impression, however, of greater assurance, subtlety, and complexity in the second novel, as if the writing of the first had strengthened and consolidated Hemingway's powers and given him new insights into this method for controlling materials from below.

Despite the insistent, denotative matter-of-factness at the surface of the presentation, the subsurface activity of *A Farewell to Arms* is organized connotatively around two poles. By a process of accrual and coagulation, the images tend to build round the opposed concepts of Home and Not-Home. Neither, of course, is truly conceptualistic; each is a kind of poetic intuition, charged with emotional values and woven, like a cable, of many strands. The Home-concept, for example, is associated with the mountains; with dry-cold weather; with peace and quiet; with love, dignity, health, happiness, and the good life; and with worship or at least the consciousness of God. The Not-Home concept is associated with low-lying plains; with rain and fog; with obscenity, indignity, disease, suffering, nervousness, war and death; and with irreligion.

The motto of William Bird's Three Mountains Press in Paris, which printed Hemingway's *in our time,* was "Levavi oculos meos in montes." The line might also have served as an epigraph for *A Farewell to Arms.* Merely introduced in the first sentence of the first chapter, the mountain-image begins to develop important associations as early as Chapter Two. Learning that Frederick Henry is to go on leave, the young priest urges him to visit Capracotta in the Abruzzi. "There," he says, "is good hunting. You would like the people and though it is cold, it is clear and dry. You could stay with my family. My father is a famous hunter." But the lowlander infantry captain interrupts: "Come on," he says in pidgin Italian to Frederick Henry. "We go whorehouse before it shuts." [6]

After Henry's return from the leave, during which he has been almost everywhere else on the Italian peninsula *except* Abruzzi, the mountain-image gets further backing from another low-land contrast. "I had wanted," says he, "to go to Abruzzi. I had gone to no place where the roads were frozen and hard as iron, where it was clear cold and dry and the snow was dry and powdery and hare-tracks in the snow and the peasants took off their hats and called you Lord and there was good hunting. I had gone to no such place but to the smoke of cafés and nights when the room whirled and you needed to look at the wall to make it stop, nights in bed, drunk, when you knew that that was all there was."

Throughout Book I, Hemingway quietly consolidates the mountain-image. On the way up towards the Isonzo from Gorizia, Frederick looks across the river and the plain towards the Julian and Carnic Alps. "I looked to the north at the two ranges of mountains, green and dark to the snow-line and then white and lovely in the sun. Then, as the road mounted along the ridge, I saw a third range of mountains, higher snow mountains, that looked chalky white and furrowed, with strange planes, and then there were mountains far off beyond all these, that you could hardly tell if you really saw." [7] Like Pope in the celebrated "Alps on Alps arise" passage, Hemingway is using the mountains symbolically. Years later, in "The Snows of Kilimanjaro," he would use the mighty peak of East Africa as a natural image of immortality, just as in *The Green Hills of Africa* he would build his narrative in part upon a contrast between the hill-country and the Serengetti Plain. When Frederick Henry lowers his eyes from the far-off ranges, he sees the plain and the river, the war-making equipment, and "the broken houses of the little town" which is to be occupied, if anything is left of it to occupy, in the coming attack. Already now, a few dozen pages into the book, the mountain-image has developed associations: with the man of God and his homeland, with clear dry cold and snow, with polite and kindly people, with hospitality and with natural beauty. Already it has its oppositions: the lowland obscenities of the priest-baiting captain, cheap cafés, one-night prostitutes, drunkenness, destruction, and the war.

When the trench-mortar explosion nearly kills Henry, the priest comes to visit him in the field-hospital, and the Abruzzi homeland acquires a religious association. "There in my country," says the priest, "it is understood that a man may love God. It is not a dirty joke." Repeating, for emphasis, the effect of the priest's first account of the highland country, Hemingway allows Frederick to develop in his mind's eye an idyllic picture of the priest's home-ground.

> At Capracotta, he had told me, there were trout in the stream below the town. It was forbidden to play the flute at night . . . because it was bad for the girls to hear. . . . Aquila was a fine town. It was cool in the summer at night and the spring in Abruzzi was the most beautiful in Italy. But what was lovely was the fall to go hunting through the chestnut woods. The birds were all good because they fed on grapes, and you never took a lunch because the peasants were always honored if you would eat with them in their houses. . . . [8]

By the close of Book I, largely through the agency of the priest, a complex connection has come clear between the idea of Home and the combination of high ground, cold weather, love, and the love of God. Throughout, Hemingway has worked by suggestion, implication, and quiet repetition, putting the reader into potential awareness, readying him for what is to come.

The next step is to bring Catherine Barkley by degrees into the center of the image. Her love affair with Henry begins as a "rotten game" of wartime seduction. Still emotionally unstable and at loose nervous ends from her fiancé's death, Catherine is a comparatively easy conquest. But in the American hospital at Milan, following Henry's ordeal by fire at the front not far from the Isonzo, the casual affair becomes an honorable though unpriested marriage. Because she can make a "home" of any room she occupies—and Henry several times alludes to this power of hers—Catherine naturally moves into association with ideas of home, love, happiness. But she does not reach the center of the mountain-image until, on the heels of Frederick's harrowing lowland experiences during the retreat from Caporetto, the lovers move to Switzerland. Catherine is the first to go, and Henry follows her there as if she were the genius of the mountains, beckoning him on. Soon they are settled into a supremely happy life in the winterland on the mountainside above Montreux. Catherine's death occurs at Lausanne, after the March rains and the approaching need for a good lying-in hospital have driven the young couple down from their magic mountain—the closest approach to the priest's fair homeland in the Abruzzi that they are ever to know.

The total structure of the novel is developed, in fact, around the series of contrasting situations already outlined. To Gorizia, the Not-Home of war, succeeds the Home which Catherine and Frederick make together in the Milan hospital. The Not-Home of the grim retreat from the Isonzo is followed by the

quiet and happy retreat which the lovers share above Montreux. Home ends for
Frederick Henry when he leaves Catherine dead in the Lausanne Hospital.

The total structure of the novel is developed, in fact, around the series
of contrasting situations already outlined. To Gorizia, the Not-Home of
war, succeeds the Home which Catherine and Frederick make together in
the Milan Hospital. The Not-Home of the grim retreat from the Isonzo
is followed by the quiet and happy retreat which the lovers share above
Montreux. Home ends for Frederick Henry when he leaves Catherine dead
in the Lausanne Hospital.

Developed for an esthetic purpose, Hemingway's contrasting images
have also a moral value. Although he has nothing to say about the images
themselves, Mr. Ludwig Lewisohn is undoubtedly correct in saying that *A
Farewell to Arms* "proves once again the ultimate identity of the moral and
the esthetic." In this critic's view, Hemingway "transcended the moral nihilism of the school he had himself helped to form" by the very intensity of his
feelings for the contrast of love and war. "The simply wrought fable," Lewisohn continues, ignoring all the symbolic complexities yet still making a just
appraisal, "has two culminations—the laconic and terrible one in which the
activity of the battle police brings to an end the epically delineated retreat of
the Italian army with its classically curbed rages and pity . . . and that other
and final culmination in Switzerland with its blending in so simple and moving a fashion of the eternal notes of love and death." The opperation of the
underlying imagery, once its purposes are understood, doubly underscores
Mr. Lewisohn's point that there is no moral nihilism in the central story of *A
Farewell to Arms.* [9]

The use of rain as a kind of symbolic obligato in the novel has
been widely and properly admired. Less apparent to the cursory reader is the way in which the whole idea of climate is related to the natural-
mythological structure. (Hemingway's clusters of associated images produce
emotional "climates" also, but they are better experienced than reduced by
critical descriptions.) The rains begin in Italy during October, just before
Henry's return to Gorizia after his recovery from his wounds. The rains continue, at first steadily, then intermittently, throughout the disastrous retreat,
Henry's flight to Stresa, and the time of his reunion with Catherine. When
they awaken the morning after their reunion night, the rain has stopped, light
floods the window, and Henry, looking out in the fresh early morning, can
see Lake Maggiore in the sun "with the mountains beyond." Towards those
mountains the lovers now depart.

Not until they are settled in idyllic hibernation in their rented chalet
above Montreux are they really out of the rain. As if to emphasize by climatic
accompaniment their "confused alarms of struggle and flight," the rain has
swept over them during their escape up the lake in an open boat. Once in

the mountains, however, they are out of the lowlands, out of danger, out of the huge, tired debacle of the war. Above Montreux, as in the priest's homeland of Abruzzi, the ridges are "iron-hard with the frost." The deep snow isolates them, and gives them a feeling of domestic safety, tranquillity, and invulnerability.

For several months the rainless idyll continues. "We lived through the months of January and February and the winter was very fine and we were very happy. There had been short thaws when the wind blew warm and the snow softened and the air felt like spring, but always the clear, hard cold had come again and the winter had returned. In March came the first break in the winter. In the night it started raining."

The reader has been prepared to recognize some kind of disaster-symbol in the return of the rains. Much as in *Romeo and Juliet,* several earlier premonitions of doom have been inserted at intervals. "I'm afraid of the rain," says Catherine in the Milan Hospital one summer night, "because sometimes I see me dead in it." In the fall, just before Henry returns to the front, they are in a Milan hotel. During a break in the conversation the sound of falling rain comes in. A motor car klaxons, and Henry quotes Marvell: "At my back I always hear Time's wingèd chariot hurrying near." He must soon take a cab to catch the train that will project him, though he does not know it yet, into the disaster of the great retreat. Months later, in Lausanne, the Marvell lines echo hollowly: "We knew the baby was very close now and it gave us both a feeling *as though something were hurrying us and we could not lose any time together.*" (Italics added.) The sound of the rain continues like an undersong until, with Catherine dead in the hospital room (not unlike that other happy one where their child was conceived), Henry walks back to the hotel in the rain. [10]

One further reinforcement of the central symbolic structure is provided by the contrast between the priest and the doctor, the man of God and the man without God. In line with the reminiscence of *Romeo and Juliet,* it may not be fantastic to see them respectively as the Friar Lawrence and the Mercutio of Hemingway's novel. The marked contrast between the two men becomes especially apparent when Henry returns to the Gorizia area following his discharge from the hospital.

The return to Gorizia is a sharp comedown. After the "home-feeling" of the hospital and the hotel in Milan, the old army post seems less like home than ever. The tenor of life there has noticeably changed. A kind of damp-rot afflicts morale. The major, bringing Henry up to date on the state of affairs, plays dismally on the word *bad.* It has been a "bad summer." It was "very bad" on the Bainsizza plateau: "We lost three cars. . . . You wouldn't believe how bad it's been. . . . You were lucky to be hit when you were. . . . Next year will be worse. . . ." As if he were not fully convinced by the Major's despair, Henry picks up the word: "Is it so bad?" The answer is yes. "It is so bad and worse. Go get cleaned up and find your friend Rinaldi."

With Rinaldi the doctor, things also are bad, a fact which has been borne in upon the major so strongly that he thinks of Rinaldi when he mentions the word *bad*. Things are not bad for Rinaldi from a professional point of view, for he has operated on so many casualties that he has become "a lovely surgeon." Still, he is not the old Mercutio-like and mercurial Rinaldi. If mercury enters into his picture at all it is because he has syphilis, or thinks he has. He is treating himself for it and is beginning to entertain certain delusions of persecution. Except for his work, and the temporary opiates of drink and prostitutes, both of which interfere with his work, Rinaldi, the man of the plain, the man without God, is a man without resources.

With the priest, the man from the Abruzzi highlands, tacitly reintroduced as a contrast for Rinaldi, things are not so bad. "He was the same as ever," says Henry at their meeting, "small and brown and compact-looking." He is much more sure of himself than formerly, though in a modest way. When Rinaldi, in the absence of the foul-mouthed captain, takes up the former indoor game of priest-baiting, the priest is not perturbed. "I could see," says Henry, "that the baiting did not touch him now."

Out of the evils of the past summer the priest has even contrived to gather a nascent hope. Officers and men, he thinks, are gentling down because they "realize the war" as never before. When this happens, the fighting cannot continue for very much longer. Henry, playing half-heartedly the *advocatus diaboli*, argues that what the priest calls "gentling down" is really nothing but the feeling of defeat: "It is in defeat that we become Christian . . . like Our Lord." Henry is maintaining that after the fearless courage of His ministry, Our Lord's gentleness and His refusal to fight against the full brunt of the experience on Calvary became the ideal of Christian meekness. If Peter had rescued Christ Jesus from the Garden, suggests Henry, Christian ethics might be something different. But the priest, who is as compact as he looks, knows otherwise. Our Lord would not have changed in any way. From that knowledge and belief comes the priest's own strength. He has resources which Dr. Rinaldi, the man without God, does not possess."[11]

The priest-doctor contrast is carried out in the sacred-versus-profane-love antithesis which is quietly emphasized in the novel. Through the agency of Rinaldi the love affair begins at a fairly low level. The doctor introduces Frederick to Catherine, and takes a jocularly profane view of the early infatuation, seeming to doubt that it can ever be anything but an unvarnished wartime seduction. On the other hand, the background symbols of home and true love and high ground suggest that the lovers' idyllic life in Switzerland is carried on under the spiritual aegis of the priest. Neither Rinaldi nor the priest appears in the latter part of the book. But when, having been driven to the lowlands by the rains of spring, Catherine enters the hospital, it is naturally enough a doctor who takes over. And though this doctor does all he can to save her life, Catherine dies.

Projected in actualistic terms and a matter-of-fact tone, telling the truth about the effects of war in human life, *A Farewell to Arms* is entirely and even exclusively acceptable as a naturalistic narrative of what happened. To read it only as such, however, is to miss the controlling symbolism: the deep central antithesis between the image of life and home (the mountain) and the image of war and death (the plain).

IV. The Female of the Species

Coleridge once made the questionable remark that in Shakespeare "it is the perfection of woman to be characterless. Every one wishes a Desdemona or Ophelia for a wife—creatures who, though they may not always understand you, do always feel [for] you and feel with you."[12] To make so inordinate a generalization, Coleridge was obliged to ignore the better than half of Shakespeare's "perfect" women who are anything but characterless.

The modern reader, brought up on similar generalizations about the heroines of Hemingway, may wish to reconsider the problem. The most frequent adverse comment on Hemingway's fictional heroines is that they tend to embody two extremes, ignoring the middle ground. This fact is taken to be a kind of sin of omission, the belief being that most of their real-life sisters congregate and operate precisely in the area which Hemingway chooses not to invade at all.

The strictures of Mr. Edmund Wilson may be taken as typical of a recurrent critical position. He puts the argument in terms of a still-to-be-written chapter on the resemblances between Hemingway and Kipling. The two writers seem to him to share in "certain assumptions about society" with particular reference to the position of women. Kipling and Hemingway show, says Mr. Wilson, "much the same split attitude toward women. Kipling anticipates Hemingway in his beliefs that 'he travels fastest who travels alone' and that 'the female of the species is more deadly than the male'; and Hemingway seems to reflect Kipling in the submissive infra-Anglo-Saxon women that make his heroes such perfect mistresses. The most striking example of this is the amoeba-like little Spanish girl, Maria, in *For Whom the Bell Tolls*. Like the docile native 'wives' of English officials in the early stories of Kipling, she lives only to serve her lord and to merge her identity with his; and this love affair with a woman in a sleeping-bag, lacking completely the kind of give and take that goes on between real men and women, has the all-too-perfect felicity of a youthful erotic dream." [13]

The relevance of this commentary is that it underscores the idea of the two extremes in Hemingway's fictional treatment of women. In one group are the "deadly" females. Their best-realized (because most sympathetically presented and most roundly characterized) representative is Brett Ashley. The horrible example would presumably be someone like Margot Macomber, who is really and literally deadly. In varying degrees—and the fact that it is a matter of degree ought to be noticed—these women are selfish, corrupt, and predatory. They are "bad" for the men with whom they are involved. At the other extreme would stand the allegedly docile and submissive mistress-types, of whom Catherine Barkley and Maria are the conspicuous examples. These, for Mr. Wilson, are incredible wish-projections, youthfully erotic dream-girls, or impossibly romantic ideals of wife-hood. They bear, it seems, little resemblance to the women with whom one is acquainted. Where now, Mr. Wilson seems to be asking, are the day-by-day vagaries, the captious bickerings, the charming or enraging anfractuosities which combine to produce the "normal" or "real" married state? The greater number of the female kind obviously occupy some realm intermediate between the Becky Sharps and the Amelia Sedleys, between the pole of Goneril and Regan and the pole of Ophelia and Desdemona. By his failure, or his tacit refusal, to depict realistically the occupants of this realm and to use them as the heroines of his fiction, Hemingway has somehow failed in his obligation to present things as they are.

This point of view naturally affects Mr. Wilson's judgment of *A Farewell to Arms*. On the whole he finds the novel to be "a less serious affair" than Hemingway's previous work. Catherine Barkley and Frederick Henry, at least during the period of their Swiss idyll, strike him as "not in themselves convincing as human personalities." For him their relationship is merely an idealization, "the abstraction of a lyric emotion."[14] Mr. Cowley evidently shares this view. "To me," writes Mr. Cowley, "[Catherine] is only a woman at the beginning of the book, in her near madness"—as if, perhaps, some degree of emotional instability were a criterion of credibility in the portrait of a fictional heroine.[15]

For those who find it hard to accept Mr. Wilson's view of Catherine as an abstraction and of Maria as an amoeba, four practical points might well be made. The first has to do with the relation of Brett Ashley and Catherine Barkley to what Mr. Wilson might call the Great Infra-Anglo-Saxon tradition of fictional heroines. It is of some interest to observe that Mr. Wilson's strictures on the heroines of Hemingway could be applied with equal justice, not only to the heroines of Kipling but also to a considerable number of other heroines throughout the history of English and American fiction. Hemingway shares with many predecessors an outlook indubitably masculine, a certain chivalric attitude not without ironic overtones, and a disinclination to interest himself in what may be called the prosaisms of the female world.

The second point is that through a method of comparative portraiture, Hemingway carefully establishes a moral norm of womanly behavior. Then, whether by ethical intent or by temperamental attitude, he uses the established norm as a means of computing various degrees of departure from it. Depending on their own views in this area, readers may find Hemingway's "norm-women" less interesting and less credible than their "abnormal" cousins. For the inveterate reader of fiction and narrative poetry it is perhaps a psychological truism that the *femme fatale,* the general type of the temptress, seems more "interesting" than the stable heroine.

In the early work of Hemingway the point is well illustrated by the contrast between Brett and Catherine. There are, to begin with, certain resemblances. Like Brett, Catherine is an Englishwoman; like Brett, she is beautiful, tall, and blonde. She talks as Brett does, stressing certain words which in print are italicized. Like Brett, she has lost her own true love early in the war, and her emotions, like her way of life, have become confused as a result of the bereavement. But here the resemblances stop.

Brett's neurosis drives her from bar to bar, from man to man, and from city to city. None of it is any good: her polygamy, with or without benefit of justices of the peace, leads only to more of the same, as one drink leads to another in the endless round. Brett is not "good" for the men she knows. Romero wants her to let her hair grow out, to become more feminine, to marry and live with him. The basic abnormality at work in Brett opposes such feminization. She is the short-haired companion of men, wearing a man's felt hat, calling herself a "chap." She does not really like other women, and neither has nor wishes to have any real friends among them. She is never happier than in the Pamplona wineshop, the center of raucous masculine singing, as if she were a half-woman half in love with damnation.

Catherine Barkley, on the other hand, is all woman. At once dependent and independent, she half-mothers, half-mistresses Frederick Henry. She wants no other life than with him, no other man than he. She drinks little and displays none of Brett's geographical restlessness. She is temperamentally monogamous. Where she is, home is. Even the red-plush hotel room in Milan (which for several minutes makes her feel like a whore) is changed by her presence until she herself can feel at home in it. "In a little while," says her lover, "the room felt like our own home. My room at the hospital had been our own home and this room was our home too in the same way." Trying at first to help her out of the harlot-feeling, Henry kisses her and assures her, "You're my good girl." "I'm certainly yours," says Catherine, wryly. But she is also, and preeminently, a "good girl"—even more so, for example, than Hardy's Tess, who was so designated on the title page.[16] As if Hemingway were looking back for contrast to the Circean figure of his first novel, Rinaldi refers to Catherine as "your lovely cool . . . English goddess." But she is a woman, not a goddess. She rescues, pities, comforts, companions, and sustains, just as she in turn is rescued from the "craziness" induced by her lover's death when she has finally involved herself sufficiently in Henry's growing love. Her hair is long; she dresses like a woman and gets on well with other women like her friend Ferguson. Yet she is evidently happiest alone with her husband. She would be unhappy and possibly frightened on the wine-cask in Pamplona. She is at ease in Milan in the midst of a war because she is a young woman in the midst of love. Like Maria, she is a completing agent for the hero, and is in turn completed by her association with him. But Brett, on the other hand, is an agent of depletion, as she herself realizes, and as her unselfish renunciation of Romero is presumably meant to show.[17]

The third point to be made about Hemingway's heroines is that they are, on the whole, an aspect of the poetry of things. It is perhaps a sign of an attitude innately chivalric that they are never written off, as sometimes happened in Kipling, as mere bundles of rags, bones, and hanks of hair. Even Margot Macomber, in the bottomless slough of her bitch-hood, is seen to be "damned beautiful." The treatment of Catherine, like that of Brett, shows in Hemingway a fundamental indisposition to render his heroines "reductively." And if one argues that he nowhere seems to commit himself to the emancipation of women, or to become in the usual sense of the term an ardent feminist, the answer would be, perhaps, that his women are truly emancipated only through an idea or ideal of service. His heroines, to make the statement exactly, are meant to show a symbolic or ritualistic function in the service of the artist and the service of man.

The final point grows naturally out of the preceding ones. It is, in brief, that all of Hemingway's heroines, like all of his heroes, are placed in a special kind of accelerated world. We do not see them puttering in their kitchens, but only dreaming of that as a desirable possibility. They are never presented as harassed mothers; their entire orientation tends to be, in this connection, premarital. Wars and revolutions, the inevitable enemies of peace and domesticity, set them adrift or destroy their lives. Yet they contrive to embody the image of home, the idea if not the actuality of the married state, and where they are, whatever the outward threats, home is.

Mr. Wilson's feeling that Catherine is not convincing as a human personality, his belief that her love affair with Frederick Henry is an "abstraction of lyric emotion," may be partly explained by the fact that a majority of the characters in the first two novels are oddly rootless. With a few notable exceptions like Robert Cohn, Brett Ashley, or the priest from Abruzzi, they seem on the whole to possess no genealogies or previous biographies. We know nothing about Henry's background, and next to nothing about Catherine Barkley's. Like Jake Barnes, Bill Gorton, and Dr. Rinaldi, they seem to come from nowhere, move into the now and here, and depart again for nowhere after the elapsed time of the novels. They have substance and cast shadows, but they lack the full perspective and chiaroscuro that one finds among most of the people in *For Whom the Bell Tolls.* We are seldom permitted to know them in depth. The inclination is to accept them for what they do more than for what they are. They are the men and women of action, the meaning of whose lives must be sought in the kind of actions in which they are involved, very much, again, as in *Romeo and Juliet.*

This feeling about the characters can be accounted for in two different ways. One has to do with Hemingway's esthetic assumptions as of 1928–1929; the other is a natural consequence of the kind of stories he chose to tell. His working assumption that character is revealed through action will, if rigorously adhered to, produce the kind of fiction in which characterization-in-depth is in a measure sacrificed to the exigencies of narrative movement. Even there, however, it is advisable to notice that a close reading of any of the early books reveals far more in the way of nuances of light and shade, or in subtle shifts of motivation, than one at first imagined was there. This half-concealed power is easily explained by what is now acknowledged in all quarters: Hemingway's carefully controlled habit of understatement. As for the second explanation, it might be pointed out that nearly all of the important characters in the first two novels are "displaced persons"—either men fighting a war far from their former home-environments, or aliens in foreign lands whose ties with nearly everything they have known before are now severed—for better or for worse, but severed.

These two explanations, the esthetic and the "geographical," may throw some further light into the reasons behind Mr. Wilson's strictures. If Hemingway had not yet met head-on the problem of characterization-in-depth, perhaps it was unfair to ask a writer who had done so much so brilliantly that he should do so much more. He had developed a memorably individualized style-whittled it, as MacLeish said, from the hard wood of a walnut stick. He showed an unerring ability to keep his narratives in motion. Finally, he had achieved mastery of that special combination of naturalistic and symbolic truthtelling which was the despair of those who could (and so frequently did) imitate his style and his narrative manner.

In the absence of other evidence, it is probably wisest to assume that Hemingway knew what he was doing. That he could draw a character fully, roundedly, and quickly is proved by a dozen minor portraits in the first two books—Cohn's acidulous mistress, for example, or Brett's friend Mippipopoulos [*sic*], or the wonderful old Count Greffi, with whom Henry plays at billiards and philosophy in the hotel at Stresa, or the Milanese surgeon who does the operation on Henry's leg after the affair of the trench mortar, a surgeon who seems, and is, four times as good as the three old-maiden doctors who have wisely wagged their heads an hour before and advised Henry to wait six months for the operation. These are only four examples, but they are enough to show that the ability to draw character was by no means lacking in the Hemingway of 1929. If he went no deeper into the backgrounds of his displaced persons, he went as deeply as he needed to do for the purposes of his narrative. And the paring-out of the superfluous had always been one of his special addictions.

There is, finally, a *tendenz* in *A Farewell to Arms* which helps to account for the opinion that Hemingway has somehow failed in his attempt to present Catherine as a credible characterization. In a large and general way, the whole movement of the novel is from concretion towards abstraction. This became apparent in our consideration of the wonderfully complex opening chapter, and the importance of the observation is enhanced by what happens in the closing chapters of the book. The fact that the whole story is projected in actualistic terms ought not finally to obscure the symbolic mythos on which it is built and from which a great part of its emotional power derives. Catherine may be taken as an English girl who has a Juliet-like liaison with a young American officer. Similarly, one may read the novel as a naturalistic narrative of what happened to a small group of people on the Italian front during the years 1917–1918.

In the central antithesis between the image of life, love, and home (the mountain), and the image of war and death (the plain), Catherine however has a symbolic part to play. It is indeed required of her that she should become, as the novel moves on towards its denouement, more of an abstraction of love than a down-to-earth portrait of an actual woman in love and in pain. The truly sympathetic reader may feel that she is a woman, too. But if she does move in the direction of abstraction, one might argue that the *tendenz* of the novel is in this respect symbolically and emotionally justified. For when Frederick Henry has closed the door of the hospital room in order to be alone with his dead wife Catherine, he learns at once, as if by that act, the finality and totality of his loss. It is the loss of a life, of a love, of a home. Saying good-bye is "like saying good bye to a statue." The loved woman has become in death an abstract unvital image of her living self, a marble memorial to all that has gone without hope of recovery. Her death exactly completes the symbolic structure, the edifice of tragedy so carefully erected. This structure is essentially poetic in conception and execution. It is achieved without obvious insistence or belaboring of the point, but it is indubitably achieved for any reader who has found his way into the true heart of the book. And it is this achievement which enables Hemingway's first study in doom to succeed as something far more than an exercise in romantic naturalism. Next to *For Whom the Bell Tolls*, it is his best novel.

Notes

1. Hemingway, *Men at War*, introd., p. xx.
2. Details on the composition are drawn from the following letters: EH to MP, 3/17/28, 3/21/28, 6/7/28, ca. 9/5/28, 9/28/28, 1/8/29, 1/10/29, 1/22/29, 6/7/29, 6/24/29. Also EH to Bridges, 5/18/29; and MP to EH, 5/24/29, and

7/12/29. At the time he began *FTA*, Hemingway had been for some time at work on another novel—"a sort of modern Tom Jones," which was up to nearly 60,000 words when he dropped it in favor of the story of Frederick Henry and Catherine Barkley. On Thanksgiving Day, 1927, he told Perkins that he had completed 17 chapters of the *Tom Jones* work and was only a third through. He had decided to change the narrative method to the third person, having "got tired of the limitations" imposed by first-person narrative. But *FTA*, like *SAR*, used the first-person method. Hemingway did not begin to employ the third person consistently until the middle 1930's.

3. See Hemingway's introduction, dated June 30, 1948, to the illustrated edition of *FTA*, New York, Scribner's, 1948, pp. vii–viii. Hemingway seems to be in error when he gives the impression that the original publication date was "the day the stock market crashed"—that is, October 30, 1929. The book had been published September 27th. For an excellent review of *FTA* following publication, see Malcolm Cowley, *New York Herald Tribune Books*, October 6, 1929, pp. 1 and 6.

4. The *Romeo and Juliet* comment is quoted by Edmund Wilson in "Ernest Hemingway: Bourdon Gauge of Morale," which first appeared in the *Atlantic Monthly* 164 (July 1939), pp. 36–46. The essay was collected in *The Wound and the Bow*, New York, 1941, and reprinted by J. K. M. McCaffery, ed., *Ernest Hemingway, The Man and His Work*, New York, 1950, pp. 236–257. Further page references to this essay will be to the McCaffery reprint only.

It is of some interest to notice that Bertrand Russell on an American lecture tour denounced the novel as a piece of Victorianism. See Irene and Allen Cleaton, *Books and Battles*, New York, 1937. Compare further the opinion of Oliver Allston (Van Wyck Brooks) that *FTA* is another version of the Evangeline story. See *The Opinions of Oliver Allston*, New York, 1941, p. 173.

Boston and Italy had other opinions. The serialization of the novel began in *Scribner's Magazine* in May 1929 (Vol. 85, pp. 493ff.) and ran to October (Vol. 86, pp. 20ff). One startling event of the summer was the banning of the June and July issues from public sale on the orders of Chief of Police Michael H. Crowley of Boston. The result, however unhappy for censorship, was increased sales for the book. A poet in *The Daily Oklahoman* felt that

> *Scribner's* may have larger circulation
> Since Boston with its codfish and its beans
> Deems Hemingway a menace to the nation.

Both the novel and the film were banned in Italy by Mussolini's government. It was felt that they showed Italian military valor in an ugly light. The film, which Hemingway resented as a falsification of his intention, was released in December 1932. Samuel Putnam notes that up to 1947 Hemingway was still popular with Italian anti-fascists. (*Paris Was Our Mistress*, p. 132.)

FTA is the only one of Hemingway's works to appear in three media. The novel was successfully dramatized by Lawrence Stallings, and presented at the National Theatre, September 22, 1930. See *New Republic* 64 (October 8, 1930), pp. 208–209.

5. On Catherine's bad luck, see *FTA*, pp. 342, 350.

6. *FTA*, pp. 9, 13.

7. *FTA*, p. 48.

8. *FTA*, p. 78.

9. *Expression in America*, New York, 1932, p. 519.

10. *FTA*, pp. 135, 165, 267, 326, and 332 show, in order, the various premonitions and the obligato use of rain. Malcolm Cowley was one of the first of Hemingway's critics to point to his symbolic use of weather. See *The Portable Hemingway*, New York, 1944, introd., p. xvi.

11. On the low morale among the Italian troops, see *FTA*, pp. 174–175. On Rinaldi's affliction, see p. 181. On the priest's firmness, see pp. 183–184.

12. Coleridge, *Table Talk*, in *Works*, ed. Shedd, vol. 6, p. 349.

13. McCaffery, *op. cit.*, p. 254, note.

14. *Ibid.*, p. 242.

15. Malcolm Cowley to CB, 10/20/51.

16. On Catherine's connection with the "home-feeling," see *FTA*, p. 163. Rinaldi's remark on her goddess-like qualities is on p. 71.

17. Mr. Theodore Bardacke has an interesting essay on "Hemingway's Women" in McCaffery, *op. cit.*, pp. 340–351. Among its contributions is a discussion of Hemingway's "symbolic" use of long and short hair as a mark of femininity or the relative lack of it. The point is of special interest in connection with Maria, who has been raped and shorn by the fascists. The growing-out of her hair is a reminder of her gradual return to mental and physical health under the double tutelage of Pilar and Roberto.

SHERIDAN BAKER

Frederic Henry and the Undefeated

When Scribner's published *The Sun Also Rises* on October 22, 1926,
Hemingway had already separated from Hadley Richardson, to whom with
their three-year-old son, John Hadley Nicanor (namesake of bullfighter
Nicanor Villalta), he dedicated the book; and the first phase of Hemingway's
career was almost over. The defeated Jake Barnes was to give way to a new
undefeated hero, only to recur again in the half-defeated Frederic Henry.
"The Undefeated" itself had been written in March, 1925, immediately after
Hemingway returned to Paris from Austria exuberant over the acceptance
of *In Our Time*, before Pamplona and *The Sun Also Rises*. But Hemingway's
undefeated loser was to continue and eventually triumph in *The Old Man
and The Sea*, a type of character running somewhat counter to Nick and
Barnes and Henry.

Hemingway had mailed off the manuscript of *The Sun Also Rises* on April
24, 1926. On Sunday, May 16, alone in Madrid, snowed out of the bullfights,
he had, as he told Plimpton, written three stories in one day:

First wrote "The Killers," which I'd tried to write before and failed.
Then after lunch I got in bed to keep warm and wrote "Today Is
Friday." I had so much juice I thought maybe I was going crazy and
I had about six other stories to write. So I got dressed and walked

Ernest Hemingway: An Introduction and Interpretation (New York: Holt, Rinehart and
Winston, 1967): pp. 56–73. Copyright © Sheridan Baker.

to Fornos, the old bullfighters' café, and drank coffee and then came back and wrote "Ten Indians." This made me very sad and I drank some brandy and went to sleep.

Later in the spring he had published "Banal Story," probably written late in 1925, a journalistic, torrents-of-spring report about a writer in a cold room, an ad for a literary magazine, and the death by pneumonia of Maera, whose fictive death Hemingway had portrayed from his first impressions of bullfighting. He had spent the summer in Spain, following the fights and thinking of a book on bullfighting, a project first mentioned to Maxwell Perkins of Scribner's in 1925. In July, "To-day Is Friday" had been published as a pamphlet in New Jersey. In December, 1926, two months after *The Sun Also Rises*, "The Undefeated"—already published in German, English, and French—appeared in *The Best Short Stories of 1926*.

In 1927, Hemingway's stories began to appear in American magazines; and he began a long epic novel. In early spring, a ten-day trip through Italy by Model T produced a report for the *New Republic* (May 18) entitled "Italy—1927"—good, oblique journalism to be renamed "Che ti Dice La Patria" for the coming volume of fiction, an early symptom of the political stirrings of Italian memories for *A Farewell to Arms*. In March "The Killers" was published in *Scribner's Magazine* (also selected for *Best Short Stories of 1927*) and in April, "In Another Country"; in July, "Fifty Grand"; in August, "Hills Like White Elephants," the last of the stories for *Men Without Women* to appear in advance.

The spring of 1927 had seen Hemingway divorced from Hadley Richardson and married to Pauline Pfeiffer, within the Catholic Church. A further manifestation of Hemingway's subterranean Christianity appeared, perhaps a reaction both from Jake Barnes's wistful Catholicism and the rough affirmation of "To-day Is Friday." Hemingway published in Ezra Pound's *Exile* magazine (Spring, 1927) a "poem" that seemed to plead that he had not dropped out of the advance guard after all. Under the misprinted title of "Notheomist Poem," the text reads:

> The Lord is my shepherd, I shall not
> want him for long.

And a footnote explains: "The title 'Neo-Thomist Poem' refers to temporary embracing of church by literary gents—E. H." Hemingway, with his newly embraced Catholic bride, now settled in Key West, Florida—a home in America at last, but at its extreme, fugitive tip.

* * *

Men Without Women appeared on October 14, 1927, collected from the magazines, with four unpublished stories: two competent (A Simple Inquiry," "A Pursuit Race"), two splendid ("Ten Indians," "Now I Lay Me"). A month later, on Thanksgiving Day, Hemingway wrote Perkins that he had seventeen chapters, about one third (60,000 words) of what was intended to be "a sort of modern *Tom Jones.*" His reading of Fielding, swept into *The Torrents of Spring*, had turned his thoughts to the big epical novel, which he was soon to abandon and later to denounce (in *Death in the Afternoon*): "all bad writers are in love with the epic." He had been trying to write his epic in the first person (obviously not understanding much about epics), and had decided to change everything to third person, having "got tired of the limitations" that had served in *The Sun Also Rises* and would serve again in *A Farewell to Arms.*

Men Without Women, containing some of Hemingway's best stories, nevertheless does not, as a book, equal *In Our Time*. The title merely catches at the masculine deprivation or masculine resentment or masculine independence variously to be found in most of the stories. The title, as Carlos Baker has noted, merely gives an opportune twist to Ford's *"Women and Men,"* the second work in The Three Mountain's Press's series, of which *In Our Time* has seen the sixth and last. The book balances Hemingway's two emerging modes, which might be called the autobiographical and the observational, roughly the first and the third person between which his "epic" was equivocating, the defeated and the undefeated. In *Men Without Women*, the two modes alternate and engage each other somewhat as two halves of a deck of cards: on the one hand, "In Another Country" and "Now I Lay Me"; on the other, "The Undefeated" and "Fifty Grand." The book begins with "The Undefeated" and ends, like a copy of *In Our Time*, with Nick and symbolic trout streams, in "Now I Lay Me." "The Killers," for all its power, is a hybrid, an observation of the tough world that shifts to a revelation of Nick's inner agony.

The rest of the stories, good and indifferent, fall between, down to "Banal Story," just before the end, which perhaps should have dropped out of sight completely. (Edmund Wilson and W. M. Frohock, however, consider it among Hemingway's best.) "A Simple Enquiry" is an efficient study of a homosexual major, which suffers by comparison with D. H. Lawrence's similar "The Prussian Officer" (published in 1914). "Canary for One" is autobiographical, another and poorer "Out of Season," with a sharp last line. "An Alpine Idyll" and "A Pursuit Race" are unattractive but able stories of isolation and self-destruction.

"Hills Like White Elephants" is better, a study of the destructiveness of the selfish, and a study in Hemingway's ultimate terseness. A man wants his consort to have an abortion so that they can be just as "we were before."

The girl knows that the world, with hills like the skin of white elephants, "isn't ours anymore." No matter which way they turn, the man's wish has hurt them beyond repair. Of the story, Hemingway remarked to Plimpton: "I met a girl in Prunier where I'd gone to eat oysters before lunch. I knew she'd had an abortion. I went over and we talked, not about that, but on the way home I thought of the story, skipped lunch, and spent the afternoon writing it." Robert McAlmon indicates (in Knoll's redaction) that a hint of the story had been in Hemingway's mind since the Rapallo days at Pound's, early in 1923, for about five years:

> One night in Rapallo the lot of us were talking of birth control, and spoke of the cruelty of the law which did not allow young unmarried women to avoid having an unwanted child. Recalling an incident of college days I told a story of a girl who had managed to have herself taken care of. Her attitude was very casual. "Oh, it was nothing. The doctor just let the air in and few hours later it was over."

"Two years later," continues McAlmon, with his usual inaccuracy, he saw Hemingway's story "in some magazine": "I didn't see the point of the story and reread it and encountered the phrase 'Let the air in.' Later Hemingway informed me that my remark suggested the story." The story is indeed cryptic. The indirection of Hemingway's talk with the girl in Prunier is there; the casual girl of McAlmon's anecdote has turned numb, confronting the casual attitude of her lover; and, of course, there is a great deal more in the story, from white-skinned, fetal oysters to Hemingway himself.

"To-day Is Friday" is Hemingway's first experiment with the drama. Three Roman soldiers are talking in the wineshop of a Hebrew (who is named "George," as is the manager of Henry's lunchroom in "The Killers," written an hour or so before). They discuss the routine crucifixion they have just performed. Hemingway probably intended a shocker, but the play's positive Christianity is empowered by its rough inarticulation. The second soldier, at the lowest rung of understanding, wonders why Christ did not come down off the cross. The first soldier, a good drinker and man of experience, knows "That's not his play." He has illegally "slipped the old spear into him" to end His suffering and reward His bravery. He continues to repeat: "He was pretty good in there to-day." The second soldier calls the first a "regular Christer," and when, as they walk away, the first soldier defends the obsequious George as a "nice fella," the second soldier replies: "Everybody's a nice fella to you to-night." Christ's suffering has taken effect, even at this level of understanding. The third soldier can understand no more than that he has a "gut-ache" and feels "like hell to-night." This is the pagan world, the hellish world, suggesting a spiritual dimension it cannot understand but can partly comprehend. This is Hemingway's earthbound Christianity, that of Nick—who cannot get beyond "on earth" as he prays, two stories further along—and that of Jake Barnes and Frederic Henry, whose thoughts fly up from their earthbound souls. It is also Hemingway's first use of Christianity as a symbology for brave Man crucified by the world, as Young says, and as Waldmeir has seen it in *The Old Man and the Sea*.

"The Undefeated" is a big and fine story, the best of Hemingway's bull-fighting in fact or fancy, free from the nonsense of *Death in the Afternoon*, surpassing in its thoroughness the picture of Romero in *The Sun Also Rises*. It is in the new mode, projected out and away from the secret autobiography, fiction solidly created from Hemingway's admiration of Manuel Garcia, known as Maera. Indeed, Romero's exhibit of undefeat in his fight with Cohn is no accident, for Romero has a great deal of Maera in him, as well as of Niño de la Palma. Hemingway remembers, in *Death in the Afternoon*, "the last night of feria when Maera fought Alfredo David in the Café Kutz." The aging Manuel Garcia of the story (called "kid" and "Manolo" by his friends) is the first of Hemingway's undefeated losers, connecting his first sketch of Maera with the Old Man of his last novel, whose friend is the boy Manolin.

Hemingway has shifted his attention from the Nicks to the less sensitive friends of the Nicks, those able to live in the world: Bill of "The Three-day Blow," Tommy of "The Light of the World," Bugs of "The Battler," George of "The Killers," Bill Gorton, Romero, Count Mippipoplous, Count Greffi. Not that the essential pattern has changed. The hero is still paired with a friend more able than he, and more worldly wise. But the pair has moved one whole step toward the right, from defeat to undefeat. And the hero is now distinctly a man of lower class and lower intelligence. Garcia is the "little one with the white face"; his friend is the huge Zurito, ten years older, now retired, still the best picador alive. (The real Zurito, in *Death in the Afternoon*, was "the last and one of the greatest of the old-time picadors.") After moments that equal those of the great Belmonte, Garcia, booed by the crowd, and gored, finally kills his bull after five tries. As he goes into oblivion on the operating table, Zurito lets him keep his pigtail, the sign of the fighter, and assures him he was "going great."

It is a fine and moving story, completely presented. The feel and smell and excitement of the bullring are all there, created with remarkable reality from the bullfighter's point of view. The grandeur of undefeat shines from the tawdry surroundings—the heartless manager whose heart can yet light up for a second, the pathetic horses, the useless picadors, the hard crowd up there in the darkness, the jargonal reporter—with the solid Zurito to show that Garcia's dauntless end was unnecessary, and the young Hernandez to show that his beginning was happy. And because the story is cut down to Garcia's size—he cannot read, cannot find words for his thoughts—we have the reality of bullfighting as Hemingway was able to achieve it only occasionally, when he himself did not try to find words to defend all that lies beyond the only defensible area: a man's bravery, skill, and dedication.

The story comes from details firmly caught in Hemingway's imagination, details recorded and imagined in his first report to the Toronto *Star Weekly* and in his first bullfighting sketches—the dark interior from which the bull emerges, the bull turning like a cat, the gored matador and the "kid" who must try five times, only to sit vomiting before the dead bull as the crowd throws things, the "whacked" horses, the little bullfighter pelted and shorn of his pigtail, the fictional Maera first "bumped," then gored and dying on the operating table. All this comes together with the real Maera's great afternoon (in *Death in the Afternoon*) with a dislocated wrist and a bull "made out of cement." All has been re-projected from the point of view of a new imaginary Maera, a man much older, smaller, less skillful, less intelligent than the real Maera, in a triumphant extension of Hemingway's first imaginary projection of him. The young gypsy's excellent banderillaring is also an imaginative transfer of one of Maera's famous skills.

"Fifty Grand," which follows the superb "defeated" interlude of "In Another Country," is another story of an undefeated loser, and again, one of Hemingway's greatest stories. "The Undefeated" is tragic; "Fifty Grand" is comic. It is unique among Hemingway's stories in that the "I" is not the hero but a "character" (Jerry Doyle, the prizefighting hero's trainer). The narrative angle is similar to that of "My Old Man," except that the "I" is neither innocent nor instructed. But his limited intelligence turns all the tawdry details comic and frank, as against the reader's broader perceptions. The picture of the tough world and of Jack Brennan, homebody, worrywart, tightwad, fighter, emerges amusingly and gallantly as Doyle's tight lips give us the wisdom of the ring as if it were the wisdom of the world: "Jack got a good hand coming down through the crowd. Jack is Irish and the Irish always get a pretty good hand. An Irishman don't draw in New York like a Jew or an Italian but they always get a good hand."

Doyle's observations and omissions constantly give marvelous flashes of character and detail to solidify the boxing world, in which the champion moves:

> "What do you make it?" Jack asked the fellows who were weighing.
> "One hundred and forty-three pounds," the fat man who was weighing said.

Something in the colloquial rhythm, something in the weighty reply, something in the narrator's simple assumption that we know all about "weighing" and the fat man who does it, makes that solid flesh immortal.

This is the world that Hemingway first attempted in high school in "A Matter of Colour," and in his postgraduate course at the Chicago gym. But unlike the high-school story, "Fifty Grand" turns a tricked ending into a supreme test of wits and courage. The brave and amusing Brennan, the classic boxer who can out-gouge anyone in the clinches, the homebody who fights for a living, is to be seen again in Harry Morgan of *To Have and Have Not,* the buccaneer alone against a buccaneering world. Jack Brennan, as with the bullfighter before and Morgan after, was modeled on a man Hemingway admired: Jack Britton, who, as Hemingway was to tell Lillian Ross, "kept on his toes and moved around and never let them hit him solid."

* * *

Underneath the growing manuscript of Hemingway's modern *Tom Jones,* his third-person observation of the world, the old inner cry persisted. Early in March, 1928, Hemingway began his final telling of the story of the nurse in Milan, dropping the epic completely. He began *A Farewell to Arms* in Paris, continued during the spring and summer in Key West, wrote a good deal of the book in Havana, went on in Arkansas and Kansas City, and finished the first draft in Wyoming in August, six months later. In another five months, on January 22, 1929, he wrote Perkins that revision was complete. In May, *A Farewell to Arms* began to appear monthly in *Scribner's Magazine,* Hemingway changing galley proof all the way. Book proof arrived in Paris on June 5. Hemingway mailed it back on June 24, finally achieving a "new and better ending" after thirty-nine rewritings. Scribner's published it on September 27, 1929.

A Farewell to Arms is a welling up of the concern with birth and death with which Hemingway had begun *In Our Time,* together with his surrogate hero, Nick, wounded into separate peace, man against a senseless world. The Caesarian delivery of Hemingway's second son, Patrick, at the end of June, 1928—when the first draft was nearing completion—colored the Caesarian (and the paternal anxiety) with which Hemingway ends the book, and with which he had dealt in the first story of *In Our Time.* His father's suicide during the rewriting underlined the tragic, as his "Introduction" to the 1948 edition was to reveal:

> I remember all these things happening and all the places we lived in and the fine times and the bad times we had that year. But much more vividly I remember living in the book and making up what happened in it every day. Making the country and the people and

the things that happened I was happier than I had ever been. Each day I read the book through from the beginning to the point where I went on writing and each day I stopped when I was still going good and when I knew what would happen next. The fact that the book was a tragic one did not make me unhappy since I believed that life was a tragedy and knew it could only have one end. But finding you were able to make something up; to create truly enough so that it made you happy to read it; and to do this every day you worked was something that gave a greater pleasure than any I had ever known. Beside it nothing else mattered.

Hemingway's "making up" what happened is frequently a recapturing of country traversed before. Nick, wounded and propped against the church, and his friend Rinaldi became Lieutenant Frederic Henry and his roommate Rinaldi, now non-combatants, ambulance officer and surgeon. The unnamed soldier under bombardment at Fossalta who prays "Oh Jesus Christ get me out of here . . . please, please, please . . . I'll do anything you say" becomes young Henry, who, when blown up at night, says "Oh God get me out of here" and who prays, later, when his wife is dying: "Please, please, please don't let her die. God please make her not die. I'll do anything you say if you don't let her die."

Hemingway's Italian retreat from Caporetto, which he knew only by report, revives the Greek retreat from Adrianople (as Malcolm Cowley has detected), and revives it in the language both of his Toronto dispatch and of his revision for *In Our Time*. The Maritza River that "was running yellow almost up to the bridge" becomes the Tagliamento flooded "close under the wooden planking." The Thracian road is now Italian. Here is *In Our Time*: " . . . carts loaded with everything they owned. The old men and women, soaked through, walked along keeping the cattle moving. . . . The women and children were in the carts, crouched with mattresses, mirrors, sewing machines, bundles." Remembering other details reported to Toronto ("This main stream is being swelled from all the back country"—"Chickens dangle by their feet from the carts"), Hemingway now re-creates the Italian retreat:

> In the night many peasants had joined the column from the roads of the country and in the column there were carts loaded with household goods; there were mirrors projecting up between mattresses, and chickens and ducks tied to carts. There was a sewing-machine on the cart ahead of us in the rain. They had saved the most valuable things. On some carts the women sat huddled from the rain and others walked beside the carts keeping as close to them as they could.

As we have noted, the Thracian retreat taught Hemingway to saturate disaster with rain, as he does throughout the book.

Lieutenant Henry is almost an anthology of Lieutenant Nick (not to mention Jake Barnes and the "joke" Italian front). "In bed I lay me down my head," thinks Henry; and he has trouble sleeping without a light, prays hopelessly, has faith only during the fears of the night. He has a skull fracture, shuts off his thoughts, says of the war: "I'll tell you about it if I ever get it straight in my head." He is wounded in knee and calf; he exercises on machines in a Milan hospital to which he walks daily, looking in the shops; he knows his medals are undeserved; and, later, Italians shout at him, as at Nick, "*A basso gli ufficiali!*" The Italian major's advice to Nick sounds like an unheeded warning against Henry's tragedy: a man must not marry, for, "if he is to lose everything, he should not place himself in a position to lose that." As many have noted, Henry repeats Nick's very first words about making a "separate peace."

Of course, the story is significantly different from Nick's, and from the one first sketched about the nurse in *In Our Time*. Henry, an architectural student in Italy, joins the Italian ambulance corps because he can speak Italian. His roommate, Rinaldi, introduces him to Catherine Barkley, a Scotch nurse of the British Voluntary Aid Detachment. She carries the riding crop of a childhood fiancé recently killed in France. Henry makes advances; she slaps him, embraces him, says they will lead a strange life. "What the hell," thinks Henry. He is wounded by an explosion of a mortar shell while eating macaroni and cheese in an ambulance drivers' dugout. Catherine transfers to the Milan hospital, Henry falls in love in earnest, and Catherine becomes pregnant.

Henry returns to the front (October 4, 1917—Hemingway has again, as in *The Sun Also Rises*, put the story one year ahead of his personal life). He is just in time for the Italian retreat from Caporetto, from which, his trucks and men lost one by one, he finally deserts by leaping into the Tagliamento when battle police try to shoot him as a spy. In civilian clothes, he joins Catherine in the Italian Alps, from which they escape to Switzerland, rowing all night across a stormy lake. They wait for the baby, finally delivered, dead, as Catherine dies, and Henry walks back to the hotel, alone, in the rain.

Robert Penn Warren, triangulating from Hemingway's other work, has admirably described what this is supposed to mean. The story does catch, as Warren says, the long rumble of disintegrating Christian and social faith that reached a crescendo in World War I. Henry wants some kind of faith like that of the priest in the officers' mess, who comes from mountains where a man may love God, and religion "is not a dirty joke." Henry will find his faith in the religion of love, and will learn, as the priest says, to sacrifice and to serve. Henry learns, says Warren, that personal love is doomed by all the accidents of a blackguard universe, that the whole is "just a dirty trick" after all—"But this is not to deny the value of the effort, or to deny the value of the discipline, the code, the stoic endurance, the things that make it true—or half true—that 'nothing ever happens to the brave.'"

Unfortunately, this does not fit Henry, as it does fit Manuel and Hemingway's other undefeated losers. Henry is not wholly one of the "disciplined": he finds that his officering is first unnecessary, then ineffective, then meaningless. Even the disciplined Rinaldi goes glum, his surgical skill no longer adequate protection from the diseased world. Henry is not one of the brave: he knows his batting is only average. Henry may have learned "the value of effort," though Hemingway is far from intent on the demonstration. Henry does say, "It has only happened to me like that once," as he looks back on the story he is telling, exactly as Nick looks back in "Now I Lay Me," when all was long ago and he has never married. In this single remark, Henry indicates that he has learned the full value of what he has lost. But Warren's "effort" can mean only the effort to make love last, which is something different from "the discipline, the code, the stoic endurance." James Light and others who laud Henry's stoicism merely extend Warren's misreading.

Henry is not one of the undefeated, nor is he one of the defeated so sweetly drawn in the alienated Nick and the sleepless Nick, so commendably drawn in Barnes. Henry is still capable of action, and his own action defeats him, contrary, I think, to what Hemingway intends and Warren reads. Jake Barnes is a rugged name and man, whom war has prepared for Brett's slaughter. Nick Adams has the very name of Man, but war has nicked him and knocked him out. And in his defeat he eventually invites, I believe, a faint sneer from his creator, who calls him a condescending "Nicholas." "Frederic Henry" has the same faint scorn in it, the faintly effeminate ring already heard in the "Henry" on the lips of the Doctor's wife, in "Henry" Braddocks and in the chauffeur Henry of *The Sun Also Rises,* and in other recurrent Henrys. As Young suggests, Hemingway may have adapted the name from Stephen Crane, whose own frequent and slightly patronized Henrys culminate in Henry Fleming (a name virtually the reverse of "Frederic Henry") of *The Red Badge of Courage.* Hemingway may have seen the name as a kind of personal anagram, half-conscious and self-accusatory: "Henry" compressed from "Hemingway," with "Frederic" another first name calling for defense. We will see the same thing in the naming of Francis Macomber—in a story that may, as Young suggests, derive its plot from Crane's *Red Badge.* Even a *k* on "Frederic" would have toughened it slightly. Is Henry's name "Frederico Enrico or Enrico Federico?"—an Italian messmate asks (Rinaldi calls him "Federico," without the *r*). To be sure, Hemingway may have been thinking of Frederic Manning, soldier and avant-garde writer in Paris, whose *The Middle Parts of Fortune* (published in 1929, contemporaneously with *A Farewell to Arms*) Hemingway was to read each year on the anniversary of Hemingway's (and Henry's) wounding. Again, we may think of *Henry IV,* whence big-game hunter Wilson's brave motto, and even of Frederick the Great. But Hemingway and the modern world have undermined the glory in those names. "Frederic Henry" is a strange name for a modern hero, alongside the Nicks and Jakes and Jacks.

Hemingway's uncertainty, uncontrolled because not thoroughly understood, follows Henry to the end. In spite of feminine shadows, Henry is an astounding lover, a man's man, well-liked by barkeep and count, able at doing "those things that gave you a false sense of soldiering"; slightly contemptuous of the real soldier, slightly contemptuous of his own job, too, yet disappointed to see how well it runs without him. He is an officer—an officer in an army not an army, somewhat behind the lines of a secondary front: in the war but not of it. There is with Henry, from the beginning, a sense of uneasiness, of disillusion, about one's role.

There is, indeed, a strange confusion of male and female which, though poetic and almost choreographic, probably goes deeper than Hemingway knew. In the beginning, cartridge boxes on the belts of muddy troops "bulged forward under the capes so that the men, passing on the road, marched as though they were six months gone with child"; and at the end, Catherine out walking on the road "did not look big with the cape . . . ." In the beginning, we have Henry and Rinaldi, his roommate who kisses him and calls him "baby" in the Italian manner; in the end, Catherine and Henry. The book begins, on the masculine side of the dance, as if a married couple and not a group of men—indeed as if a wife—were looking out at the war: "In the late summer of that year we lived in a house in a village that looked across the river and the plain to the mountains. . . . Troops went by the house and down the road. . . ." The second chapter begins with identical domesticity, even more cloistered: "we" are now living "in a house in Gorizia that had a fountain and many thick shady trees in a walled garden and a wistaria vine purple on the side of the house." This is indistinguishable from the domesticity of Catherine and Henry at the end: "That fall the snow came very late. We lived in a brown wooden house in the pine trees on the side of the mountain. . . ." At the end, the magic of the mountains, as Carlos Baker says, is at work. But at the beginning, the untutored reader may be surprised when he finally comes upon the soft-voiced narrator looking at the snow out of the window of a bawdy house, an officer drinking with another officer. At the beginning, whether we like it or not, the anonymous Frederic Henry sounds very much like a woman.

At the end, when Henry is supposed to be disciplined and stoic and filled with valuable effort, we find that he is in fact unmanned by Catherine, defeated by Catherine, as Theodore Bardacke has pointed out, in his "Hemingway's Women," just as surely as Barnes is unmanned vis-à-vis Brett. Hemingway's basic distrust of women has unstrung his lyre. The nurse who threw him over will not wholly convert into the lady true unto death. Catherine of the long blond hair, which first catches Henry's eye, which tents their kisses in bed, is not so womanly as Hemingway seems to suppose. She is uncomfortably similar to the sleek British Brett of Jake's hospital tour. Young has already noted their similar backgrounds as nurses with lovers killed in the war. Catherine is also narrow of hip; she wants to bob her hair, to forget maternity. She makes Henry her plaything, having him grow a beard (on which he asks instructions), wanting him to grow his hair a little longer: "... and I could cut mine and we'd be just alike only one of us blonde and one of us dark." Make me a boy again just for tonight! She wants "to be you too"; she wants "us to be all mixed up." She does not really want him to go skiing with the men; and Henry replies, "I won't ever go away. . . . I'm no good when you're not there. I haven't any life at all any more." When Catherine says that she will cut her hair when she is thin again, and become "a fine new and different girl" for him to fall in love with:

> "Hell," I said. "I love you enough now. What do you want to do? Ruin me?"
> "Yes. I want to ruin you."
> "Good," I said, "That's what I want too."

What Henry thinks in his last phase, he does not record. He tries not to think. We do learn that the beard makes him self-conscious in the shadow-boxing mirror at the gym, and that it makes him seem in the hospital mirror "a fake doctor with a beard." But he likes it; it gives him "something to do." Catherine likes it: "It looks so stiff and fierce and it's very soft and a great pleasure." It is a perfect symbol for Henry's disguised effeminacy, fierce yet false, really soft to please a woman. Henry is much the war-numbed Nick, also much the man forbearing with a woman with child, giving and serving at last as the priest said he would. But he is unmanned nevertheless; and the beard (as with Hemingway's own) makes a compensation too obvious. Awake one night, he hears Catherine, also lying awake, mention her first "craziness." He lies "awake for quite a long time thinking about things and watching Catherine sleeping, the moonlight on her face."

Life with the beautiful Catherine does arouse uneasy thought. She remains something of a puzzle to the reader. Edmund Wilson and Malcolm Cowley and others have found her unsatisfactory, a masculine daydream on paper; and Carlos Baker has only called up other unsatisfactory heroines in her defense. Cowley, indeed, has hit the startling truth when he says that she is credible only at the beginning—"in her near madness." Actually, Catherine, who continues to say that she is "all right now" and no longer "crazy," retains uncomfortable touches of madness—among which, her very protestations—until pregnancy takes its benign effect. Hemingway records a clinical history he seems not to understand, just as he fails to see through the twilight of his hero.

Catherine is afraid of the rain, because she sees herself dead in it. On the other hand, she is strangely blithe, living in the moment, careless of contraception, of marriage, of pregnancy, of going A.W.O.L., of Henry's deserting, of danger, of crossing a stormy lake with little concern. She has no religion, none of Henry's feeling that perhaps one should. She goes into sudden reverie, thinking her first sexual experience the same as her madness:

She came back from wherever she had been.

"I had a very fine little show and I'm all right now. You see I'm not mad and I'm not gone off. It's only a little sometimes."

When she tells Henry she is pregnant, she suddenly goes "away a long way" and comes "back from wherever she had been"—a phrase to knell ominously at the end when, after temporary anesthetic, she "came back from a long way away."

And with all the cheeriness, she is paranoid: "We work very hard but no one trusts us"—"there's only us two and in the world there's all the rest of them. If anything comes between us we're gone and then they have us." This, the two "alone against the others," Henry eventually takes for his own, now needing Catherine to keep him from fears of the night. Henry and Hemingway take this strange insulation of Catherine's as "so much courage" that the world must finally break her. To be sure, Catherine is attractive scene by scene, and perfectly credible, with her ability to make a cot a home, her daintiness of nightgown, her pleasant spirits; but she remains ephemeral because neither Henry nor Hemingway can add her scenes accurately. Hemingway has unwittingly, I think, written the story that also defeated F. Scott Fitzgerald in *Tender is the Night,* though Fitzgerald at least knew what he was attempting: the story of a man unmanned in trying to serve the charming fey.

Perhaps the real source of our uneasiness (and of Hemingway's) is Henry himself. Hemingway writes a story about manhood and self-respect lost for a love that ends in death, and he thinks he has written of a transcendent love crushed by a meaningless world, and of a man learning to take the ultimate loss. Henry is ruined by woman, not by the world; and he is enough of the man of action to be vaguely haunted by a mistake neither he nor Hemingway can admit, though they suggest its pressure.

For Henry's "separate peace," contrary to several distinguished opinions, is not that announced by young Nick to his Rinaldi. Nick had been joking, as he notes with satisfaction that the battle is succeeding on up the street and that the stretchers soon will come. He and Rinaldi are no longer "patriots"—

apparently the term, in the slightly anarchistic Italian army, for the eager soldier, the military apple-polisher of any army. Like swallow-tailed ambassadors, Nick and Rinaldi have made a "separate peace," in a phrase then current among the uneasy allies. Nick is joking because they have been knocked out of the war and out of patriotism by enemy gunfire. Their peace has been not at all of their own making. Lieutenant Henry's peace, however, is of his own making. He is hale and on his feet. He deserts a disintegrating army, angry, to be sure, and with considerable provocation. But he has taken the action. Now, in civilian clothes, he is in a train with some scornful aviators (shades of Jake Barnes!). They leave. He does not want to read the paper: "I was going to forget the war. I had made a separate peace. I felt damned lonely. . . ."

Henry has deserted, saving himself through anger and for love. He knows that the unpatriotic Piani will return to the unit, more constant though with much less danger. Henry's conscience bothers him, but soon Catherine absorbs even this:

> It was clouding over outside and the lake was darkening.
> "I wish we did not always have to live like criminals." I said.
> "Darling, don't be that way. You haven't lived like a criminal very long. And we never live like criminals. We're going to have a fine time."
> "I feel like a criminal. I've deserted from the army."
> "Darling, *please* be sensible. It's not deserting from the army. It's only the Italian army."
> I laughed. "You're a fine girl. Let's get back into bed. I feel fine in bed."

Henry's symbolic resignation from society, which we accept with lessened qualms, Warren points out, because it is only the Italian army, leaves Henry the misgivings he can forget only in Catherine's arms. Like the war-numbed Nick, he stops his mind from thinking; but with Nick it was horror, and with Henry it is guilt. "Abstract words such as glory, honor, courage, or hallow were obscene beside the concrete names of villages, . . . the numbers of regiments and the dates." True. But as Henry attempts to reject the society that has mouthed the words (and has kept paying his sight-drafts without question), he cannot forget, as Hemingway himself could not, that he bore no honored nor courageous number, that he was only a pseudo-officer, that his medals were slightly spurious. Henry is enough of an undefeated man of action to leave him, and us, uneasy about his defeated inaction at the end. Catherine's death, which leaves him utterly alone in the rain, cannot quite weigh as an indictment of the world and its wars, nor as a lesson for Henry, nor as a splendor of irrational ironies, hardly even as a tragedy of young life wasted in the world's tangle—the *Romeo and Juliet* that Hemingway and Carlos Baker have hoped it to be. The meaning simply drifts away, uncertainly, in the rain.

But the book has a poetry that almost holds it together: *A Farewell to Arms*—the lonely, lyric *A*, the heraldic diction. The title is poetic, indeed, being also the title of a poem by the Elizabethan, George Peele, who regretfully bids both the arms of glory and the arms of love farewell, as Philip Young and Jerome L. Mazzaro have pointed out. Professor Harry Levin has thought that the title came from Richard Lovelace. And though Lovelace can show no phrase even close, no such pun on the arms of love and war, Hemingway's sweet goodbye would certainly have been stronger and truer if, indeed, his Henry had flown to Warre and Armes, and not from them, if he had tried to rejoin his scattered unit though a Hell of carabinieri should bar the way, though he should have been disgracefully shot, knowing that he could not love his Dear so much loved he not Honour more.

But the song goes flat only after the flight to Switzerland, and we realize that a peg must have slipped unnoticed. Minute by minute, the song is, in Warren's word, hypnotic, as it sings of what it is like to be in a war in a world adrift, and to know the excitements of love made reckless in consequence. The march of the seasons, chapter by chapter, the ominous march of the rain, the two alone in the night against the flashes of war, yes, it is good:

> That night a bat flew into the room through the open door that led onto the balcony and through which we watched the night over the roofs of the town. It was dark in our room except for the small light of the night over the town and the bat was not frightened but hunted in the room as though he had been outside. We lay and watched him and I do not think he saw us because we lay so still. After he went out we saw a searchlight come on and watched the beam move across the sky and then go off and it was dark again. A breeze came in the night and we heard the men of the anti-aircraft gun on the next roof talking.

Hemingway has in fact used poetry itself for his poetic effects: Henry quotes Marvell's famous couplet (learned from the man who made it famous, T. S. Eliot, as Donna Gerstenberger has shown and Hemingway himself has indicated in *Death in the Afternoon*):

> But at my back I always hear
> Time's wingèd chariot hurrying near.

And toward the end, the lovers feel "as though something were hurrying us and we could not lose any time together." The little pre-Elizabethan lyric about the western wind and the small rain and love's arms is even more intricately suffused through Henry's thoughts of Catherine during the retreat, as Charles R. Anderson has shown in his "Hemingway's Other Style." Hemingway's characteristic reiteration of word, phrase, and picture are beautifully and darkly expanded so that the essential lyric cry of self is braided with harmonics from beginning to end. And the construction is nicely balanced: "pregnant" troops at the beginning, pregnant Catherine at the end; statues in the hospital as Henry meets Catherine, Catherine dead in the hospital like a statue, as he leaves her.

As with the exposition, so with the scenes—Catherine in the red plush room, Henry and the pompous doctors:

> "Do you want to keep your knee, young man?"
> "No," I said.
> "What?"
> "I want it cut off." I said, "so I can wear a hook on it."

The secondary characterizations are perfect: Rinaldi, and Valentini the other surgeon, and Ferguson, and Count Greffi (one of Ezra Pound's old men with "beautiful manners"), and the wonderful Italian ambulance drivers—the kind of idiomatic portraiture Hemingway first struck in "Out of Season," and continued in "Now I Lay Me." The whole retreat from Caporetto is as vivid as anything Hemingway ever wrote, subtly touched with reminders of love sacred and profane, the soldier's only solace (as Anderson says): the harlot of the fluttering tongue, the frightened virgins, the inexplicit dream of Catherine. The book is full of the kind of writing and seeing that would make its author happy every day: the "sudden interiors of houses that had lost a wall through shelling"; troops that "moved smoothly, almost super-naturally" over a bridge, before Henry sees that they are on bicycles; or this: "I sat up straight and as I did so something inside my head moved like the weights on a doll's eyes and it hit me inside in back of my eyeballs."

Yet, as Edmund Wilson said some time ago and I am surprised to discover, *A Farewell to Arms* is a lesser book than *The Sun Also Rises*, even a lesser love story. The romantic cry is not so true, nor even so sad, since Henry leaves us trying to blame the world for private deficiencies as well as for Catherine's death, and a still, small Tiresian voice warns us against trying to smoke the bounder out. The little major of "In Another Country" was completely convincing, as was the unwarranted death of his young wife. His is a world of some cruel whim, and his cry that one should not marry and expose oneself is right from the heart. But Henry is so unmanned by his wife, as the major is not, that toward the end we can almost read a resentful cryptogram, to the effect that men can remain undefeated only without women.

MICHAEL S. REYNOLDS

Going Back

> So we walked along through the street where I saw my very good friend
> killed, . . . and it all seemed a very sad business. I had tried to recreate
> something for my wife and had failed utterly. The past was as dead as
> a busted victrola record. Chasing yesterdays is a bum show—and if you
> have to prove it go back to your old front.
>
> —Ernest Hemingway "A Veteran Visits Old Front"
> (*TDS*, July 22, 1922)

When Frederic Henry, hero of Hemingway's *A Farewell to Arms*, lived
in the house "that looked across the river and the plain to the mountains,"
it was the late summer of 1915. Italy had just entered the European War,
and Ernest Hemingway had just turned sixteen in upper Michigan. In the
spring of 1918, Catherine Barkley died in childbirth in Lausanne, Switzerland; in April, 1918, Ernest Hemingway drew his last pay check from the
Kansas City Star and left for his own war experience in northern Italy.[1]

When he reached Italy in 1918 for his shortlived tour as a Red Cross
ambulance driver, the Italian front bore no resemblance to the front at
which Frederic had served for two years as an ambulance driver in the Italian army. In June, 1918, American Red Cross Ambulance Section Four, to
which Hemingway was assigned, was stationed at Schio in the Dolomite

In *Hemingway's First War: The Making of* A Farewell to Arms (Princeton, N. J.: Princeton
University Press, 1976): pp. 3–19. Copyright © 1976 Princeton University Press.

foothills. Although there was a major Austrian offensive in June, there was little action at Schio. Hemingway drove Section Four ambulances for only three weeks. In July he asked to be transferred to the canteen operation along the more active Piave river front. At Fossalta di Piave, on July 8, 1918, he was blown up by an Austrian trench mortar. He had been in the war zone for about one month, and he was not to return to it actively in that war.[2]

Carlos Baker has remarked that Hemingway was acutely conscious of *place*, and that he was painfully accurate in his geographic descriptions.[3] Mary Hemingway has described the careful checking of street names and distances that Hemingway put into *A Moveable Feast*.[4] Hemingway himself said that his concern was for "the way it was," which he loosely defined as "the people, the places, and how the weather was." Against this concern it is difficult to balance his lack of firsthand knowledge of the Italian front of 1915–1917. He had not seen the Tagliamento river when he wrote *A Farewell to Arms*; he had not walked the Venetian plain between Codroipo and Latisana. It was not until 1948 that he saw Udine.[5] He may never have seen Gorizia, the Isonzo river, Plava, or the Bainsizza plateau; he certainly had not seen them when he wrote the novel. His return trip to Fossalta di Piave in 1922 and his skiing trip at Cortina d'Ampezzo in 1923 did not take him to the terrain of the novel. His 1927 trip to Italy with Guy Hickock did not cover the war zone of 1915–1917.[6] Not only had Hemingway not experienced the military engagements in which Frederic Henry takes part, but he had not seen the terrain of Books One and Three of *A Farewell to Arms*. Yet the geography is perfectly accurate and done with the clarity that made its author famous for his descriptions of place.

Because the Caporetto section (Book Three) is so powerfully written, most critics have confined their remarks about military descriptions to this portion of the book, being content to make generalizations about the remainder of the military activity in the novel. Book Three has been widely recognized for its narrative excellence, and early reviewers like Malcolm Cowley, Percy Hutchinson, and H. S. Canby responded to Hemingway's power in this section.[7] Canby called the description of the retreat a "masterly piece of *reporting*" (my emphasis).[8] Yet none of these men had served on the Italian front and should not be expected to notice minor inaccuracies if they existed.

Later critics, more knowledgeable about Hemingway's biography, knew that he had not participated in the retreat; but they also knew that he had covered the Greek retreat in the Greco-Turkish War (1922) as a journalist. It was an easy assumption that Hemingway had transposed his Greek experience to the Friulian plain of northern Italy: steady rain, muddy roads, stumbling refugees. What this assumption fails to account for is the considerable amount of specific detail in Book Three of *A Farewell to Arms* that has nothing to do with muddy roads or refugees.

One would expect European readers to be more critical. Yet one French reviewer wrote: "The one aspect of the last war which has least interested writers is the defeat. . . . There has been need for an American witness on the Alpine front who could reveal to us, in its abject horror, the Italian rout near Caporetto: . . . If Hemingway has not dedicated all his book to this debacle, . . . one can believe that he had to obey autobiographical motives."[9]

Italian critics, some of whom took part in the Caporetto retreat, were unable to find any fault with Hemingway's history or geography. The Italian fascist government under Mussolini found the account of Caporetto so painful, and presumably so accurate, that *A Farewell to Arms* was banned in Italy until after World War Two. In 1930 one Italian reviewer saw the novel as unvarnished autobiography: "[The novel] narrates autobiographically his experience as an officer on the Italian front after he, although a foreigner, enlisted in our army as a volunteer, more through the desire to do like everyone else (he was already in Italy as an architecture student) than through ideological dedication; and then of his flight as a deserter after Caporetto . . . every page of the books resembles a sheet torn from a notebook. . . . One hears the eulogy of the Duke of Aosta pronounced in words so banal and nasty as to move anyone who remembers the Duke and those years at all well to protest. . . . *the time is objectively precise, with references to dates and 'historical' episodes*, but it has no color, no duration . . . diary composition comes to mind . . . rather too scrupulous and unified." (My emphasis)[10]

Twenty-five years later another Italian critic, reading the book more sympathetically and more nostalgically, was no less convinced of the historic and geographic accuracy: "Four-fifths of the work unfolds in Northern Italy, in Milan and above all among the hills, mountains and plains of the Veneto which are particularly dear to my heart. *Every landscape evoked in the now famous novel, every place cited, is familiar to me. . . . The novel . . . evokes the climate of the first two years of the war until the disaster of Caporetto with extraordinary vivacity. . . . All that his protagonist narrates has an undeniable sound of authenticity. . . .* After the intoxication of the days in May (*which he does not mention but in which he* [Hemingway] *certainly must have taken part to be led to enlist and leave for the front during his stay in Italy*) he found himself in a country in which the war was not felt but only submitted to as a calamitous circumstance *. . . this actually was . . . the climate of Italy between the summer of 1915 and the autumn of 1917. The picture painted by Hemingway is exact. . . . one who wishes to know what the defeat was like in the minds of officers and soldiers of the Second Army after Caporetto can read* A Farewell to Arms. Perhaps in no other book are the tragic days relived with such intensity. . . . Only one who truly loves the country, who has suffered there and lived there intensely can describe the Venetian countryside, or speak of the disaster of Caporetto as Ernest Hemingway has done." (My emphasis)[11]

In 1954 Alberto Rossi, who had collaborated on several translations of Hemingway novels into Italian, reviewed Charles Fenton's *The Apprenticeship of Ernest Hemingway*. Rossi reminded his Italian readers that Hemingway's considerable talents are above all "his ability to present a situation as actually lived with a few well-chosen touches; one tends instinctively to identify the character who narrates with the author himself, and thus to attribute to the author the intention of affirming, as authentic and experienced by him, all the details of his own story." But Rossi had great difficulty in believing that Hemingway had not taken part in the retreat from Caporetto: "That the work was in effect one of imagination and not of history, however evident this seems, was not an affirmation which could satisfy everyone's curiosity." He was perplexed by the accuracy he could not account for biographically: "It is no less evident that for certain parts of that novel his imagination was not working on data of direct experience; and among these is the impressive evocation of the retreat."[12]

Even after Malcolm Cowley, in the introduction to the *Portable Hemingway*, pointed out that the author had not taken part in the Caporetto retreat, American critics failed to question Hemingway's accuracy. The main stream of Hemingway criticism has followed either Carlos Baker into romantic and biographic criticism or Philip Young into psychological analyses, all of which were encouraged by the virile public image Hemingway cultivated. One need only to read through the massive bibliography of Hemingway criticism to see how limited most second- and third-generation criticism has become and how debilitating it has been for the novels.[13]

As early as 1922, Hemingway had begun to formulate a method of dealing with reality. In a feature story for the *Toronto Daily Star*, "A Veteran Visits Old Front," he told how depressing it was to return to the scene of battles he had taken part in, for the country was so changed that it ruined the memory. It would have been better to have visited a battle site he had not known: "Go to someone else's front if you want to. *There your imagination will help you out and you may be able to picture the things that happened*" [my emphasis].[14] This same idea appears in the deleted coda to "Big Two-Hearted River" (c. 1924):

> *The only writing that was any good was what you made up, what you imagined.* . . . You had to digest life and then create your own people. . . . Nick in the stories was never himself. He had made him up. Of course he'd never seen an Indian woman having a baby. That was what made it good. [My emphasis][15]

In a 1935 *Esquire* article Hemingway gave a somewhat fuller statement on the point:

> Good writing is true writing. If a man is making a story up it will be true in proportion to the amount of knowledge of life he has and how *conscientious* he is; so that when he makes something up it is as it truly would be. . . . Imagination is the one thing beside honesty that a good writer must have, the more he learns from experience the more truly he can imagine. *If he gets so he can imagine truly enough people will think that the things he relates all really happened and that he is just reporting.* [My emphasis][16]

In 1948, when he wrote his own introduction for an illustrated edition of *A Farewell to Arms*, Hemingway made no pretense of having experienced the historical events of the novel firsthand:

> I remember living in the book and making up what happened in it every day. Making the country and the people and the things that happened I was happier than I had ever been. . . . Finding you were able to make something up; to create truly enough so that it made you happy to read it.[17]

And in 1958, when he was interviewed by the *Paris Review,* Hemingway restated his position with the same simplicity he had used in 1922:

> Q: Have you ever described any type of situation of which you had no personal knowledge?
> A: That is a strange question. . . . A writer, if he is any good does not describe. *He invents or makes out of his knowledge personal and impersonal.* [My emphasis][18]

Over a thirty-six-year span, Hemingway's attitude toward his profession remained constant on the point of "making it up." Yet no one ever took him very seriously, for he had been typed as an autobiographic writer when he published *The Sun Also Rises.* His statements about invented action on the basis of knowledge "personal and impersonal" appeared either simpleminded or some sort of ruse. They were neither.

In his terse disciplinary sketches written in 1922–1923, Hemingway had already developed an objective style that treated the experience of others as his own. Of the eighteen sketches, called "chapters," collected in the 1924 edition of *in our time,* eight were based on second-hand information. Two of the sketches were based on the war experiences of his British friend, Captain

E. E. Dorman-Smith, at the fighting around Mons. Another (Chapter 16) described the goring and death of the matador Maera. At the time Hemingway had never seen a bullfight, and Maera was very much alive. Hemingway based his description on conversations with Mike Strater and Gertrude Stein. Chapter 6, which describes the inglorious execution of the deposed Greek cabinet ministers, was based on a newspaper clipping. The ninth chapter, which describes the shooting of the cigar-store bandits, was based on a story in the *Kansas City Star* from Nov. 19, 1917. The hanging of Sam Cardinella (Chapter 17) probably came from either police-station or city-room gossip from the Kansas City days. The description of the King of Greece in his garden (Chapter 18) was based on information related to Hemingway by an acquaintance who had an informal interview with the king.[19] From the beginning Hemingway felt free to use second-hand sources.

After Hemingway showered Stephen Crane with praise in his introduction to *Men at War,* critics began to note thematic and structural similarities between *The Red Badge of Courage* and *A Farewell to Arms.* What was carefully ignored by the critics was the reason why Hemingway said he admired Crane's novel:

> Crane wrote [*The Red Badge of Courage*] before he had ever seen any war. But he had read contemporary accounts, had heard the old soldiers, they were not so old then, talk, and above all he had seen Matthew Brady's wonderful photographs. Creating his story out of this material he wrote that great boy's dream of war that was to be truer to how war is than any war the boy who wrote it would ever live to see. It is one of the finest books in our literature and I include it entire because it is all as much of one piece as a great poem is.[20]

Hemingway's praise is neither for Crane's structure nor for his theme; the praise is for the technique and the verity. In 1928, when he was writing his first war novel, Hemingway already knew about Crane's research method in *The Red Badge of Courage.* While working on the *Transatlantic Review* in 1924, Hemingway served as a sub-editor under Ford Madox Ford. Ford had known Crane during the Brede Manor days in England, and later Ford both wrote and lectured on the young American writer. One of the things that Ford knew about Crane, and that was not public knowledge, was the way in which Crane had researched his war novel. During Hemingway's association with Ford in 1924, he must have heard the anecdote, probably more than once. Crane's research methods that Hemingway chose to praise—reading histories, talking to veterans, and looking at pictures—were the same methods that Hemingway used on *A Farewell to Arms.*

As early as 1922, Hemingway had already done sufficient historical reading to pose as an expert on a war in which he had served only briefly and that he later admitted he did not understand. When he wrote his *Toronto Daily Star* feature, "A Veteran Visits Old Front" (July 1922), he created the flat tone of the seasoned campaigner, alluding to many more events than he had experienced:

> I remember . . . looking out the window down at the road where the arc light was making a dim light through the rain. It was the same road that the battalions marched along through the white dust in 1916. They were the Brigata Ancona, the Brigata Como, the Brigata Tuscana and ten others brought down from the Carso, to check the Austrian offensive that was breaking through the mountain wall of the Trentino and beginning to spill down the valleys that led to the Venetian and Lombardy plains. They were good troops in those days and they marched through the dust of early summer, broke the offensive along the Gallo-Asiago-Canove line, and died in the mountain gullies, in the pine woods on the Trentino slopes, hunting cover on the desolate rocks and pitched out in the soft-melting early summer snow of the Pasubio.
>
> It was the same old road that some of the same brigades marched along through the dust in June 1918, being rushed to the Piave to stop another offensive. Their best men were dead on the rocky Carso in the fighting around Goritzia,[21] on Mount San Gabrielle, on Grappa, and in all the places where men died that nobody ever heard about.

When he wrote those words Hemingway had never seen the Carso, Gorizia, or Mount San Gabrielle. When the road turned dust at Schio in 1916, he was preparing for his senior year in high school. The journalist must always be the expert, and he had already developed a keen sense of the insider's information. He had learned that hard facts create an immediate sense of authenticity. Those were not just soldiers on any road—they were specific brigades who died at specific places. In order to write this article, Hemingway had done extensive reading on the art of war, which he continued throughout his life. He may not have known in 1922 how much he would need that reading in 1928 when he came to write *A Farewell to Arms*, but in the manuscript of the novel, historical facts, dates, places, and events roll from the writer's pencil with facility and accuracy.

In that 1922 visit to Schio, Hemingway realized a truth that he passed on to his readers and that he remembered when he tried to make fictional sense of his own war experience:

> Don't go back to visit the old front. If you have pictures in your head of something that happened in the night in the mud at Paschendaele, or of the first wave working up the slope of Vimy, do not try and go back and verify them. It is no good. The front is different from the way it used to be. . . . Go to someone else's front if you want to. There your imagination will help you out and you may be able to picture the things that happened. . . . The past was as dead as a busted victrola record. Chasing yesterdays is a bum show—and if you have to prove it go back to your old front.[22]

If he functions in the realist/naturalist tradition, a writer is always chasing yesterdays. In writing *A Farewell to Arms*, however, Hemingway went back to someone else's front and recreated the experience from books, maps, and firsthand sources. It is his only novel set on terrain with which he did not have personal experience; in it, his imagination, aided by military histories, has recreated the Austro-Italian front of 1915–1917 more vividly than any other writer.

Hemingway, the public man, may have been just as much of a romantic as some readers would see him, and many of his plots may have smelled of the museums, as Gertrude Stein thought. But as an artist, Hemingway was able to approach his material in those early years with an objectivity that never allowed personal experience or friendships to interfere with his fiction. Like most twentieth-century innovators, he found himself his own best subject, but to mistake his art for his biography is to mistake illusion for reality. In *Green Hills of Africa* no reader can believe that the dialogue is a reportorial account of what was actually said, or that there is no artistry in Hemingway's arrangement of the action. Even in *A Moveable Feast*, Hemingway warns the reader: "If the reader prefers, this book may be regarded as fiction. But there is always some chance that such a book of fiction may throw some light on what has been written as fact."[23]

To read any of Hemingway's fiction as biography is always dangerous, but to read *A Farewell to Arms* in this manner is to misread the book. Hemingway himself was particularly anxious, during those early years, for Scribner's to keep biographical statements about him out of print. In letters to his editor, Max Perkins, he urged that the critics and readers be allowed to make up their own lies (Feb. 14, 1927). He belittled his own war experiences, telling Perkins that the medals had been given to him simply because he was an American attached to the Italian army. One medal, he insisted, was awarded for action on Monte Maggiore when he was three hundred kilometers away in a hospital at the time. He did not want anyone to think him a faker, a liar, or a fool (Feb. 19, 1929). Perkins agreed to correct misinformation that Scribner's had unknowingly given out to the media and to restrain the publicity department in the future, remarking that usually authors were so intent on such publicity that it had not occurred to him that Hemingway might be sensitive on the point.

Like most of his central characters, Hemingway in 1928–1929 preferred to exist in the present tense, with as little reference to the past as possible, particularly his private past. Later, when biographical critics like Fenton and Young began to probe into his private life, Hemingway resented it bitterly. In a letter to Carlos Baker, he said that biographies of living writers were destructive in several ways. Because all writers wrote out of their own experience, the premature biographer was nothing more than a spoiler, ruining experiences that the writer might have turned into fiction. All writers, he insisted, write about living people; that is, they use them for the base upon which they build their fictional characters. Biographical critics were forcing him to create characters no longer credible because he had become so conscious of covering up the original.[24]

Readers have always wanted to see the heroes as projections of their author, and critics have generally promoted the parallel. Hemingway, however, in the Twenties never encouraged the parallelism. He admitted to using real prototypes for characters, like Cohn in *The Sun Also Rises*, but he felt that most of the characters he used did not read books.[25] Unfortunately, *The Sun Also Rises* was read as a thinly veiled who's who of Paris and Pamplona, and Hemingway was never able to convince his critics afterwards that he did not do this all the time or that his central character was not himself. In 1926, he told Scott Fitzgerald that in spite of what he and Zelda always thought, "Cat in the Rain" was not a story about Hemingway and Hadley. He explained that the two characters were a Harvard graduate and his wife whom he had met in Genoa.[26]

To read *A Farewell to Arms* as biography is to believe that Hemingway learned nothing from *The Torrents of Spring* and *The Sun Also Rises*, where the use of real people had caused him considerable difficulty. In the correspondence with Maxwell Perkins during the galley-proof stage of *The Sun Also Rises*, Perkins asked him to make numerous small changes to avoid libel suits. After much bargaining, Hemingway obscured references to Glenway Wescott, Hilaire Belloc, Joseph Hergesheimer, and Henry James. In *The Sun Also Rises* there is still a passing remark about "Henry's bicycle," which in the manuscript referred to Henry James's apocryphal groin injury similar to the one of Jake Barnes. Perkins advised Hemingway: "As for Henry James, you know how we feel about it. . . . this town and Boston are full of people who knew him and who cannot regard him as you do, i.e. as an historical character. There are four right in this office who were his friends. . . . Then as to the fact of a groin injury, I have inquired into it and it is at most, extremely doubtful. Van Wyck Brooks who questioned everyone who knew James, does not believe it, nor anyone here. There are a variety of rumors, and many obvious lies, but no certainty."[27] Hemingway removed James's name, finally admitting that it was a mistake to put real people in a book. He vowed not to make the same mistake again. That same year, 1926, John Dos Passos criticized Hemingway's use of actual people and names in his writing. Hemingway agreed with Dos Passos. He explained that in *Torrents of Spring* he was satirizing that type of writing, but concluded that it was still a bad thing to do.[28]

When Hemingway began the holograph manuscript of *A Farewell to Arms* in the spring of 1928, he consciously avoided actual names and people wherever he could. He could not altogether eliminate prominent names in an historical novel, but people like King Emmanuel and the Duke of Aosta are mentioned only in passing and are kept well offstage. The central characters were based on real people, but they were not meant to be those people. Hemingway used people he knew as models much as a painter will use a model. Frederic Henry is not Ernest Hemingway at the Italian front, for Frederic is no nineteen-year-old novice. Catherine Barkley may possess some of the physical features of a nurse in Milan but she also resembles several other women Hemingway had known.

Guy Hickok, who read the novel in manuscript, recognized something of Hemingway's second wife, Pauline, in the character of Catherine: "How is Pauline as a blonde? She talks a lot like Catherine as a brunette. Hennaed-up she would be Catherine if you could stretch her up height-wise a few inches."[29]

Scott Fitzgerald, however, was determined to see Ernest doing the same sort of novel he had done in *The Sun Also Rises:* "You are seeing him Frederic in a sophisticated way as now you see yourself then but you're still seeing her as you did in 1917 through a 19-year-old's eyes—in consequence unless you make her a bit fatuous occasionally the contrast jars—either the writer is a simple fellow or she is Elenora Duse disguised as a Red Cross nurse. In one moment you expect her to prophesy the second battle of the Marne—as you probably did then."[30]

Apparently Hemingway had discussed the plot of the novel with Fitzgerald before he began writing it, but he did not let the older author criticize the manuscript as he had done with *The Sun Also Rises*. Fitzgerald did not see the war novel until it was in typescript. Yet it is interesting to note that Fitzgerald assumes that Hemingway was in Italy in 1917 and that the experience of the book is largely autobiographical. Although Hemingway did not correct Fitzgerald's assumption, neither did he encourage anyone to read the novel as autobiography. The best part of the novel, he later told Perkins, was invented.

NOTES

1. Carlos Baker, *Ernest Hemingway: A Life Story* (New York: Scribner's, 1969), pp. 20–38.

2. *Ibid.*, pp. 41–56.

3. Carlos Baker, *Hemingway: The Writer as Artist*, 4th ed. (Princeton: Princeton University Press, 1972), p. 49.

4. Philip Young, *Ernest Hemingway: A Reconsideration* (New York: Harcourt Brace, 1966), p. 290.

5. Carlos Baker, "Hemingway's Italia," *NYTBR* (Jan. 23, 1966), p. 2.

6. Baker, *A Life Story*, p. 184.

7. Malcolm Cowley, "Not Yet Demobilized," *NYHTBR* (Oct. 6, 1929), p. 6; Percy Hutchinson, "Love and War in the Pages of Mr. Hemingway," *NYTBR* (Sept. 29, 1929), p. 5; Henry S. Canby, "Chronicle and Comment," *Bookman*, 70 (Feb., 1930), p. 644.

8. Canby, p. 644.

9. Denis Marion, "L'Adieu aux Armes," *Nouvelle Revue Française*, 41 (Oct., 1933), p. 632.

10. Umberto Morra, "*A Farewell to Arms* di Ernest Hemingway," *Solaria*, 2 (1930), rpt. in *Antologia di Solaria*, ed. Enzo Siciliano (Milan: Editore Lerici, 1958), pp. 377–380.

11. Giacomo Antonini, "*Addio alle Armi* Venticinque Anni Dopo," *La Fiera Letteraria*, 9, no. 1 (March 21, 1954), pp. 1–2.

12. Alberto Rossi, "Ernest Hemingway e la guerra italiana," *La Nuova Stampa*, Anno x, num. 261 (Nov. 2, 1954), p. 3.

13. Audre Hanneman, *Ernest Hemingway: A Comprehensive Bibliography* (Princeton: Princeton University Press, 1967).

14. Ernest Hemingway, "A Veteran Visits Old Front," *Toronto Daily Star* (July 22, 1922), p. 7.

15. Quoted in Baker, *A Life Story*, pp. 131–132.

16. Ernest Hemingway, "Monologue to the Maestro: A High Seas Letter," originally published in *Esquire*, 4 (October, 1935), 21, 174a, 174b; rpt. in *By-Line: Ernest Hemingway*, ed. William White (New York: Scribner's, 1967), p. 215.

17. Hemingway, "Introduction," *A Farewell to Arms*, illustrated ed. (New York: Scribner's, 1948), pp. vii–viii.

18. George Plimpton, "The Art of Fiction, XXI: Ernest Hemingway," *Paris Review*, 5 (Spring, 1958), p. 85.

19. See Baker, *Writer as Artist*, p. 12; Baker, *A Life Story*, pp. 108–110; M. S. Reynolds, "Two Hemingway Sources for 'In Our Time,'" *Studies in Short Fiction*, 9 (Winter, 1972), pp. 81–84.

20. Ernest Hemingway, ed., *Men at War* (New York: Crown Publishers, 1942), p. xvii.

21. There is an Italian spelling for the town: *Gorizia;* and an Austrian spelling: *Goritzia.* In 1922, Hemingway used the Austrian spelling. In the first draft and holograph revisions of the AFTA manuscript, he used the Austrian spelling throughout.

The change to the Italian spelling occurred in the typescript. By the time the novel was serialized in *Scribner's Magazine* the spelling was *Gorizia*.

22. Hemingway, "A Veteran Visits Old Front," *TDS* (July 22, 1922), p. 7.
23. Hemingway, Preface, *A Moveable Feast* (New York: Scribner's, 1964).
24. Hemingway letter to Carlos Baker, June 11, 1953.
25. *Ibid.*
26. Hemingway letter to Scott Fitzgerald, Feb., 1926.
27. Perkins letter to Hemingway, July 20, 1926.
28. Hemingway to Dos Passos, Feb. 16, 1927.
29. Guy Hickok to Hemingway, July 26, 1929.
30. Scott Fitzgerald to Hemingway, undated, 1929.

BERNARD OLDSEY

The Sense of an Ending

The final act of enclosure in *A Farewell to Arms* consists of less than one page of print, just under two hundred words. In its own way, however, as a dramatic piece of tightly rendered fiction, it proves to be as structurally sound and effective as the evocative "overture" (Chapter I) with which the novel opens.[1] Long admired critically, this conclusion has become one of the most famous segments in American fiction—having been used in college classrooms across the land as a model of compositional compression, and as an object lesson in auctorial sweat, in what Horace called "the labor of the file." The undocumented story of how hard Hemingway worked to perfect the ending of *A Farewell to Arms* approached the level of academic legend. Some tellers of the tale said he wrote the conclusion fifty times, some as high as ninety; others used the safer method of simply saying Hemingway wrote it, rewrote it, and re-rewrote it. Carlos Baker, in his otherwise highly detailed biography, says of the matter only that "Between May 8th and 18th [1929] he rewrote the conclusion several times in the attempt to get it exactly right."[2] In their inventory of the papers available to them at the time, Philip Young and Charles Mann mention only one alternate conclusion separately, and what appears to be either one or two others attached to the galleys for the periodical publication of the novel.[3] One of these is the version Baker published in a collection called *Ernest Hemingway: Critiques of Four Major*

In *Hemingway's Hidden Craft: The Writing of A Farewell to Arms* (University Park, Pa.: Penn State University Press, 1979), pp. 71–83. Copyright © 1979 Penn State University Press.

Novels under the heading of "The Original Conclusion of *A Farewell to Arms*."[4] For reasons that will become clear later, this version should be referred to more precisely as "The Original *Scribner's Magazine* Conclusion," for although it was indeed the first to be set in galleys for that publication, it was preceded in composition by at least one other version in handwritten form, and probably more.[5]

As the papers now indicate, Hemingway deserved to be taken pretty much at his word when he told George Plimpton he had written the conclusion thirty-nine times. Depending upon a number of small variables, and upon what one is willing to call an attempt at conclusion, there are between thirty-two and forty-one elements of conclusion in the Hemingway Collection of the John F. Kennedy Library.[6] These appear in typescript and in handwritten form, and run from one or two sentences to as many as three pages in length. Some of the short elements show up again in the fuller attempts, helping to produce combination endings that consist of fragments arranged in varying alignments. There is, of course, no guarantee that Hemingway did not write even more variations: some could have been lost, destroyed, forgotten. But those that exist in the Hemingway Collection represent a rich fund of critical information capable of revealing the process of rejection-selection that the author went through to reach "the sense of an ending."[7] Not only can we see in this scattered process the thematic impulses which run through the novel and which the author was tempted to tie off in many of these concluding attempts; but we find in it the figurative seven-eighths of Hemingway's famous "iceberg" that floats beneath the surface of the art object. In one sense, most of the concluding attempts that are to be examined here may be considered as artistically subsumed under what finally became *the* ending of *A Farewell to Arms*. Understanding them should lead to a better understanding of it, and the novel as a whole.

All of the conclusions in the Hemingway Collection presuppose Catherine's death. Hemingway chose to present the actual death in understated, summary fashion at the very end of the penultimate section of the last chapter: "It seems she had one hemorrhage after another ... and it did not take her very long to die."[8] Presumably, that summarization did not take much writing effort. In itself Catherine's death, although beautifully prepared for in the first three quarters of the last chapter, is not one of Hemingway's moments of artistic truth—like the flat cinematic projection of Maera's death in *In Our Time*, or the elaborate mythic flight of Harry in "The Snows of Kilimanjaro." It contains none of the asyntactical eloquence of Frederic's near-death, when he feels his soul slip out of his body like a handkerchief from a pocket and then return to corporeal life (p. 57). This is, after all, Frederic Henry's story, and it is his reaction to Catherine's death that had to be depicted with revelatory force. All of the variant conclusions that Hemingway wrote for the novel are attempts to epitomize Henry's traumatized perception—from which, years later, the story unfolds.

Most of the variant attempts fall into natural clusters that can be referred to as: (1) The *Nada* Ending, (2) The Fitzgerald Ending, (3) The Religious Ending, (4) The Live-Baby Ending, (5) The Morning-After Ending, (6) The Funeral Ending, (7) The Original *Scribner's Magazine* Ending, and (8) *The* Ending. But a final grouping of (9) Miscellaneous Endings is needed initially to accommodate five brief attempts that have little in common with each other or any of those in the previously mentioned categories.

These five are all single-page holographs, four mere fragments. Two echo material in Chapter I by mixing rain with the thought of many men and women dying in wartime; and they conclude that knowing about the death of many is no consolation to someone mourning the death of a specific person. Another reaches back to Henry's nearly fatal wounding, as he compares the traumatic effect of Catherine's death on him with that produced by the physical wound: in both instances the numbness wears off and only pain remains. Still another of these miscellaneous attempts makes use of the old saying "See Naples and die," concluding bitterly that Naples is a hateful place, a part of that unlucky peninsula which is Italy. The last, and most interesting, of these attempts briefly entertains the notion of suicide: the narrator realizes he can end his life just as arbitrarily as he writes finis to his narrative; but he decides not to and later is not "sorry" about his decision. Through the first four of these attempts, and a number of others later, we can observe Hemingway trying to find the right linear motif with which to tie off the novel—climatological, psychological, or geographical. With the introduction of suicide in the fifth, however, we are reminded that the end of any novel, not just this, is in a sense a prefigurement of the novelist's death. All of the attempts to conclude a novel mirror the life choices of the creator; and the conclusion of a life can be as arbitrary and/or artistically appropriate as the conclusion of a novel.

"The *Nada* Ending" is represented by three fragmentary attempts to express Henry's sense of being-and-nothingness after Catherine's death. His mind is stunned and produces only a negative response, a form of *nada*. He senses that everything is gone—all their love—and will never be again. But at the bottom of one of these handwritten fragments an added note declares, with some of the ambiguity found at the end of "A Clean, Well-Lighted Place," that "nothing" is lost. The bluntest of the three attempts simply states that there is nothing left to the story, and that all the narrator can promise is that we all die.[9] This nihilistic attitude echoes Henry's earlier statement made to a hungry animal nosing around a garbage can: "There isn't anything, dog." And it is this same negative tonality, expressed dramatically, which dominates the ending Hemingway eventually devised for the novel.

Although related to the *nada* group, "The Fitzgerald Ending" deserves separate discussion because of the peculiar editorial circumstances surrounding it. As is now well known, F. Scott Fitzgerald helped Hemingway considerably in choosing the proper opening of *The Sun Also Rises*. What has not been well known is that he also advised Hemingway editorially on a number of matters in *A Farewell to Arms:* Item 77 in the Hemingway Collection consists of nine handwritten pages of Fitzgerald's comments on the typescript of the novel.[10] He so admired one passage in the book that he noted it in the typescript as being "one of the most beautiful pages in all English literature"; and later, in his last note on the novel to Hemingway, he wrote: "Why not end the book with that wonderful paragraph on p. 241 [pp. 258–259 in print]. It is the most eloquent in the book and would end it rather gently and well." The passage referred to is that in which Henry, in Chapter XXXIV, contemplates how the world "kills the very good and the very gentle and the very brave," and concludes "If you are none of these you can be sure it will kill you too but there will be no special hurry." Hemingway did try to use the passage as an ending, once by itself in holograph and once with other elements in polished typescript. As we know, he rejected both possibilities and kept the passage intact within the novel. In a letter to Hemingway (dated June 1, 1934), defending his own *Tender Is the Night,* Fitzgerald shed much light on his own sense of an ending, as well as Hemingway's and Joseph Conrad's:

> The theory back of it I got from Conrad's preface to *The Nigger,* that the purpose of a work of fiction is to appeal to the lingering aftereffects in the reader's mind. . . . The second contribution . . . was your trying to work out some such theory in your troubles with the very end of *A Farewell to Arms.* I remember that your first draft—or at least the first one I saw—gave a sort of old-fashioned Alger book summary . . . and you may remember my suggestion to take a burst of eloquence from anywhere in the book that you could find it and tag off with that; you were against this idea because you felt that the true line of a work of fiction was to take a reader up to a high emotional pitch but then let him down or ease him off. You gave no aesthetic reason for this—nevertheless, you convinced me.[11]

"The Religious Ending" represents one of Hemingway's least negative variants and perhaps the most potentially incongruous. Had any form of this conclusion been retained, *A Farewell to Arms* would have emerged with a much different emphasis in theme—one depending heavily upon a passage (in Chapter III) that has puzzled many readers. This is the place where Henry tries to express the evanescent wisdom of the priest: "He had always known what I did not know and what, when I learned it, I was always able to forget.

But I did not know that then, although I learned it later" (p. 14). What is the *it* which Henry learns, and when does he learn it? The usual interpretation stresses *it* as love: the priest's love of God, Frederic's love for Catherine; and the connection between agape and eros. But Hemingway's experiments with religious conclusions for the novel reveal the *it* of the priest as transcending any mundane love, which can be snuffed out by death. Under these circumstances, the *it* that Henry learns "later" is that everything will be all right if, as these fragments indicate, "you believe in God and love God." No one, the narrator concludes, can take God away from the priest, and thus the priest is happy. With such a conclusion the priest would have emerged as the supreme mentor of this *Bildungsroman,* not Rinaldi, Count Greffi, or even Catherine. However, a question imbedded in two of these religious attempts helps to explain why this kind of conclusion was rejected. Henry wonders how much of what the priest has is simply luck, how much is wisdom—and how do you achieve what the priest has if you are not "born that way"? It is, eventually, a question of deterministic grace.

Another fairly positive ending that Hemingway dropped is one in which Frederic and Catherine's child lives, instead of dying as it does in the novel. Two of these "Live-Baby Endings" were written to be inserted into the penultimate section of the last chapter, to precede Catherine's death. But the third makes it clear that Hemingway attempted to provide an ending in which the fact of birth, of new life, mitigates death. In this version Henry finds it difficult to talk about the boy without feeling bitter toward him, but concludes philosophically that "there is no end except death and birth is the only beginning." Stoic as these words may sound, they nevertheless tend to mitigate the deeper gloom produced in the novel by the death of both mother and child. In several senses "The Live-Baby Ending" would have meant another story; and with a touch of editorial wisdom reflecting that of the author, Henry realizes "It is not fair to start a new story at the end of an old one. . . ."

The concluding element Hemingway worked on longest and hardest was one built on a delayed reaction, "The Morning-After Ending". In holograph and typescript form, ten variations on this conclusion exist as more or less discrete elements; five are incorporated into combination conclusions, including "The Original *Scribner's Magazine* Ending," as published by Baker, and both the "original" and "first-revised" conclusions, as represented in Michael Reynolds' *Hemingway's First War*.[12] In all of these Frederic returns, after Catherine's death, to the hotel where they had been staying: after some time he falls asleep because he is so tired; waking to a spring morning, he sees the sun shining in through the window and for a moment is unaware of what has happened. The moment of realizing Catherine is gone—something of a dull, truncated epiphany—is rendered in two ways. In most versions, including those published by Baker and Reynolds, Henry merely experiences a delayed response—"then suddenly to realize what had happened." But in other versions his recognition of his predicament is stimulated by a burning light bulb: seeing it still lit in the daylight brings double illumination. Through this simple device, Hemingway placed Frederic Henry among those other protagonists of his who, like children, have trouble with the dark—including the Old Man in "A Clean, Well-Lighted Place," the Lieutenant in "Now I Lay Me," and Nick Adams in "A Way You'll Never Be," who confesses, "I can't sleep without a light of some sort. That's all I have now." His words could stand for Frederic Henry in these versions of the conclusion. He too, earlier in the novel, gives utterance to nocturnal blues: "I know that the night is not the same as the day: that all things are different . . . the night can be a dreadful time for lonely people once their loneliness has started. But with Catherine there was almost no difference in the night except that it was an even better time" (p. 258). Without Catherine, all that is left is a light bulb burning in the night, announcing on the morning after that she is dead.

In one instance Hemingway employed "The Morning-After Ending" as a transitional device to achieve "The Funeral Ending". The initial material of this one-page holograph is essentially the same as that described in the Baker version, but this variant does not end with the flat statement of "that is the end of my story." Instead, Hemingway here makes one of his first attempts to conclude with an obverse-iteration method: Henry says that he could tell about his meeting with the undertaker and "the business of burial in a foreign country," but, the implication is, as the sentence trails off, he will not. The same kind of obverse iteration is incorporated into the two other attempts at this funeral conclusion: people die and they have to be buried, but the narrator does not have to tell about the burying, or the resulting sorrow. Henry tells us—somewhat reversing the earlier notion of suicide—that in writing "you have a certain choice that you do not have in life."

It is impossible to state with certainty what the exact order of composition was for all the variant elements of conclusion, since they are undated.[13] But there are good indications that the combining form of "The Original *Scribner's Magazine* Ending" was the penultimate version. For one thing, most of the variations in this group (five of eight) are highly polished typescripts. For another, these versions combine many of the previously mentioned attempts as contributing elements—including the "morning-after" idea, as well as the funeral, suicide, lonely nights, the Fitzgerald suggestion, and the obverse-iteration method of stating-but-not-stating what happened after that particular night in "March nineteen hundred and eighteen." Most significantly, one version of this combining conclusion very nearly became the ultimate one—to the extent of having been set in galleys for the serial publication of the novel.

Hemingway scribbled a note to hold matters on this conclusion, how-ever, and then eventually supplanted it with the dramatic version that we now have. If he had not done so, *A Farewell to Arms* would have ended in the old-fashioned manner of tying up the loose narrative ends in summary fashion. For in the original galley version Frederic Henry says that he could, if he wanted to, tell his reader many things that had happened since that night when Catherine died. He could tell how Rinaldi was cured of syphilis (answering the question of whether Rinaldi did indeed have the disease); how the priest functioned in Italy under Mussolini (indicating that this is a story being told years after its occurrence); how Simmons became an opera singer; how the loudly heroic Ettore became a Fascist; and how the loyal Piani became a taxi driver in New York. A variant of this conclusion places Piani in Chicago instead of New York and hints that something unpleasant happened to the socialist-deserter Bonello in his home town of Imola. In all of the variants of this combining ending, however, Henry decides he will not tell about all of these people, or about himself, since that time in 1918, because all of that would be another story. This story ends with Catherine's death, or more specifically with the dawn of his awakening to that fact on the morning after.

Hemingway reached this point in his search for an ending by August 1928. He made some galley adjustments on this combination ending early in June 1929. But he still was not satisfied; the last phase of his search began, and on June 24, 1929, almost ten months after completion of the first full draft of the novel, Hemingway reached "*The* Ending".[14] Tracing through all of the elements of conclusion for *A Farewell to Arms* in the Hemingway Col-lection is like accompanying the captain of a vessel who has been searching through uncharted waters for a singularly appropriate harbor: then suddenly after all this pragmatic probing there appears the proper terminus to his voy-age, and yours, something realized out of a myriad number of possibilities. In less figurative terms, "*The* Ending" emerges suddenly as the product of what Mark Schorer has aptly called "Technique as Discovery."

Even in the very last phase of this process Hemingway continued to write and rewrite to discover what should be said on the final page of the novel as a result of what had been said in the preceding three hundred and forty pages. Including the ultimate choice, there are extant five holographic variants of "*The* Ending." They are closely related, and they remind us that Hemingway once said the most difficult thing about writing was "getting the words right." With cross-outs, replacements, realignments, these final five efforts demonstrate technique as discovery in the most basic sense of getting the words right, which leads to getting the right message, the right form.

All five are basically alike in form and substance. They are all examples of the dramatic method of showing, rendering, rather than telling. They all contain the descriptive element of the rain, the dramatic action of clearing the hospital room and taking leave of Catherine's corpse, and the narrative reflection that none of it is any good. All include the most important sentence in the actual conclusion: "It was like saying good-by to a statue." But they all state these matters in slightly different ways, using different positions for various phrases and ideas, achieving different emphases and effects. For example, Hemingway moved the sentence about "saying good-by to a statue" around like a piece in a puzzle: in one instance he tried for maximum effect by restating it as the very last sentence of the novel, but evidently thought that too obvious and placed it eventually in its penultimate position, where it is now followed by the line that runs "After awhile I went out and left the hospital and walked back to the hotel in the rain."

Kenneth Burke reads that last sentence as a small masterpiece of understatement and meteorological symbolism: "No weeping here," he declares; "Rather stark 'understatement.' Or look again, and do you not find the very heavens are weeping in his behalf?" Burke finds here an echo of Verlaine's line "It rains in my heart as it rains on the town."[15] This critical hunch receives support from the most interesting variant of "*The* Ending," which takes from the heavens a touch of religious consolation. In this version, out of Frederic Henry's reflections, comes a brief line obviously modeled on the Beatitudes: "Blessed are the dead that the rain falls on. . . ." It has poetic lilt and fits in beautifully with the weather imagery throughout the novel; and at first the reader is inclined to think Hemingway made the wrong decision in dropping it from the final ending. But further consideration reveals a sense of craft wisdom. Having previously rejected "The Religious Ending" that features the happiness of the priest, and having depicted the inefficacy of Henry's prayers for the dying Catherine, the author here remained artistically consistent. In eliminating even this nub of religious consolation, he obtained the flat, nihilistic, numbing conclusion that the novel now has.[16]

Here again, in this last instance of rejection as in all of the preceding instances, we are reminded that Hemingway's best fiction is the product not only of *what has been put in* but also of *what has been left out*. "Big Two-Hearted River" is perhaps the most obvious example of this propensity in Hemingway's work; it took critics years to fill in the deliberate gaps in that story, by borrowing information from other pieces of Hemingway's fiction, in order to get a full reading of what they sensed was a powerful work of suppressed drama. Hemingway intuitively understood that sublimated words form part of any message as uttered, providing as they do a psychological tension and an emotional context for that utterance. He spoke of trying to achieve "a fourth and even a fifth dimension" in his fiction, and formulated a synecdochic theory for the-thing-left-out: "I always try to write on the principle of the iceberg. There is seven-eighths of it underwater for every part that shows. *Anything you know you can eliminate and it only strengthens your iceberg.* It is the part that doesn't show."[17] Examining some forty attempts at conclusion for *A Farewell to Arms* provides a rare inside view of that theory: it reveals what the author knew, the submerged, suppressed part of the message. Moreover, it opens to critical view an auctorial process of exclusion-inclusion, an exercise of willed choice, that closely parallels the life-choices of the protagonist-narrator. Thus we can see that the published conclusion is possessed of an extraordinary tension and literary power because it sublimates, suppresses, and/or rejects the same things that Frederic Henry does—including religious consolation; hope for the future and the continuance of life (as reflected in "The Live-Baby Ending" and in the summary of characters in the combination endings); the eloquence of courage and beauty (expressed in "The Fitzgerald Ending"); and even the negative solution of suicide (suggested in one of the miscellaneous endings). In this instance, everything that the author and the protagonist knew and eliminated went into strengthening this tip of the iceberg.

Conceived as it was in the spirit of rejection, the conclusion of *A Farewell to Arms* is in and of itself a compressed exemplification of the process of rejection and negation. The only thing that Hemingway retained from all the preceding attempts at ending the novel is the core of "The *Nada* Ending." He eventually wrote finis to the story by bringing its materials down to a fine point of "nothingness," and thus left the reader with the same message Frederic Henry gives the hungry dog in the last chapter: "There isn't anything, dog." Within the short space of the one hundred and ninety-seven words that comprise the conclusion, Hemingway uses *nothing* three times and a series of some thirteen forms of negation, in various phrases like "No. There is nothing to do," "No. . . . There's nothing to say," and simply "No, thank you." In the process, Frederic Henry rejects the attending physician's explanation of the Caesarean operation, his offer of aid, and the nurse's demand that he stay out of Catherine's room. But the most powerful form of rejection occurs in the final paragraph of the book, when Henry says his last farewell to arms: "But after I got them [the nurses] out and shut the door and turned off the light it wasn't any good. It was like saying good-by to a statue." He rejects the corpse; it rejects him. Even in this ultimate scene of nullification Hemingway uses his principle of omission in a subtle manner: he says nothing about Frederic's embracing or kissing the statue-like corpse, although it is a rare reader who does not interpolate some such act. Also, Hemingway does nothing here to remind the reader that with Catherine Lieutenant Henry had come to accept the night, the darkness, and found that with her it was an "even better time" than the day. But now Henry deliberately turns off the light, as though to test his alliance with Catherine, and finds that the warmth and companionship of love are inoperative, defunct. We can thus understand why, in many of the combination endings, Henry is described as sleeping with the light bulb turned on in the hotel room. Night will never be "a better time" for him again.

NOTES

1. As discussed earlier [in Oldsey's book], pp. 65–66.

2. Carlos Baker, *Ernest Hemingway: A Life Story* (Princeton: Princeton University Press, 1969), p. 201. In his *Hemingway: The Writer as Artist* (Princeton: Princeton University Press, 1952), Baker declares, "There is a persistent tradition that the present ending was rewritten seventeen times before Hemingway got the corrected galley-proof aboard the boat-train," p. 97.

3. Philip Young and Charles W. Mann, *The Hemingway Manuscripts: An Inventory* (University Park: Pennsylvania State University Press, 1969), pp. 11–12. Item 5-F in this inventory describes a three-page manuscript ending in which the baby lives; Item 5-H mentions only that there are "Different versions of ending" attached to the four galleys set for the *Scribner's Magazine* publication of the novel; and Item 5-J merely adds that "four more endings of the novel" are attached to two galleys dated June 4, 1929. If this information seems somewhat vague, it should be said in fairness to Young and Mann that their inventory was meant to be an "interim report," as they declare in their preface, "and not the much more elaborate catalogue . . . that should be made when the papers have reached their permanent repository."

4. (New York: Scribner's, 1962), p. 75.

5. See Hemingway Collection, specifically Item 64 and Item 70: the first is the manuscript of the novel as first completed; the second is a series of drafts for an ending (some forty pages in manuscript and typescript). See also Michael Reynolds, *Hemingway's First War: The Making of "A Farewell to Arms"* (Princeton: Princeton University Press, 1976), pp. 46–48.

6. Item 64 and Item 70, as mentioned in note 5 above.

7. Used with a slightly contradictory connotation in the title of this chapter, this phrase is borrowed from Frank Kermode's challenging analysis of apocalyptic literary endings: *The Sense of an Ending: Studies in the Theory of Fiction* (New York: Oxford University Press, 1967).

8. *A Farewell to Arms*, Modern Standard Authors edition (New York: Scribner's, 1953), p. 343.

9. This variant has been published in Reynolds' study, p. 294.

10. See Philip Young and Charles W. Mann, "Fitzgerald's *Sun Also Rises:* Notes and Comment," *Fitzgerald/Hemingway Annual 1970* (Washington D.C.: NCR Microcard Editions, 1970), pp. 1–9. See also Item 77 of the Hemingway Collection, which contains Fitzgerald's comments on an early form of the novel, most probably Item 65, the original typescript and setting copy of *A Farewell to Arms*.

11. As reprinted in George Perkins' *The Theory of the American Novel* (New York: Holt, Rinehart and Winston, 1970), p. 334.

12. See note 5 and Reynolds, pp. 46–48.

13. There is a date established for Item 64, the manuscript copy of the novel (see note 14 below), but the great bulk of the variants, found in Item 70, are not dated.

14. See Reynolds, pp. 50, 285.

15. Kenneth Burke, *A Grammar of Motives* and *A Rhetoric of Motives*, a double-volume edition (Cleveland: World, 1962); this citation is from the second volume, p. 850.

16. As the author of this study recently discovered, there is another good reason for Hemingway's dropping this line: it is used by Fitzgerald in the last chapter of *The Great Gatsby*, in the funeral scene: "Dimly I heard someone murmur 'Blessed are the dead that the rain falls on,' and then the owl-eyed man said 'Amen to that' in a brave voice." Whether the line is original or not with Fitzgerald, Hemingway would have looked overly dependent in using it for similar effect in conclusion.

17. In George Plimpton's interview with the author, "Ernest Hemingway: The Art of Fiction XXI," *Paris Review* 18 (Spring 1958), p. 84.

MILLICENT BELL

Pseudoautobiography and Personal Metaphor

Autobiographic novels are, of course, fictions, constructs of the imagination, even when they seem to incorporate authenticating bits and pieces
of personal history. But all fiction is autobiography, no matter how remote
from the author's experience the tale seems to be; he leaves his mark,
expresses his being, his life, in *any* tale. *A Farewell to Arms* can illustrate
both of these statements.

Ernest Hemingway's novel is not the autobiography some readers have
thought it. It was not memory but printed source material that supplied
the precise details of its descriptions of historic battle scenes on the Italian
front in World War I. The novel's love story is no closer to Hemingway's
personal reality. He did go to Italy and see action, but not the action he describes; he did fall in love with a nurse, but she was no Catherine Barkley. A
large amount of the book fulfills the principle expressed in the deleted coda
to "Big Two-Hearted River": "The only writing that was any good was what
you made up, what you imagined." Still, there is much that must represent
authentic recall in the book. Innumerable small details and a sense of general conditions in battle, the character of the Italian landscape, the Italian
soldier, the ambulance corps—all impressed themselves upon Hemingway
in 1918 in the Dolomite foothills near Schio as surely as they might have
further east around the Tagliamento a year earlier. And there are fetishes

---

In *Ernest Hemingway: The Writer in Context*, ed. James Nagel (Madison: University of
Wisconsin Press, 1984): pp. 113–129. Copyright © 1984 by the Board of Regents of the
University of Wisconsin System. University of Wisconsin Press.

of autobiography, trophies of the personal, chief among these the famous wounding at Fossalta, which Hemingway often recalled.

Why is this last episode reproduced so exactly as it happened—the shell fragments in the legs, the sensation of dying and coming to life, the surgical sequel? In the coda, Nick—who is Hemingway—had "never seen a jockey killed" when he wrote "My Old Man"; "he'd never seen an Indian woman having a baby" like his namesake in "Indian Camp." But Hemingway had been wounded just as Frederic is. The answer may be that it was a trauma obsessively recurring to mind, irrepressibly present in his writing because of its crucial, transforming effect upon his life. Still, in the novel the wounding is not at all transforming, does not provide the occasion for the "separate peace" declared by Nick at a similar moment in chapter 6 of *In Our Time,* often incorrectly thought to be the novel's germ. It does not even cause the novel's hero to suffer from sleeplessness afterward, the consequence of a similar wounding for the narrator of "Now I Lay Me," written only two years before *A Farewell to Arms.* Perhaps in life as in the novel the wounding was simply a very striking experience, the young man's first brush with death. But as an authentic, indelible memory it was deliberate evidence, in any case, that the fiction was not all made up. Perhaps, then, the authentic wounding is chiefly a sign, a signature of the author's autobiographic contract with himself.

Hemingway's style, his realist pose, suggests, guilefully, that much more has been borrowed directly from experience than is actually the case. Perhaps the testimonial incorporation of the real, which guarantees autobiographic realism, may also be mimicked. When the "real" is made up to become the "realistic," when the seemingly accidental detail appears to have been stuck into the narrative for no other reason than that it happened, than that it was there, the writer has deliberately made it look as though he is yielding to memory and resisting the tendency of literature to subdue everything to a system of connected significance. In *A Farewell to Arms,* as elsewhere in his writing, Hemingway made the discovery of this secret of realist effect, and his art, which nevertheless presses toward poetic unity by a powerful if covert formalist intent, yet seems continually open to irrelevance also. The result is a peculiar tension requiring the strictest control. Only a manner which conceals implication as severely as Hemingway's can nevertheless suggest those coherences, those rhythmic collocations of mere things, in the manner of imagist poetry, pretend notation of what the witnessing eye might simply have chanced to see. And this restraint is reinforced by deliberate avoidance of the kind of comment that might impose significance or interpretation. It is even further strengthened by the often-noted qualities of Hemingwayan syntax, the simple or compound declaratives lacking subordination, and the vocabulary high in nouns and verbs and low in qualifiers. The frequency of the impersonal passive voice that presents events simply as conditions, as in the many sentences that begin with "There were," suppresses not only the sense of agency but the evaluating presence of the observer. If, despite these effects, there is often poetic meaningfulness it is also true that the poetic is sometimes renounced altogether and the realistic detail maintains its irrelevance, refusing any signification in order to affirm the presence of the actual, whether or not truly remembered, reported, historical.

But this stylistic contest only reflects the struggle of the writer between the impulses to tell it "as it was" and to shape and pattern a story; it is not that struggle itself. The "realistic" style is, in fact, most conspicuous and most successful in the most "invented" parts of the book, the war scenes. It is not so evident in those other scenes where Hemingway draws upon memory—the Milan and Switzerland sections. Hemingway had been a patient in the Red Cross hospital in Milan and had spent convalescent weeks in the city; and he had taken vacation tours in the Alpine lake region. But the action situated in those places in the novel has no authenticity to match that of the great Caporetto chapter in which Frederic participates in events Hemingway had not. Still, it is the war scenes, probably—to turn our paradox about once more—that express Hemingway's deepest feelings by way of metaphor, his sense of the war as an objective correlative of his state of mind. The love affair located in familiar, remembered scenes fails of authenticity though it takes something from the writer's experiences with his nurse, Agnes von Kurowsky, and something from his love for Hadley Richardson, and even Pauline Pfeiffer's caesarian operation; it succeeds less well than the invented war scenes in achieving either the effect of realism or the deeper autobiography of metaphor. It is as the latter that it can, however, be explained.

Any first-person story must imitate the autobiographic situation, but there is particular evidence that Hemingway gave his narrator his own sense of the difficulty of reconciling *Wahrheit* and *Dichtung*. The novelist's struggles to achieve an appropriate ending to his book are visible in the manuscript drafts at the John F. Kennedy Library. They show that his chief problem was that he felt both that a novel needed formal closure and also that life was not "like that." He rejected, in the end, the attempt to pick up dropped threads and bring Rinaldi and the priest back into the narrative from which they had been absent since the end of chapter 26, a little beyond the novel's midpoint. It may be argued that these two *companions de la guerre* are felt even in their absence, that there are no dropped threads, the priest in particular being absorbed into the transformed conception of love which the American lieutenant and the English nurse discover in the later portions of the book. But there is really no such absorption; Frederic and Catherine remain very much what they were at the beginning, this mentor and the skeptical doctor both being left behind. Of the "three people of any importance in this story" to whom Hemingway referred in the rejected opening for chapter 10, only Catherine persists. Hemingway must have decided this made an ending—the tightening isolation of his hero requires the loss of the larger human world—but in one of the discarded drafts he permits Frederic to express the misgivings of his creator. "I could tell how Rinaldi was cured of the syphilis. . . . I could tell how the priest in our mess lived to be a priest in Italy under Fascism," the pseudoautobiographic narrator observes. But he knows that a story must end somewhere. That he realizes that his closure cannot be complete is due to his awareness that life does not have endings.

> Things happen all the time. Everything blunts and the world keeps on. You get most of your life back like goods recovered from a fire. It all keeps on and then it keeps on. It never stops for you. Sometimes it stops when you are still alive. You can stop a story anytime. Where you stop is the end of that story. The rest goes on and you go on with it. On the other hand you have to stop a story. You have to stop at the end of whatever it was you were writing about.

The rejected passage can be read not merely as a device to excuse the odd shape of the novel but as a reflection of Hemingway's personal dilemma, his desire to respect the claim of art and also to get back his own past like "goods recovered from a fire."

Getting back his life by writing fiction was not, in this case, a matter of endings, of plot. The indeterminacy of remembered experience does not matter, because the coherence of events is not so important as the unity of the mind which is the container for them. If Hemingway was to fulfill the autobiographic expectation, the promise made by authentic transcriptions like the Fossalta wounding, it would not be by trying to tell, literally, "the story" of his past. The novelist wrote about himself, and perhaps never so truly as in *A Farewell to Arms*, but he did so by projecting, lyrically, an inner condition. Mood and tone, not events, provide unity, and these were more intensely the concomitants of the present life of the writer than of his younger self. The novel is about neither love nor war; it is about a state of mind, and that state of mind is the author's.

That plot is not dominant in *A Farewell to Arms* has not been properly recognized. Critics who have stressed the prevalence of poetic metaphors in the novel have failed, on the whole, to see that such patterns establish its "spatial" composition, minimize progressive effects. In fact, an unvarying mood, established by the narrative voice, dominates everything it relates, bathes uniformly all the images and levels events which are seen always in one way only. That the principal descriptive elements—river, mountains, dust or mud, and above all, rain—are all present in the opening paragraphs suggests not so much that later scenes are being predicted as that the subsequent pages will disclose nothing that is not already evident in the consciousness that has begun its self-exhibition.

The famous wounding is no turning point in the journey of that consciousness. But even the later "separate peace" in chapter 32 after Frederic's immersion in the Tagliamento is not really a change of direction, a peaking of the plot, though Hemingway's hero does say as he lies on the floor of the flatcar that takes him to Milan, "You were out of it now. You had no more obligation." In chapter 7, even before his wounding, it should be remembered, he has already said, "I would not be killed. Not in this war. It did not have anything to do with me." It is impossible to tell at what point this narrator has acquired his conviction of separateness amounting to alienation from the events which carry him along the stream of time.

By the time he turns away from the war at the Tagliamento in October 1917, Frederic will have had two years in which to acquire the apathy of war weariness. But this is not his malady. Already on the opening page, in 1915, the voice that speaks to us exhibits that attitude psychoanalysts call "blunting of affect," the dryness of soul which underlies its exquisite attentiveness. One has heard of the "relish of sensation" implied in this and other passages of descriptive writing by Hemingway. But "relish" is too positive a word for the studied emotional distance from the perceived world which is in effect here. For the view from Gorizia across the Isonzo, toward the passing troops and the changing weather, this narrator seems hardly to feel anything beyond a minimal "things went very badly." An alienated neutrality governs the reiterated passives, the simple declaratives. "There were big guns. . . . There was fighting. . . . There were mists over the river. . . . There were small gray motor cars." The next year (chapter 2) is the same. "There were many victories. . . . The fighting was in the next mountains. . . . The whole thing was going well. . . . The war was changed." The different character of military events makes for no change in the tone. We are prepared for the personality who emerges into view as he describes his leave. He had not gone to Abruzzi but had spent drunken nights when "you knew that that was all there was," and he had known the "not knowing and not caring in the night, sure that this was all . . . suddenly to care very much," swinging from not caring to caring and back again, from affectlessness to affect and then again to its loss. If there is something that transcends this alternation, the ecstasy of either love or religion, it is so fugitive as to be almost unnameable: "If you have had it you know. . . . He, the priest, had always known what I did not know, what, when I learned it, I was always able to forget."

"Always" is an important word here. There is no hint that Frederic has at any time had a beginning in illusion, that he ever started out like Stephen Crane's Henry Fleming in *The Red Badge of Courage* (something of a model for *A Farewell to Arms*) with a naive belief in exalted meanings. The well-known passage "I was *always* embarrassed by the words sacred, glorious, and sacrifice, and the expression in vain" is not the culmination of a process by which these concepts have withered. His embarrassment goes as far back as he can remember. He has had it always. "Gino was a patriot," Frederic continues, "so he said things that separated us sometimes, but he was also a fine boy and I understand his being a patriot. He was born one." And the opposite attitude, disbelief in such things, may also be inborn. Rinaldi has told Frederic that for him "there are only two things"—drink and sex—and his work. Frederic hopes that he will get other things but the doctor says, "No. We never get anything. We are born with all we have and we never learn." If Frederic may be conceived of as having been also born with all he has, this explains why he is described as having enlisted in the ambulance corps for no reason at all, unlike Hemingway who was swept into the wave of American enthusiasm to aid the Allies. Frederic just happened to be already in Italy when the war broke out. He had been studying architecture. He has never had any belief in the big words. "Why did you do it?" asks Catherine, referring to his enlistment. "I don't know. . . . There isn't always an explanation for everything," he answers.

And yet this sufferer from blunted affect can fall in love. It is one of the "givens" of the story, though it seems to demand a capacity which, like the emotion of patriotism, he was born without. "When I saw her I was in love with her," he says when Catherine appears again at the hospital. "I had not wanted to fall in love with anyone. But God knows I had." Catherine, as well, had experienced this hardly credible conversion. Although we never get so direct a view of her mental operations— this is Frederic's story, after all—she appears, in the earlier scenes, to be as incapacitated as Hemingway's other English nurse who has lost a fiancé in the war, Brett Ashley. There is more than a hint that she too suffers the dissociation of feeling from sensation that accounts for her unfocused sexuality when Frederic first makes love to her. But now she feels. The raptures of both lovers, however, are curiously suspect.

Frederic has only delusively attached himself to an otherness. Far from the war's inordinate demand upon his responses, he has been converted to feeling in the isolation of his hospital bed, where, like a baby in its bassinet, he is totally passive, tended and comforted by female caretakers, the nurses, and particularly by this one. The image is regressive, and the ministering of Catherine, who looks after all his needs, including sexual, while he lies passive, is more maternal than connubial. The relation that now becomes the center of the novel is, indeed, peculiar enough to make us question it as a representation of adult love. More often noted than Frederic's passivity is the passivity of Catherine in this love affair, a passivity which has irritated readers (particularly female readers) because it seems to be a projection of male fantasies of the ideally submissive partner. It results from her desire to please. She is a sort of inflated rubber woman available at will to the onanistic dreamer. There is, in fact, a masturbatory quality to the love of each. The union of these two is a flight from outer reality and eventually from selfhood, which depends upon a recognition of the other; the selfhood that fails to find its definition in impingement upon the world at large and the establishment of distinction from it eventually proves incapable of recognizing the alien in the beloved and therefore the independent in itself. The otherness that Frederic and Catherine provide for one another is not enough to preserve their integral selves, and while the sounds of exteriority become more and more muffled in the novel, their personalities melt into one another. It is for this reason that Hemingway's novel, far from being the *Romeo and Juliet* he once carelessly called it, is more comparable to *Antony and Cleopatra*, a play which shows that the world is not well lost for love, though nothing, of course, can be further from the masterful images of Shakespeare's adult lovers than Hemingway's pitiful pair.

Affective failure, then, shows itself not merely in the war sections of the novel but in the parts where one would imagine it to have been transcended, the love story of Catherine and Frederic. Catherine constantly reminds her lover of her resolution not to offer him otherness but to collapse her own selfhood into his. She asks what a prostitute does, whether she says whatever the customer wants her to, even "I love you." She will outdo the prostitute: "But I will. I'll say just what you wish and I'll do what you wish and then you will never want any other girls, will you. . . . I want what you want. There isn't any me any more. Just what you want." The idyll of their Milan summer is spent in such games as this: "We tried putting thoughts in the other one's head while we were in different rooms. It seemed to work sometimes but that was probably because we were thinking the same thing anyway." She refuses his offer to marry her, and when he says "I wanted it for you" replies, "there isn't any me. I'm you. Don't make up a separate me."

Their solitariness *à deux* is only emphasized by their occasional contacts with others who are outside the war, those met in the Milan cafes or at the racetrack who are not the true alienated but the self-serving and parasitic, and even by their encounter with the genuine war hero, Ettore, who is wounded in the foot, like Frederic, and has five medals, and whom they cannot stand. After she becomes pregnant, Catherine says, "There's only us two and in the world there's all the rest of them. If anything comes between us we're gone and then they have us." When the time comes for him to leave for the front, they walk past a couple embracing under a buttress of the cathedral, and she will not agree that they are like themselves. "'Nobody is like us,' Catherine said. She did not mean it happily." Not surprisingly, they both are orphans of a sort. Catherine has a father but "he has gout," she says to Frederic; "You won't ever have to meet him." Frederic has only a stepfather, and, he tells her, "You won't have to meet him." When they are waiting for the birth of their baby in Switzerland, she asks him about his family: "Don't you care anything about them?" He replies, "I did, but we quarrelled so much it wore itself out."

Book 3, the justly praised Caporetto section, returns Frederic to Gorizia where others have spent a different sort of summer. Rinaldi, depressed, over-worked, perhaps syphilitic, says, "This is a terrible war, baby," drinks too much, and is impatient of Frederic's acquisition of a "sacred subject." The priest tells him how the terrible summer has made the major gentle. No one any longer believes in victory. But Frederic confesses that he himself believes in neither victory nor defeat. He believes, he says, "in sleep." It is more than a joke, even though in a moment he apologizes that "I said that about sleep meaning nothing." The regressive process, the withdrawal from reality, the surrender of complex personal being, the limitation of relationship to that with another who is really only a mirror of self approaches more and more the dreamless sleep of apathy, the extremity of ennui. There is a suggestion of the pathologic in the "I was deadly sleepy" with which the chapter ends.

The retreat is reported by a sensibility already asleep, by an emotional apparatus already itself in retreat from the responsibilities of response. "The houses were badly smashed but things were very well organized and there were signboards everywhere." However much this sounds like irony to us, irony is not intended by the speaker, who does not mean more by saying less. His downward adjustment of feeling is the one often made by soldiers—or by concentration camp victims, or long-term prisoners—by which emotions are reduced to the most rudimentary since the others have become insupportable. His battle-weary companions express their own reduction by a preoccupa-tion with food. The entire retreat is a massed legitimization of apathy and a symbol of it.

Frederic's affectlessness is climaxed by his "cold-blooded" shooting of one of the Italian sergeants who has refused to obey his order to move the stalled ambulance. "I shot three times and dropped one," he observes, as though describing the pursuit of game, and Bonello then takes the pistol and "finishes him," as a hunting companion might finish off an animal still quivering where it has fallen. One may say that this is simply war—Sherman's war—and feeling has no place in it. But this does not make it less shocking that the perceiving hero is so matter-of-fact. Even Bonello expresses a mo-tive: he is a socialist, and all his life he has wanted to kill a sergeant, he tells Frederic, who expresses no personal motive at all, and who has never felt that it was his war. Yet for giving up his part in it he has also no special motive. His case is not like that of the demoralized soldiers who are flinging down their arms and shouting that they want to go home. He cannot go home. And now a profoundly significant flash of memory comes to him as he rests in the hay of a barn:

The hay smelled good and lying in a barn in the hay took away all the years between. We had lain in the hay and talked and shot sparrows with an air-rifle when they perched in the triangle cut high in the wall of the barn. The barn was gone now and one year they had cut the hemlock woods and there were only stumps, dried tree-tops, branches and fireweed where the woods had been. You could not go back.

The "separate peace" was made long ago. Again we must note the reference to a congenital disengagement when he says with what only looks like a newly acquired minimalism, "I was not *made* to think, I was *made* to eat. My God, yes. Eat and drink and sleep with Catherine." Removing his uniform after his escape, he strips himself of the last vestige of social self. He no longer can interest himself in the war news, as he had in the earlier Milan section, and does not give us summaries of military events. "I had a paper but I did not read it because I did not want to read about the war. I was going to forget the war" he says at the beginning of chapter 34. It is now that he says, "I had made a separate peace." "Don't talk about the war," he tells the barman at the hotel. And he reflects, "The war was a long way away. Maybe there wasn't any war. There was no war here. Then I realized it was over for me." But how committed to this war has he ever been?

The rest is a "fugue" in the technical psychiatric sense of a period during which the patient, often suffering loss of memory, begins another life from which all his past has been drained. Thus, the "all for love" that remains for Frederic and Catherine is qualified by the lovers' knowledge that the whole empire of normal being has been surrendered. "Let's not think of anything," says Catherine. The lover boasts that he has no wish to be separate from his beloved: "All other things were unreal." He tells her, "My life used to be full of everything. Now if you aren't with me I haven't a thing in the world." Their universe of two is reducing itself further, and their games continue to suggest this constriction. He might let his hair grow longer, she suggests, and she might cut hers short so that even their sexual difference may be lessened. "Then we'd both be alike. Oh, darling, I want you so much I want to be you too." He says, "We're the same one," and she, "I want us to be all mixed up. . . . I don't live at all when I'm not with you." He replies, "I'm no good when you're not there. I haven't any life at all any more."

These scenes are a drift toward death, which is why the novel must end in death, Catherine's and the baby's, though Hemingway considered allowing the child to survive. Such a survival would have contradicted all that has gone before by introducing a new otherness when its parents are losing the otherness of each other. The two lovers already live on the margin of life. Count Greffi is an even more mythological figure than Mippipopolous in *The Sun*

Also Rises, whom he resembles. The very old man, so close to death, is a fit sentinel upon that border they are about to cross before they pass, by a symbolic boat voyage, out of Italy. Their Switzerland is not on the map, notwithstanding the fact that it resembles the Switzerland of Hemingway's vacation tours. In their chalet, wrapped in the cottony blanket of the winter snow, cared for by their good-natured landlord and his wife, whose lives have a reality with which they make no connection, and in contact with no one else, they are united as before in his hospital bed. Their destiny is out of their own hands as they become, quite literally, patients awaiting surgery, playing bedgames. Perhaps Frederic will pass the time by growing a beard. Their loss of connection with human modes of being produces fantasies of an animal identity, like that of the fox they see in the snow who sleeps with his brush wrapped about his face, curled in the regressive fetal position. What would they do if they had tails like the fox? They would have special clothes made, or "live in a country where it wouldn't make any difference" to have a fox's tail. Catherine says, truly, "We live in a country where nothing makes any difference. Isn't it grand how we never see anyone?" The country is, of course, the country of the dead, toward which she is bound.

If indeed "all fiction is autobiography," no special demonstration is required to support the idea that *A Farewell to Arms* expresses the author's inner being, his secret life. Yet there is particular reason to suppose this in the case of this novel which is the presentation of a state of mind, a mood and condition of being. These, it may be arguable, belonged to the writer himself at the time of writing. As a war novel, it is curiously late. In 1929, American society was preoccupied with other things than its memories of the battles of the First World War. Hemingway, already the author of a novel dealing with a later period and married for the second time, had come a long way from the naive nineteen-year-old of 1918. Any such analysis is speculative, but there is reason to suppose that for the writer as for Frederic Henry the barn was gone where he had lain in the hay as a boy: "You could not go back." This realization must have been particularly acute when this novel was being written. Since 1925 his life had been one of personal turmoil. He had found himself in love with Pauline Pfeiffer, forced to decide between her and the woman whom he still claimed also to love and who had been, he would declare, a faultless wife. In 1927, he had remarried and, in the following year, while Pauline was pregnant, he was struggling to make progress on this second novel, plagued by various accidental disasters—an eye injury, head cuts from a fallen skylight—such as he always seemed prone to. Pauline's baby was delivered by caesarian section after a labor of eighteen hours during a Kansas heat wave. The first draft of *A Farewell to Arms* was finished two months later, but before Hemingway began the task of revision, his father, Dr. Clarence Hemingway, who had been depressed for some time, committed suicide by shooting himself in the head.

Beyond the immediate strain and horror of such events must have been their power to intensify Hemingway's most buried anxieties. His remarriage, which he did not quite understand, created a keen sense of guilt in him along with the recognition that he contained compulsive forces he was powerless to restrain. Marriage, moreover, could be destructive not only because it had resulted in pain and divorce in his own case; as a child he had seen its effects in the secret contests of will between his parents. Pauline's dangerous, agonized parturition seemed to confirm his feeling that death as readily as life was the consequence of sexuality. He may well have felt what he had imagined the Indian father to feel before cutting his throat in "Indian Camp." That early story suggests that Hemingway had always seen something terrifying in the birth process. Now he incorporated a birth process fatal to both fictional mother and child in the conclusion of his novel.

His father's suicide must have awakened further all his most inadmissible emotions, above all his feelings of hostility and guilt toward his parents. Readers of Carlos Baker's biography do not need a review of Hemingway's childhood and youth with its history of rebellions and chastisements. The spirited boy, adoring and striving to emulate his father, also incurred this father's disciplinarian severity, and young Ernest's resentment of his punishment was so intense that he would sometimes, when he was about eighteen, sit hidden in the doorway of a shed behind the house drawing a bead on his father's head with a gun while the doctor worked in his vegetable garden. Yet it was this same father who had taught him to shoot, initiated him in the craft and passion of killing animals. His feelings toward his mother, whose musical-artistic inclinations might be thought to be the source of his own impulses toward the life of art, would, in the end, prove more bitterly hostile. As he grew to manhood he felt, it would seem, more betrayed by her attempts to control his behavior, especially after the war had proved him a man and even a hero. There is the well-known incident of youthful high-jinks in the woods, shortly after his twenty-first birthday, which resulted in his expulsion from the Hemingways' summer cottage at Walloon Lake. But more hurtful must have been his parents' moralistic censure of his writing. First *In Our Time* and then *The Sun Also Rises* received their uncomprehending disapproval, against which he politely pleaded.

Beneath the politeness there was sometimes a threat. After receiving her criticism of his first novel Hemingway wrote his mother with only half-concealed scorn, "I am sure that it [the novel] is not more unpleasant than the real inner lives of some of our best Oak Park families. You must remember that in such a book all the worst of the people's lives is displayed while at home there is a very lovely side for the public and the sort of which I have had some experience of observing behind closed doors." Behind what doors but those closed upon the conflicts he had known between his parents themselves? Hemingway was prone to hint for years that he might write an Oak Park novel that would tell all: "I had a wonderful novel to write about Oak Park," he said in 1952, "and would never do it because I did not want to hurt living people." After his father's death in 1928 he wrote his mother offering her some advice about how to handle his uncle George, whom he held responsible for his father's money worries, and he also added menacingly, "I have never written a novel about the [Hemingway] family because I have never wanted to hurt anyone's feelings but with the death of the ones I love a period has been put to a great part of it and I may have to undertake it." It is a curious statement, with its slip into the plural "ones" when among his near relatives only his father had died. And was not his mother to be counted among the "ones I love?" There seems to be an unclear implication that she as much as his uncle—whom he had always disliked—might be exposed by his writing. The Oak Park novel was never written. Yet if he rejected the temptation to write about his family life—except in the hints given in such a story as "The Doctor and the Doctor's Wife"—he did not stop writing works that might convey his insight into the "unpleasant" and defy his mother's moralistic hypocrisy. And the covertly autobiographic impulse persisted.

From the time of his father's suicide, he must have felt himself to be just such an orphan, though with a living parent, as Catherine and Frederic describe themselves. "My father is the only one I cared about," he wrote Maxwell Perkins after the doctor's suicide. He then may already have believed what he later stated to Charles Scribner, that his mother had destroyed her husband, and his bitter sense of having been unloved by her fused with his identification with his father: "I hate her guts and she hates mine. She forced my father to suicide." But such liberations from filial love are never quite complete. Underneath must have been the longing for approval, for a lost infantile security. Hemingway's own sexual history, that ultimate personal expression, may have taken some shape from the mixture of need and anger which probably composed his emotions toward his mother. The need to reject as well as the need to be wanted again may explain the course of his love life, with its four marriages and, as his life advanced, its rather greater propensity of promiscuity. Promiscuity, of course, may also be based on the fear that one cannot feel at all. Beneath the intensely expressive, even violent personality of the visible Hemingway there may have been a self that was haunted by the demon of boredom. Apathy, which might seem the least likely affliction of this articulate and active man, may have been what he feared most, knowing his own inner indifference. If so, then *A Farewell to Arms* does have a special relation to the mind of the maker, is autobiographic in a metaphoric way.

Some confirmation of this view may be gained by study of Hemingway's text as the result of revision and excision in accordance with his well-known iceberg theory. In looking for the submerged element that supports a style so economic, so dependent upon implication rather than explication, one is prompted to consider the nature of what has been pruned away. Obviously, the Hemingway aesthetic promotes the elimination of the merely redundant, the detail that adds nothing, the explanation that can be supplied by the reader's own surmise, the additional episode which may thicken the reality of the story but also complicates its meaning too much. Some of this discard may well supply autobiographic clues to the intentional process by which the work was molded. Sometimes, one suspects, the rejected matter comes out of the too-exact transcript of memory.

Even before the manuscript of *A Farewell to Arms* had been studied, it was obvious that Hemingway might have planned his novel at some earlier stage to include other elements besides those finally selected. Julian Smith has argued that two stories written in 1926 just after the breakup of Hemingway's first marriage amplify the novel so precisely at certain points that they may have been conceived of as part of it at one time. One of these is "In Another Country," whose title, with its reference to Marlowe's *Jew of Malta* ("Thou hast committed— / Fornication—but that was in another country; and besides, the wench is dead"), Hemingway once considered using for the novel. The second story linked with the novel is "Now I Lay Me," entitled "In Another Country—Two" in a late draft. Both short stories fulfill the title of the collection in which they were printed in 1927, *Men without Women*, which attaches them in an interesting way to the novel begun soon after, the novel about the failure, in the end, of the sexual bridge over the gulf of solitude.

Both stories are really about marriage. In "In Another Country" the narrator, recovering from his wounds in a Milan hospital and receiving mechanical therapy—like Hemingway and Frederic Henry—is warned not to marry. An Italian major who has just lost his wife tells him that a man "cannot marry" because "if he is to lose everything, he should not place himself in a position to lose that." Had Hemingway chosen to include the story as an episode in *A Farewell to Arms* it might have served to predict Catherine's death as well as the conclusion that nothing, not even love, abides. In "Now I Lay Me" the hero has been wounded in the particular fashion and with the particular sensations Hemingway remembered from his own experience and attributed to Frederic. He does not sleep well—because of the sound of the silkworms and because he is afraid of dying—and passes restless nights thinking about two kinds of boyhood experience: trout fishing and the quarrels between his parents, with his mother's hen-pecking of his father. He is advised by his orderly to marry but does not, and does not intend to, unlike the narrator of the companion story, who tells the major that he hopes to be married.

There are any number of ways in which both stories can be related to Hemingway's personal experience, but it is clear that together they suggest a fear associated with marriage—either one will somehow kill it oneself, as he had done with his own first marriage, or it will kill you, or at least emasculate you, as his mother had emasculated his father. Despite the seemingly positive assurance of the orderly in the second story that marriage will "fix everything," the effect of both tales is to suggest that death and destruction arrive in the end. Love cannot heal the Hemingway hero who longs to return to some presexual condition in the untainted woods of boyhood.

The connection of the two stories with the novel written so soon after them is a matter of conjecture, but Hemingway's manuscript drafts of *A Farewell to Arms* may justifiably be searched for evidence of his compositional intentions and his autobiographic sources. The draft indicates that Hemingway had, for example, included a much more detailed version of the description of wounding already used in "Now I Lay Me" and also a more detailed and more emotional description of Frederic's sensations on waking up in the hospital in Milan. The final version screens out autobiographic irrelevance, for Frederic, in the draft, makes on Hemingway's behalf one of those representative comments that show him struggling against the flood of memory: "If you try and put in everything you would never get a single day done and then the one who made it might not feel it." In the end the writer made these occasions consistent with the rest of the novel as a representation of the state of mind that is the grounding of his hero's being. In the first three books, as Reynolds has observed, the revisions nearly efface Frederic as a personality. He becomes an almost completely apathetic sufferer. Though self-expression is allowed to emerge in the love affair, it does not really make for reversal of this condition, for in the place of the grand afflatus of love, the language of amorous avowal that these lovers speak is self-diminishing.

A complex revision of a crucial passage is the alteration of the conversation between Frederic and the priest in chapter 11. In the manuscript draft Frederic lists some of the things he loves, and adds at the end, "I found I loved god too, a little. I did not love anything too much." In the revision there is no such list or remark, but there is, instead, the priest's statement: "When you love you wish to do things for. You wish to sacrifice for. You wish to serve." Hemingway may be thought to have promoted by this addition the hope of moral growth in his hero, who then asks, in the printed text, "How about loving a woman? If I really loved some woman would it be like that?" He cannot answer his own question nor does the priest answer it, and though, much later, Count Greffi calls love "a religious feeling," Frederic, still dubious, can respond only, "You think so?" Can we analogize the love of God and Frederic's love of Catherine, in fact? Does human love acquire the highest possible meaning for him? Not really. He cannot be said to attain the priest's ideal of service and sacrifice. Nor does the formula apply to Catherine herself. Her death is not redemptive, is not a true Imitation of Christ. It is not voluntarily offered and does not save Frederic from anything or give him faith. Only irony attends the sequel in which the surrender of self seems the consequence of weakness rather than the bounty of strong love. The revision removes the small assertion of faith that Frederic makes, "I found I loved god too, a little," and when the priest declares, "You should love Him," the answer is simply, "I don't love much," or, as the draft has it, "I did not love anything very much," which seems a statement of affective deficiency in general, a general inability to donate emotion.

Frederic's estrangement from feeling is not the consequence of any particular wounding or of war disgust, or of any experience of adulthood, but of a deeply founded sense of loss. A passage Hemingway took out of the novel gives confirmation. It begins with the opening sentence of chapter 40, "We had a fine life," followed in the finished novel by a brief description of the way the couple spent their days during the last of their winter stay in the Swiss mountains. Hemingway decided not to use the long passage that originally followed this opening sentence in which Frederic reflects, anticipating the tragic conclusion, "wisdom and happiness do not go together," and declares his reductive certitude: "The only thing I know is that if you love anything enough they take it away from you." In this discarded passage, as in the rejected ending of the novel, Hemingway felt the need to refer once again to Rinaldi and the priest, those seemingly forgotten mentors of contrary wisdom, and it is plain that Frederic cannot accept the latter's faith, though he says, "I see the wisdom of the priest in our mess who has always loved God and so is happy and I am sure that nothing will ever take God away from him. But how much is wisdom and how much is luck to be born that way? And what if you are not built that way?" Earlier in the novel Gino is described as a patriot because he is "born that way" and Rinaldi is a skeptic for the same reason. But here, in the excised passage, Frederic speaks of himself: "But what if you were born loving nothing and the warm milk of your mother's breast was never heaven and the first thing you loved was the side of a hill and the last thing was a woman and they took her away and you did not want another but only to have her; and she was gone, then you are not so well placed." For Hemingway, too, cannot it have been true that "the warm milk of [his] mother's breast was never heaven?" Is this the underwater knowledge of self which supports the poignancy of what remains in the final text of the novel?

Hemingway's difficulties with the ending can now be seen to have been caused by something besides his desire to be true to life's inconclusiveness. His hero's emotional or philosophic *nada* threatened the very process of making sense, achieving illumination. Hemingway decided to eschew any hint of apocalypse, rejecting even Fitzgerald's suggestion that he place at the end the passage in which Frederic describes how all are finished off impartially, though the good, the gentle, and the brave go first—as dark a revelation as one could imagine, but still a revelation of sorts. What would do best, he realized, would be simply the hero's numb survival without insight, his notation without catharsis.

ERIK NAKJAVANI

Hemingway on War and Peace

You had read on and studied the art of war ever since you were a boy and your
grandfather had started you on the American Civil War.
            —Ernest Hemingway, *For Whom the Bell Tolls* (335).

Prologue

We know that Ernest Hemingway considered the Prussian warrior-philosopher General Karl von Clausewitz the "old Einstein of battles" (*By-Line* 291). From Hemingway's perspective Clausewitz, the author of *On War* (1832), a treatise on the theoretics and pragmatics of war, was "the most intelligent writer on the metaphysics of war that ever lived" (*Men at War* xiv). That is high praise, couched in simple, confident, and knowledgeable language. What we do not know is the basis of Hemingway's superlative comparison and his judgment. In his personal library at his home La Finca Vigía in San Francisco de Paula near Havana, Cuba, the wide array of books on the American Civil War, military history strategy, and war narratives in several languages attests to his own considerable intellectual and theoretical investment in the subject.[1] An examination, subsequent analysis, and critical assessment of Hemingway's own contribution to the 20th-century metaphysics of war constitute my intention in this essay. I shall mainly concentrate on Hemingway's reflections on war as

North Dakota Quarterly, Volume 68, Numbers 2–3 (Spring-Summer 2001): pp. 245–275.
Copyright © 2001 North Dakota Quarterly.

111

we find them in his preface to *A Farewell to Arms* (1949) and in introductions to *Men at War: The Best War Stories of All Time* (1942) and *Treasury for the Free World* (1946). It is our common knowledge that Hemingway gave the subject of war a privileged metaphorical position in the general thematics of his fiction. My concentration on these three prefaces would make it possible to deal with his own articulation and imbrication of metaphysical, psychological, and literary aspects of war, on the one hand, and the ethics of national and individual behavior in wartime, on the other. It leaves out his fictional concerns with such matters, which have already been extensively dealt with in Hemingway scholarship.

I. On the Inevitability and the Criminality of War

No catalogue of horrors ever kept men from war.
—Ernest Hemingway, *By-Line: Ernest Hemingway* (210)

We know war is bad. Yet sometimes it is necessary to fight. But still war is bad and any man who says it is not is a liar.
Ernest Hemingway, *Selected Letters* (480)

Hemingway's 1949 preface to the illustrated edition of *A Farewell to Arms* (1929) gives him the opportunity to express his views on the topic of war as a persistent dimension of the human condition. "The title of this book is *A Farewell to Arms*" he writes, "and except for three years there has been war of some kind almost ever since it has been written" (x). Considering the enormity of the subject, Hemingway's tone is relatively disillusioned, reticent, and almost detached, without heat or hope, but authoritative. He makes a simple statement that may be boiled down to stating that the lived history of our time is experiential proof of the inevitability of war. He only intimates that the title refers to his World War I (1914–1918) novel, a war of unprecedented mechanized violence and brutality, which was naively hailed by some as the war to end all wars. The intervening years, before and after the publication of *A Farewell to Arms,* were to belie that claim. Wars and other conflicts betrayed even the most modest measure of hope the title in one of its multiple signification might have implied—both on the planes of the individual and the particular and the national and the universal. The three years of uneasy peace to which Hemingway refers could have only been the gift of the total European war weariness and exhaustion, not at all a reassuring reason for the absence of war. After this minimal and highly compressed but essential account of two decades of European history, he then gently makes fun of the critics who irked him by regarding his interest in war as obsessive, even pathological. "Some people used to say," he chides, "why is the man so preoccupied and obsessed with war, and now, since 1933 perhaps it is clear why a writer should be interested in the constant bullying, murderous, slovenly crime of war" (x).

Thus, writing in 1949, for Hemingway nearly the whole first half of the 20th century stands accused of the "murderous, slovenly crime of war," going all the way back to the European 1908–1914 arms race, which he characteristically leaves out. What he does include is the mere mention of the virulent form of the "constant bullying" and the quasi-mystical glorification of murderous impulses in the 1933 rise of Nazi ideology. It is an ideology that regards violence as sacred within the putative prerogatives of the Aryan "master race." Hemingway might have added other bloody events he knew so much about, mainly the 1917 Bolshevik Revolution in Russia, as an armed struggle for a classless society that was to sweep away what Karl Marx and Friedrich Engels in *The Communist Manifesto*, decried as "All fixed and fast-frozen [human] relations, with their train of ancient and venerable prejudices and opinions" (12); the surge of Italian Fascism (1922) as the resurgence of the Roman Empire; and the Spanish Civil War (1936–1939). The bipolarity of these two ideologies, Communism and Fascism, found their common ground in totalitarian attitudes, but the Nazi and Fascist ideologies appeared more inclined to acclaim unbound violence as a value in itself. Violence appeared to them to yield a panacea to individual and national powerlessness. In 1935, in "Notes on the Next War," Hemingway warns:

> In a modern war there is no Victory. The allies won the war but the regiments that marched in triumph were not the men who fought the war. The men who fought the war were dead. More than seven million of them were dead and it is the murder of over seven million more that an ex-corporal in the German army [Hitler] and an ex-aviator and former morphine addict [Mussolini] drunk with personal and military ambition and fogged in a blood-stained murk of misty patriotism look forward hysterically to today. (*By-Line* 211)

Hemingway's interest as a writer in all the blood-lust and bloodletting in the 20th century is also augmented by the omnipresence of their analogues throughout human history. He reminds us that "Europe has always fought, the intervals of peace are only Armistices" (*By-Line* 212). For him, the historical background is a melancholy reminder of our foreground, a gloomy story elaborately and intricately foretold. It is the continual preparation for and perpetual occurrence of war that force Hemingway to consider war as a subject of primary interest for a writer. Persuaded that the foretold are at least forewarned, he sounds an alarm. War, as an atavistic concern, fascinates him and compels him to reflect. He would have agreed with the Chinese warrior-philosopher Sun Tzu who holds that "Military action is . . . the ground of death and life, the path of survival and destruction, so it is important to examine it" (x).

However, I find no reason to suggest that war and its metaphors and metonymies heard as echoes in Hemingway's writing are in any way an advocacy of war. It is tempting to establish a connection between intellectual, literary, and personal interests and advocacy in his case, but I believe it will prove to be wading in the shallows and ultimately a spurious undertaking. It will be so regardless of the occasions for bravery and nobility, which Hemingway greatly admired, that war provides for men. There is too much evidence to the contrary. In his introduction to *Treasury for the Free World*, he is unmistakably direct about the criminality of war:

> An aggressive war is the great crime against everything good in the world. A defensive war, which must necessarily turn to aggressive at the earliest moment, is the necessary great counter-crime. But never think that war, no matter how necessary, nor how justified, is not a crime. (xv)

In "Wings over Africa," he instructs us that "war has the essence of all of these [tyranny, injustice, murder, brutality, and the corruption of the soul] blended together and is strengthened by its various parts until it is stronger than any of the evils it is composed of can ever be" (*By-Line* 234). Thus he does not condone war as admissible or excusable—even though often war may be defensive, unavoidable, and. inevitable. For him, as we have just seen, war always conjugates all manifestations of evil in such a way as to make them more effective in their combined demonic violence.

"War is always wrong," Karl Jaspers categorically proclaims—plain and simple (115). No casuistry of just war for Jaspers. It would seem to me Hemingway would have no quarrel with such a straightforward ethical statement. Yet, from a writer's point of view, he considers war to be a significant experience. The experience of war is consequential to him even if a writer peripherally participates in it, as Hemingway did by serving with the Red Cross on the Italian front where he was gravely wounded on July 8, 1918. Accordingly, his understanding of war—as being at once unavoidable and unacceptable, even when it places itself under the sign of counter-violence—deepens and becomes exceedingly nuanced. His fictional references to matters of war testify to the scope and complexity of his comprehension of the subject, even though his own direct war experience was limited. As an exigent life-and-death experience—a veritable *extremis* or "limit-situation," as Jasper calls it—war is no doubt for many an unsurpassable and often epiphanic experience.

I would say that the dualities of Hemingway's attitude toward war and the conduct of men at war simultaneously bear marks of the antithetical Freudian and the early Christian thinking on the subject. I will go so far as to suggest that the dualities of his thought on war signal an effort to reconcile these two seemingly irreconcilable modes of thought: Christian dogmatics and Freudian psychoanalysis. The former commands: "Thou shalt love thy neighbor as thyself" and "Love thine enemies"—which, combined, speak the essence of the mysteries of the concepts of Christian love and charity. Freudian psychoanalysis considers the "neighbor" as the "stranger," the Other, and therefore as either a real or potential enemy. This dialectical shift from the thesis of Christian love to its Freudian antithesis of skepticism seems so knotty as to make a reconciliation between the two and a potential synthesis appear impossible. However, is this synthesis entirely outside the realm of at least conceptual possibility? The answer does not fall easily within our grasp. Thus it requires closer examination, analysis, and interpretation of the concepts of the Other, both as an object of our love and of our hostility or hatred, before we can conceive of a synthesis.

II. On the Metaphysics and Psychology of War and Peace

Homo homini lupus. [Man is a wolf to man.] Who, in the face of all his experience of life and of history, will have the courage to dispute this assertion?
—Sigmund Freud, *Civilization and Its Discontents* (58)

Iris Murdoch pointedly remarks that "The paradox of our situation is that we must have theories about human nature, no theory explains everything, yet it is just the desire to explain everything that is the spur of theory" (190). In relation to the concepts of war and peace, Hemingway too, feels the tug and pull of this desire—albeit that for him, as a novelist, "the spur of theory" is dominated by the density of the particular and the experiential. These characteristic polarities of his thought, his general belief in the inevitability of war, and his reluctant acceptance of it as an undeniable reality puts him in the proximity if not indeed within the parameters of Freudian psychoanalytic theory. To probe somewhat deeper into Hemingway's thought on war and to situate it within the larger context of 20th-century thought I find it helpful to review briefly its shared concerns with Sigmund Freud's similar psychoanalytic interests.

In 1909, Freud is already aware that the "aggressive instinct" needs to be included in his general theory of instincts. By 1930, he accords it a significant conceptual place as the "death instinct" in *Civilization and Its Discontents*. We find him to be initially hesitant to provide a thorough formulation of what he terms "aggressive instinct." While giving it a prominent place in animal biology, he is inclined at this time to attenuate its biological and therefore prelinguistic role in the human psyche. For "to include it in the human constitution appears sacrilegious; it contradicts too many religious presumptions and social conventions" ("Anxiety" 129). Since he was no stranger to defiance of received notions, his hesitation may have even had a more poignant source than the religious and social disapprobation: Freud was a humanist. Exposed as we have been to the thoroughgoing structuralism of the 20th century, we understand his sensitivity, ambivalence, and reserve about this subject, which is uncharacteristic of him and his courageous stance in matters clinical, theoretical, and speculative. In 1909, in the "Little Hans" case history "Analysis of a Phobia in a Five-Year-Old Boy," Freud elaborates further on his reluctance: "I cannot bring myself to assume the existence of a special aggressive instinct alongside of the familiar instinct of self-preservation and sex, and on an equal footing with them" (143). Nevertheless, during and after World War I, his reticence gradually is attenuated and then disappears altogether. By 1930, with the rise of German Nazism looming over the horizon, he is ready to proclaim:

> Starting from speculations on the beginning of life and from biological parallels, I drew the conclusion that, besides the instinct to preserve living substance and to join it into ever larger units, there must exist another, contrary instinct seeking to dissolve those units and to bring them back to their primaeval, inorganic state. That is to say, as well as Eros there was an instinct of death. (*Civilization* 65–66)

For Freud, this is a decisive moment when historical reality affirms theoretical findings. He was no doubt witnessing, reflecting on, and being influenced by powerful German ideological, political, social, and cultural upheavals in the making. Coincidentally, Hemingway too discerned these disturbing convulsions in Germany, worrying that

> those [in Germany] who had never accepted a military defeat hated those who had and started to do away with the ablest of them by the vilest program of assassination the world has ever known. They started, immediately after the war, by killing Karl Liebknecht [a founder of the German Social Democratic party] and Rosa Luxemburg [economist and revolutionary], and they killed on,

steadily eliminating revolutionary and liberal alike by an unvarying
process of intelligent assassination. (*By-Line* 182)

Intelligent assassination efficiently produces dead bodies; but, above all,
what it kills so well and so often is intelligence itself. Completely disillusioned, Freud, too, now advances the idea that all human relations are based
on irremediable aggression that, if frustrated, turns into uncontrolled and
uncontrollable violent explosions. Therefore, peaceful coexistence and coop-
eration will forever elude civilized human beings who aspire to it.

Freud theoretically defies and finally negates the two Christian com-
mandments, "Thou shalt love thy neighbor as thyself" and "Love thine enemies" on experiential, personal, collective, and historical bases. For Freud,
my neighbor is "in general unworthy of my love" and. "has more claim to my
hostility and even my hatred." This is so because my neighbor "seems not to
have the least trace of love for me and shows me not the slightest consideration" (*Civilization* 57). As, such, my neighbor shall always be a stranger to
me and I to him. Here the logic of aggression reigns supreme, and, ultimately,
the reason of the strongest proves to be the best. Freud, like Hemingway,
disillusioned by increasing Nazi and Fascist strength, finds not superior intelligence but superior force to have been the final arbiter of all matters in human history. Within this vicious circle of alterity and alienation, the "I-thou"
relationship in *caritas* is then entirely replaced by the hostile "I-it" encounter
in which I deny the subjective autonomy of my neighbor and reduce him to
an object of my aggression.

Freud seems to be generally answering Schopenhauer's old philosophical question: Is man not the "beast of prey which will pounce upon a weaker
neighbor as soon as he notices his existence? And is this fact not confirmed
everyday in ordinary life?" Freud's answer is an unsparing, Yes! Schopenhauer
further elaborates that "No animal ever torments another for the sake of tor-
menting: but man does so, and it is this that constitutes the *diabolical* nature
which is worse than the merely bestial" (*Essays* 139). In Schopenhauer's philosophy Christian love (caritas) is perverted into *Schadenfreude,* the sadistic
pleasure in someone's discomfiture or misfortune. *Schadenfreude* reveals itself
in life as the malevolent "laughter of Hell" (*Essays* 140). Nietzsche later sadly
claimed that "The whole life of the Christian is at last exactly the life from
which Christ preached deliverance" (*Will to Power* 125).

Hemingway, too, knew much about *Schadenfreude* as the drunkards' behavior in the massacre of Fascists in *For Whom the Bell Tolls* (99–129) makes
abundantly clear. His voice on these matters as a whole is in remarkable
harmony with the chorus of European disillusionment and disenchantment
with the human condition. In the essay "On the Blue River," Hemingway
wryly observes, "Certainly there is no hunting like the hunting of man and

those who have hunted armed men long enough and liked it, never really care for anything else thereafter" (*By-Line* 236). The certainty of the thrill of one man hunting another provides a striking psychological and ethical admission. It indicates a far-reaching discovery for Hemingway and a fearsome and consequential revelation for the reader. To the extent that the hunting of one man by another ushers us into an endless sadomasochistic dialectic, it clearly includes a psychical space in which the hunter and the hunted can easily metamorphose into one another. Hemingway's view of human aggressive instinct coincides with the more general psychoanalytic and philosophical theories of Freud and his philosopher predecessors Schopenhauer and Nietzsche. Human aggression merely gets stated differently by Hemingway in his own direct style of thinking and writing drawn from lived experience and imagination.

In this context, one may consider Hemingway's so-called "obsession" with war not as a symptom of his neurosis but, more accurately, as a concern with a fundamental dimension of lived history and, by extension, of all human history. He wants us to be aware that "All of history is of one piece and it is ourselves . . . " (*Men at War* xxiii). Thus if there be a neurosis, its origin must be primarily sought not in Hemingway but, above all, in the lived human history itself. Hemingway's beloved predecessors in art and literature such as Stendhal, Tolstoy, Goya, and Stephen Crane faced the same historical phenomenon: history as the long sad narratives of the collective neurosis of aggression and the psychosis of war.

III. On the Conduct of War and Just Peace

Regardless of how this war [WW II] was brought on . . . there is only one thing now to do. We must win it. We must win it at all costs and as soon as possible.

—Ernest Hemingway, *Men at War* (xi)

Hemingway appears to have considered the concept of *jus ad bellum* or "just war" as no more than a sophistical theory at best and a mendacious one at worst. It survives to our day as the Catholic Church's desire to reconcile war and Christ's commandment, "Love thine enemies," under certain conditions or circumstances (Council of Arles 314). It was a modality of *realpolitik* which later became a part of the Church's doctrine. We have already seen that Hemingway unreservedly believes war to be criminal in all its various manifestations. He finds no conditions or circumstances in which war could be sanctioned as good or legitimized as "just" as, say, Gratian and Saint Augustine did. Correlatively, for him, the only mode of *jus in bello* or just conduct in war is to win it quickly by any means possible, regardless of who or what has initially caused it. He develops a "realistic" argument to support his negation of *jus in bello*. In his introduction to the anthology of war narratives, *Men at War*, he tells us that

> The editor of this anthology, who took part and was wounded in the last war to end war [WW I], hates war and hates all the politicians whose mismanagement, gullibility, cupidity, selfishness and ambition brought on this present war [WW II] and made it inevitable. But once we have a war there is only one thing to do. It must be won. *For defeat brings worse things than any that can ever happen in a war.* (xi, my emphasis)

For me, this paragraph makes intelligible the crux of Hemingway's thought on the conduct of war: war is irrecusably evil, always and everywhere, but worse is yet the evil of defeat. Tactically, he advises, "when the moment arrives, whether it is in a barroom fight or in a war, the thing to do is to hit your opponent the first punch and hit him as hard as possible" (*Men at War* xxi). This statement has a Machiavellian cast to it; and yet it simply makes its way beyond expediency to another sphere of significant considerations. I discern in it Hemingway's absolute dread of defeat, which borders on a Hegelian master-slave dialectic. Winning a war bestows the rights of the master on the winner and ushers in a period of slavery for the loser. For Hemingway, nothing less than the essence of our humanity, that is, our freedom is at stake in losing a war. The horrific upshot of losing a war makes itself manifest in the unavoidable loss of freedom and the consequent enslavement suffered by an individual, group, tribe, race, or nation. That is precisely why Hemingway can write an unthinkable sentence such as: "The answer to the Nazi claim that Germans area superior race and other races shall be slaves is to say, and mean it, 'We will take your race and wipe it out'" (*Men at War* xxix). And mean it? The ferocity of the sentence derives from the equally unimaginable horror of slavery for Hemingway. Thus he puts forward a subcategory of the Hegelian idea of the fight to the death, which naturally issues from the master-slave conflict, its consequent dialectic, and acquires the dimension of an imperative. Hemingway can only respond to the possibility of defeat with fury and utter contempt. A human being is always better dead than enslaved. As a consequence, he simply insists that "We must win it [this war]" (*Men at War* xi), which becomes for him incantatory in its necessity, intensity, and repetition.

After all is said, it is still in the name of freedom, or the negation of slavery as a mode of human existence in its totality, that he adds: "We must win it never forgetting what we are fighting for, in order that while we are fighting Fascism we do not slip into the ideas and ideals of Fascism" (*Men at*

War xii). For Fascism absolute power denies, violates, obliterates, and eventually even *surpasses* freedom as a constituent of the human condition. I would suggest that one may interpret Hemingway's startling proposal to wipe out the German race as "We will take your Nazi ideology and we will wipe it out. We mean this." In the same mode of thinking, admitting that Germans are "practical professionals in war," he counsels:

> We can learn all their lessons without being Fascists if we keep our minds open. All we need is common sense, a quality which is often conspicuously lacking in generalship but which our own Civil War produced the great masters of. We can beat the Germans without becoming Fascists. We can fight a total war without becoming totalitarians if we do not stand on our mistakes and try to cover them. . . . (*Men at War* xiii)

This passage makes sufficiently evident the radical complexity of Hemingway's metaphysics of war, which reformulates the concept of *jus ad bellum* by removing from war the possibility of enslaving the defeated. Hemingway's reference to the American Civil War in the passage becomes noteworthy in this new reformulation. In his 1946 introduction to *Treasury for the Free World*, he refers to peacetime as "a more difficult time when it is a man's duty to understand his world rather than simply fight for it" (xiii). He considers the understanding of one's world "to be hard work [that] will involve reading much that is unpleasant to accept. But it is one of man's first duties now" (xiii). And, among other things, this unpleasant reading will make it clear to us that

> We have waged war in the most ferocious and ruthless way that it has ever been waged. We waged it against fierce and ruthless enemies that it was necessary to destroy. . . . For the moment we are the strongest power in the world. It is very important that we do not become the most hated. (*Treasury* xiii)

Again, Hemingway turns the Fascist ideology upside down by privileging freedom over absolute power. In "On the American Dead in Spain," he writes:

> The fascists may spread over the land, blasting their way with weight of metal brought from other countries. They may advance aided by traitors and by cowards. They may destroy cities and villages and try to hold people in slavery. *But you cannot hold any people in slavery.* (37, my emphasis)

What enslaving power seeks is temporary because freedom endures. "Just as the earth can never die, neither those who have been free return to slavery" ("American Dead" 37). For Hemingway, Fascism is a hating, hateful, and hated ideology, in the fullest sense of those adjectives, and doomed to failure everywhere. It is also the most pernicious because it is as contagious as a plague disguised as privilege. So "we," too, can become hated to the extent that we are vulnerable to its contagion, which can easily contaminate and corrupt a "super-power." He warns that it would "be easy for us, if we do not learn to understand the world and appreciate the rights, privileges, and duties of all other countries and peoples, to represent in our power the same danger to the world that Fascism did" (*Treasury* xiii–xiv). A terrible and terrifying possibility. He seems to agree with the ancient Taoist Chinese warrior Sun Tzu that it is best not to "celebrate victory," that "Those who celebrate victory are bloodthirsty, and the bloodthirsty cannot have their way with the world" (x). Hemingway is intensely passionate about making the conditions for a genuinely human world free from oppression a reality. He strongly admonishes that

> This is no time for any nation to have any trace of the mentality of the bully. It is no time for any nation to become hated. It is no time for any nation to even swagger. Certainly it is no time for any nation to jostle. It is no time for any nation to be anything but just. (*Treasury* xiv)

However, the just peace he proposes is as hard to attain as fighting a war and winning it, perhaps even more so in a particular sense. One may say that just peace is the Tao of overcoming without fighting—which, above all, affirms a certain existential freedom, of refusing to subject significant human activities to determinism of any kind, be it biological, instinctual, economic, or otherwise. Just peace is, then, a matter of profundities of a specific kind of education and re-education. From a psychoanalytic perspective, it is tantamount to the constructive sublimation of the "destructive instinct." Nevertheless, it must be clearly taken into account that such a sublimation, as education or re-education, is a multidimensional and difficult process. It demands that creative forces substitute freely chosen sublimates for the objects of the "destructive instinct" with which they appear to be inextricably interwoven. The determinism of the concept of "destructive instinct" opposes or modifies the fulfillment of freedom's call. Just the same, Hemingway insists upon this fulfillment. Like Plato's charioteer, Phaedrus, he intends to control two horses of great power—one dark and implacable and the other more placable and pliant—by guiding them wisely. Let us read him:

> We have fought this war and won it. Now let us not be sanctimonious; nor hypocritical; nor vengeful nor stupid. Let us make our enemies incapable of ever making war again, let us re-educate them, and let us learn to live in peace and justice with all the countries and all peoples in this world. To do this we must educate and re-educate. But first we must educate ourselves. (*Treasury* xv)

At the time (1946), this re-education was also a call to confront any victorious nation's permanent dominion over the conquered nations.

> In this new world all of the partners will have to relinquish. It will be as necessary to relinquish as it was necessary to fight. No nation who holds land or dominion over people where it has no just right to it can continue to do so if there is to be enduring peace. . . . (*Treasury* xiv)

He further warns, "There will be no lasting peace, nor any possibility of a just peace, until all lands where the people are ruled, exploited, and governed by any government whatsoever against their consent are given their freedom" (*Men at War* xxix). For Hemingway, among others, added to this complex of reasons is the emergence of the immense problematics of the atomic bomb:

> We need to study and understand certain basic problems of our world as they were before Hiroshima to be able to continue, intelligently, to discover how some of them have changed and how they can be settled justly now that a new weapon has become a property of a part of the world. We must study them more carefully than ever now and remember that no weapon has ever settled a moral problem. It can impose a solution but it cannot guarantee a just one. You can wipe out your opponents. But if you do it unjustly you become eligible for being wiped out yourself. (*Treasury* xiv)

A nagging question still persists: are we educable or re-educable in this exigent and drastic way that Hemingway suggests? Can we—either as individuals, groups, or nations—overcome sanctimoniousness, hypocrisy, vengefulness, incomprehension, even just plain stupidity? Were we capable of such rational transcendence of instinctual forces, were we able to challenge the sovereignties of major or "minor differences" (Freud, *Civilization* 61) and their attendant narcissism, were we strong enough to overcome the notion that whoever is wholly or partially not me deserves my transgression and violence, we would have never needed to resort to violence and war as a means of settling our problems in the first place. In any case, Hemingway the humanist did cherish such a hope on a good sunny day in Cuba, as did Bertrand Russell in his essay *Has Man a Future?* Perhaps he believed so in contradistinction to his own experiential knowledge—thinking against himself, as it were. Or he may have considered the refusal not to have hope a sin, regardless of the paralyzing evidence to the contrary at the time. And why not? After all, faith and hope, anticipating the nascent mystery's predawn hour, bypass the circuits of conceptual and often experiential knowledge. Even Nietzsche's Zarathustra advises: "Let work be a struggle, your peace a victory. . . . Let your love for life be your highest hope. And let your highest hope be the highest thought of life" (*Thus Spoke* 49–50). It may have indeed been so with Hemingway. In my view, work as struggle against impossible odds is constantly infused with intensities of love and life in the entirety of Hemingway's writing. As an observer (and occasionally as a peripheral participant) in different capacities in various wars and as a student of war he might have arrived at the contrary conclusion. But his hope for victory and just peace does highlight a certain hard-earned, admirable optimism in him.

One may summarily say, as far as Hemingway is concerned, once we are at war we have no other alternative but to win *at any price*. But once we have won a war and have peace, we cannot be anything but just. If Hemingway refuses to accept the conceptual and practical speciousness of "just war," he offers us a different notion as replacement: *just peace*. I consider it as his contribution to the Kantian philosophical ideal of perpetual peace. His optimism merits serious consideration, equally serious experiential and psychoanalytic arguments against it notwithstanding. I would lay it down then this way: with the notion of *just peace* Hemingway enters, at least provisionally, a zone of pure hope and freedom.

IV. On Men at War

They wrote in the old days that it is sweet and fitting to die for one's country [Horace]. But in modern war there is nothing sweet nor fitting in your dying. You will die like a dog for no good reason.
—Ernest Hemingway, *By-Line: Ernest Hemingway* (209)

My brothers in war! I love you with all my heart; I am and was of your sort. And I am also your best enemy. Then let me tell you the truth!
—Friedrich Nietzsche, *Thus Spoke Zarathustra* (48)

As we have already seen, there exists a sufficient body of evidence in Hemingway's meditations on war to make a simple, straightforward statement: Hemingway hated war. His hatred of war, however, makes a highly intricate and multi-faceted mosaic of concerns. His hatred of war should be particularly extended to the judgment he brings to men at war and those he primarily holds responsible for instigating war for ambition, venality, and sheer love of brutality. Let us begin with the judgment he renders on war profiteers. In "Wings over Africa," he expresses the conviction that "The only people who ever loved war for long were profiteers, generals, staff officers, and whores. They all had the best and finest time of their lives and most of them made the most money they had ever made" (*By-Line* 234). One may assume that for him all manner of profiteering from war is a kind of whoring. It is not too difficult, however, to imagine the real whore was the most honorable, the most honest in her intention, the least harmful to others, and the least offensive to Hemingway in his roster of the whoring profiteers and professional mercenaries. Elsewhere he writes: "I believe that all the people who stand to profit by a war and who help provoke it should be shot on the first day it starts by accredited representatives of the loyal citizens of their country who will fight it" (*Farewell* x). In mock-seriousness, he adds he would be "very glad to be in charge of this shooting, if legally delegated by those who will fight. . . . " In these reflections, he makes a clear distinction between anyone who in any way stands to profit from the war and the combatants. It is the latter whom he sees as being "amongst the finest people that there are, or just say people, although, the closer you are to where they are fighting, the finer people you meet . . . " (*Farewell* x). It is the courage and resourcefulness, the toughness and resilience—in short, the nobility and heroism of the ordinary soldier in the face of death that he so utterly admires. The soldier becomes a veritable warrior *in extremis,* a man whose life will forever be transformed by his martial experience if he survives and conducts himself well and with grace. It is "the human heart and the human mind in war" that he finds praiseworthy and instructive (*Men at War* xx). The baptism of fire will either wholly engulf the warrior or shall earn him the mantle of authenticity, in its Heideggerian sense and implications, as only the warrior elite has always come to know and to incarnate. It is all a matter of combatants facing death intelligently, bravely, even exuberantly in a war not of their own making. When slain in battle, these warriors are heroes that the Norse mythology assigns to Valhalla, the paradise of heroes. It is exactly to such potential warriors that Hemingway addresses himself—if not as a former brother-in-arms at least as a participant in war and then as an older, wiser commentator. In a paragraph in *Men at War,* Hemingway offers to the book's potential World War II warrior-readers a lyrical narrative of being wounded in World War I:

When you go to war as a boy you have a great illusion of immortality. Other people get killed; not you. It can happen to other people; but not to you. Then when you are badly wounded the first time you lose that illusion and you know it can happen to you. After being severely wounded two weeks before my nineteenth birthday I had a bad time until I figured it out that nothing could happen to me that had not happened to all men before me. Whatever I had to do men had always done. If they had done it then I could do it too and the best thing was not to worry about it. (xiii–xiv)

This is a multi-layered narrative of elegiac elegance and depth. The illusion of immortality partakes of a deep-running narcissism, which, incidentally, markedly influences Hemingway's writing as a whole. It signals a regression to "The fantasy from childhood of a secret valley of no death, like beliefs in the Elysian Fields, or joining our ancestors or the company of immortals, is eloquent testimony to the strength and influence of our striving toward narcissism which eludes the real impairment or injury" (Rocklin 216). The soldier all too quickly wakes up from this dream of immortality and has to face the verities of combat. What awaits him is the nightmarish reality of history's "killing fields" and the warrior's stoic acceptance of it and willing participation in it. As William James has put it: "Ancestral evolution has made us all potential warriors; so the most insignificant individual, when thrown into an army in the field, is weaned from whatever excess of tenderness towards his precious person he may bring with him . . . " (283). For both Hemingway and James, war signifies a process of divestment of narcissism, whose virulent outbursts our history has continually recorded and has mostly rationalized and glorified. It is the acceptance of war and its vicissitudes as an inextricable part of human existence that eventually dissipates the quasi-hallucinatory narcissism and gives birth to the true warrior within whose ranks Hemingway aspired to inscribe his own name. The warrior loses the illusion of immortality to the extent that his narcissistic fantasy of a precious and immortal self commences to lose its grip on his psyche. From a Nietzschean vantage point, it is at this very juncture that Hemingway appears as both "brother" and "enemy" to would-be warriors he counsels. His kinship is with the disillusioned, mortal warrior against the naive, narcissistic, immortal soldier. To the World War II potential warrior-readers of *Men at War*, he points out:

This book will not tell you how to die. This book will tell you, though, how all men from the earliest times we know have fought and died. So when you have read it you will know that there are no worse things to be gone through than men have been through before. (xi)

He speaks directly from experiential knowledge and his words carry a considerable existential and psychological insight. There is a strange and striking fraternity among warriors of all time who stoically endure the unendurable, which the act of reading can evoke and affirm. Hemingway speaks from the depth of this fraternal feeling. Trusting these fraternal bonds and understandings, he recommends as profoundly enlightening, helpful, and healing the narratives of men at war bearing away the unspeakable violence, from the earliest time in history to our own. He regrets that he was

> very ignorant at nineteen and had read little and I remember the sudden happiness and the feeling of having a permanent protecting talisman when a young British officer [E. E. "Chink" Dorman-Smith] I met when in the hospital first wrote out for me, so I could remember them, these lines:
> *"By my troth, I care not: a man can die but once; we owe God a death . . . and let it go which way it will, he that dies this year is quit for the next"* [from Shakespeare's *Henry IV*].
> That is probably the best thing that is written in this book and, with nothing else, a man can get along all right on that.

Hemingway regrets that "there was no really good true war book during the entire four years of the war [1914–1918]" except in poetry (*Men at War* xiv). A really good book might have revealed how in a war

> worrying does no good . . . A good soldier does not worry. He knows that nothing happens until it actually happens and you live your life up until then. Danger only exists at the moment of danger. To live properly in war, the individual eliminates all such things as potential danger. Then a thing is only bad when it is bad. It is neither bad before nor after. Cowardice, as distinguished from panic, is almost always simply a lack of ability to suspend the functioning of the imagination. (*Men at War* xxvii)

Perhaps one can equate "worrying" in this passage with anxiety in its clinical, definitional sense; that is to say, as catastrophic anticipation of the deeply suppressed annihilative threat to the self that, with the help of a highly sensitized imagination, is aroused from its slumber, exceeds itself and subsequently operates as an autonomous unconscious force within consciousness. As such, it makes itself known as a psychic state beyond conscious control.

Freud connects it with the castration complex. For Melanie Klein, it has its origin in the ruthlessness of the death instinct and is thereby experienced as an intimation of death itself. Both theories indicate a fantasy of aggression that has risen to a way of being replete with intimations of non-being, an ontological state and its antithesis, turning inward now rather than outward in its multiplicity of forms. In yet another register, Jacques Lacan properly categorizes it as *"aggression suicidaire narcissique"* (*Écrits* 187).

Along with psychoanalyst Rollo May, I would go a step further and place Hemingway's notion of a soldier's "worrying" or anxiety under the over-all umbrella of existential experience of "the threat of imminent non-being," which "is always a threat to the foundation, the center of my existence" (50). As such it is a specific "ontological" concern that differentiates it from mere "panic" or fear:

> Fear . . . is a threat to the periphery [of one's] existence; it can be objectivated and the person can stand outside and look at it . . . Fear can be studied as an affect among other affects, a reaction among other reactions. But anxiety can only be understood as a threat to *Dasein* [existence]. (May 51)

And for men at war, it is the temporal element of anxiety, as a break in the continuity of everyday life, which Ludwig Binswanger recognizes and designates as "suddenness," that is most salient. In this context, Binswanger tells us that "It is this type of temporal orientation that permits the element of suddenness to assume such enormous significance; because suddenness is the time quality that explodes continuity, hacks it and chops it to pieces, throws the earlier existence out of its course and exposes it to the Dreadful, to the naked horror" (204). War is preponderantly the realm of "sudden-ness," that is, the unpredictable and therefore of the dreadful and the hor-rific. Unpredictability surging up from nowhere, so to speak, makes war at once inordinately simple and terrifyingly complex. As a result, the difficulty of the simple things in war and their attendant anxiety are their particular temporal dimension, that is, suddenness and its consequent tearing apart of the fabric of human life.

Clearly, Hemingway is experientially, emotionally, and intellectually fully cognizant of the psychological ramifications of the triad of fear, cata-strophic anticipation, and anxiety. His recommendation to the intelligent and imaginative warrior is the willed and willing suspension of that highly prized capacity: imagination. Now imagination is constituted by and is constitu-tive of a certain mode of psychic wholeness that comprises a lived space and time. Let us call it an imaginal spatio-temporal continuum. It is within this continuum that intelligence, sensitivity, sensibility, emotional empathy, connectedness, and psychical cohesiveness dwell. In short: imagination, perpetually unfolding within its own continuum as it does, is what properly renders us human. The suspension of our imagination demands a restructuring of the imaginal spatio-temporal continuum—a task so exigent as to seem impossible without negating one's own lived or ego identity. But then the strength to will the suspension of imagination is tantamount to preternatural bravery of the warrior elite, which simultaneously enriches and impoverishes the warrior as a human being. Hemingway's thinking here is not too far from James's, who argues: "Far better it is for an army to be too savage, too cruel, too barbarous, than to possess too much sentimentality and human reasonableness. If the soldier is to be good for anything as a soldier, he must be exactly the opposite of a reasoning and thinking man" (283). A reasoning and thinking man is by definition an imaginative man as well. Such a man will find it considerably troublesome believing that "Any act that helps my side win the war is right and good, and any act that hinders it is wrong and bad" (Gray 132). Yet a true warrior needs to act spontaneously on that basis under extreme circumstances—an operation that, as we have already seen, requires at least a provisional shutting down of the imaginative processes. When the warrior has acquired the "ability to suspend the functioning of the imagination," he may then discover that

> To win a war you have to do things that are inconceivable in peace and that are often hateful to those who do them. Afterwards some people get used to them. Some get to like them. Every one wants to do everything, no matter what, to get it [war] over with. (*Treasury* xv)

As James puts it, "the immediate aim of a soldier's life is . . . destruction and nothing but destruction; and whatever constructions wars result in are remote and non-military" (83–84). James and Hemingway appear then to be establishing a new pragmatic vocabulary for reflection on the metaphysics of war and the conduct of men at war. Hemingway's military pedagogy intentionally remains mostly at the level of the experiential and the pragmatic. It provides the basis for a theory of combat that one may refer to as conceiving the inconceivable by suspending the imagination. It becomes a matter of accepting the fantasy of annihilation as a real possibility. A warrior, as a "fighting man or *Homo furens*," still needs to manage to belong to the genus *Homo sapiens* and not be degraded to "something less than a man" (Gray 26–27). Ultimately, great warriors are capable of fully reconciling themselves with Dylan Thomas' well known line: "After the first death, there is no other" (197). Thomas' poetic logic brings to mind the passage about dying in Shakespeare's *Henry IV*—bearing witness at once to total rebellion and total stoicism, to oblivion and immortality. From this specific angle, a warrior's profession is not only *"le métier triste"* but also, to a large extent, *le métier mystique* as well.

V. On the Metaphysics and Psychology of War and Writing

No one has more right to write of these actions that saved Madrid than Gustav Regler. He fought in all of them.
> —Ernest Hemingway, preface to Gustav Regler's
> *The Great Crusade* (vii)

War is the father of all good things [Heraclitus]. War is also the father of good prose.
> —Friedrich Nietzsche, *The Gay Science* (145)

Hemingway considered war a significant experience for a writer. In *Green Hills of Africa*, thinking of Tolstoy, he acknowledges "what a great advantage an experience of war was to a writer." Further magnifying the scope of this advantage, he pronounces war "as one of the major subjects and certainly one of the hardest to write truly of." He resents that "those writers who had not seen it were always very jealous and tried to make it seem unimportant, or abnormal, or a disease as a subject, really, it was just something quite irreplaceable that they had missed" (*Green Hills* 70). In a long passage in *Men at War*, he pays homage to Stendhal as a writer who begins with this irreplaceable experience and then invents a "true" and unforgettable account from it:

> The best account of actual human beings behaving during a world shaking event is Stendhal's picture of young Fabrizio at the battle of Waterloo. That account is more like war and less like the nonsense written about it than any other writing could possibly be. Once you have read it you will have been at the battle of Waterloo and nothing can take that experience away from you. You will have to read Victor Hugo's account of the same battle, which is a fine, bold, majestic painting of the whole tragedy, to find out what you saw there the as you rode with the boy [Fabrizio]; but you will have actually seen the field of Waterloo already whether you understood it or not. You will have seen a small piece of war as closely and clearly with Stendhal as any man has ever written of it. It is the classic account of a routed army and beside it all of Zola's piled on detail in his "Debacle" is dead and unconvincing as a steel engraving. Stendhal served with Napoleon and saw some of the

greatest battles of the world. But all he ever wrote about war is the
one long passage from "Le [sic] Chartreuse de Parme". . . . (xx)

Needless to say, what Hemingway admires in Stendhal is the latter's having seen "a war in serving with Napoleon," who "taught him to write."
According to Hemingway, Napoleon "was teaching everybody then;
but no one else learned" (*Green Hills* 7). Stendhal learned because, as
Nietzsche has remarked, Stendhal "may well have had more thought-
ful eyes and ears than any other Frenchman of *this* century" (*Gay Science*
149)—a keen observation wonderfully put. It may be reasonably inferred
that Hemingway put Stendahl's meiotic account of the battle of Waterloo
in the exclusive category of "good and true books" because it issues from
the experience of war and is no mere propaganda of one kind or another.
These "true books" are written by writers who are of such "great probity
and honesty as a priest of God" (*Men at War* xv). It is this rare combination
of experience of seeing a war and absolute artistic integrity and honesty
that allows Stendhal to reduce the details of what he observed to their
absolute necessary minimum, but no further. The rigorous pressures of
Napoleonic wars teach Stendhal to produce an imaginative iconic compression of the essence and truth of the battle of Waterloo as, say, only
Goya could have done. For, above all,

> A writer's job is to tell the truth. His standard of fidelity to the
> truth should be so high that his invention, out of his experience,
> should produce a truer account than anything factual can be. For
> facts can be observed badly; but when a good writer is creating
> something, he has time and scope to make it of an absolute truth.
> (*Men at War* xv)

I should add here that Hemingway's appreciation of Stendahl's prowess as
a writer, which can create artistic absolute truth, is almost a direct endorse-
ment of his own aesthetics and stylistics—albeit in an encapsulated form—
as he at least partially practiced it, for example, in *A Farewell to Arms*. On a
certain mythological plane, the war here serves the warrior-writer at once as
Hermes Trismegistus and Niké.

At first glance, this juxtaposition, of writing as an individual creative act
and war as a collective, destructive enterprise, may prompt some readers to
dismiss it as contrived, unconvincing, and morally suspect—if not altogether
an appalling boast unworthy of a great writer. The immediate contemporary
temptation will be to disregard Hemingway's seemingly idiosyncratic view of
the literary history of war as so much sadomasochistic bombast and relegate
it to the long regrettable list of crypto-Fascist justifications of blood lust.

Immediately and in the abstract, this deceptive and dismissive attitude may be justified. Further reflection, however, militates against this well meaning but misleading initial reaction to a seemingly fundamental contradiction. Today, psychoanalysis alone seems to be able to shed some light on the crepuscular psychic place where this contradiction dwells in Hemingway and to offer an analysis of its structures that makes it visible and intelligible. Freud boldly assures us that Eros and the death instinct "seldom—perhaps never—appear in isolation from each other, but are alloyed with each other in varying and very different proportions and so become unrecognizable to our judgment" (*Civilization* 66). Later he comments, "It must be confessed that we have much greater difficulty in grasping that [death] instinct, we can only suspect it, as it were, as something in the background behind Eros, and it escapes detection unless its presence is betrayed by its being alloyed with Eros" (*Civilization* 68). Thus we are dealing with psychic structures that contain alternative antagonistic but complementary movements; thereby we do not simply love or hate but "love-hate" or "hate-love," as it were, at the same time. Similarly, we do not simply create but simultaneously create and destroy or destroy and create. In other words; the Mephistophelean destructive impulse to reverse the process of creation in all things created also calls forth its constructive opposite. Each of these antithetical impulses calls the other forth and allies itself with it or they already coexist.

For my part, I will say that the most instructive aspect of Hemingway's metaphysics of war and Freud's psychoanalytic insights that one may acquire here is to consider war largely as a secondary process. This insight allows the death instinct to be apprehended as an unconscious primary process to be experienced and sublimated in wars that are always consciously legitimized in one way or another. War makes the unacceptable "world destructive instinct" often acceptable, even highly desirable, to the superego through the agency of state and social sanction. A given group, state, society, or culture may condone and encourage supreme violence as a legitimate *praxis* in wars and conflicts to such an extent that the individual becomes a member of a "group in fusion" through violence, to use the Sartrean terminology. Individual and group violence sublimate the ever present destructive instinct as the love of one's people, country, and state, dragging in their wake destruction and self-destruction as well as the latent libidinal creative and reparative forces. The latter makes the continuation and often, curiously enough, the prosperity of human life, even for the vanquished, in post-war periods viable. The post-World War II economic recovery and expansion of Germany and Japan bear witness to the truth of this contradiction.

Now, if we return to the province of the arts, we also become aware, as did Hemingway, that similar processes are at work in them. As psychoanalyst Anthony Storr brings to our attention, "This same aggressive impulse which can lead to strife and violence also underlies man's urge to independence and achievement" (78). In an extraordinary way, much like the aggressive pursuit and consummation of sexual love, each artistic achievement demands that artists aggress to some degree against the very sources that nourish their art. This creative aggression is much more discernible in plastic arts such as sculpture and painting in which the natural order of matter undergoes the violence of artistic transformation and manifests the ubiquitous inscription of human "work" upon it as its ontological signature. It is less detectable in the art of writing or music in which creative violence makes itself known respectively as an act of aggression against the immense powers of language and of absolute silence or relative silences. The nature of the writer's violence against the real or adopted "mother tongue" by violating its phonological, lexical, syntactic, and semantic structures and norms in the name of a new linguistic creation is shrouded in all the ambiguities of love and aggression the adult shows toward the lost mother of infancy. The innovative writer's aggression against language falls into the category of what Lacan properly calls *"aggressivitié"* in contradistinction to pure violence and destruction. Even the James Joyce of *Finnegans Wake* does not seek to destroy the English language as such. Nonetheless, it is still a mode of warfare in which he engages. In "The Origin of the Work of Art," referring to Heraclitus' thought on war as the father and king of all, Martin Heidegger writes:

> In the tragedy nothing is staged and displayed theatrically, but the battle of the new gods against the old is being fought. The linguistic work, originating in the speech of people, does not refer to this battle; it transforms the people's saying so that now every living word fights the battle and puts up for decision what is holy and what unholy, what great and what small, what brave and what cowardly, what lofty and what flighty, what master and what slave. (43)

What Heidegger discloses in the preceding passage is this: the infinite spider's web of psychic forces that we call the human mind is all of the same piece. Each part of it is intricately interwoven with the rest, and touching it at any given point affects the whole and puts us concurrently in contact with all the rest. Touch the unholy and you are defiantly brushing against the holy; speak of the Devil and the Good Lord is within hearing distance. That is why Claude Lévi-Strauss can claim that "there is no incompatibility between artistic refinement and extremely cruel manners," which "profoundly disturbs" him (182). It is indeed disturbing because it is true.

I would propose, then, that Hemingway's belief in the "great advantage an experience of war" offers writers indicates his intuitive grasp of the dynamics

of this complex synthesis of libidinal creation, sadistic destruction, and masochistic self-destruction—and how, oddly, one always calls the others forth. As
an extreme situation, war reveals something of the nature of the writers' own
imaginary work as a secondary process which is thoroughly permeated by sadomasochistic elements. So for writers, war generally synthesizes the unconscious,
preconscious, and conscious states and the immensities of the eventual effects
of their synthesis in intersubjective and intrasubjective life. One may assign
to them a place within the Jungian archetypal patterns because this synthesis
of war and writing (and before writing, between war and oral tradition), has a
recurrent history. The Freudian and Jungian views of individual and collective
unconscious satisfactorily become connected here in Hemingway's views on
writing and war and lay claim to vaster domains of experience. In this light, the
commonalities between the origin and history of development of the arts and
creative writing and the metaphysics and psychoanalytics of war become more
discernible and comprehensible.

Despite such comprehension, it does not directly follow that war experience makes it *easier* for a writer to write. For Hemingway, quite the opposite
seems to have been the case. In a plaintive tone, he tells the Russian critic
Ivan Kashkin that war is "complicated and hard to write about truly." He
then adds:

> For your information in stories about the war I try to show *all* the
> different sides of it, taking it slowly and honestly and examining it
> from many ways. So never think one story represents my viewpoint
> because it is much too complicated for that. (*Letters* 480)

This shifting viewpoint, representing war as a kind of Hegelian truth-in-
becoming, whose aim is to surpass the circuits of received ideas and the logic
of the predictable, needs to realize and expand itself in the imaginal continuum. The upshot of it is that the writer does not merely catch a glimpse
of war as history's truth within the boundaries of a certain culture imposed
upon it. What is even more important is the writer's refusal to consider
the truth of the individual participation in war as solely predetermined by
cultural prejudices and their supporting ideologies. Hemingway writes: "I
would like to be able to write understandingly about both deserters and
heroes, cowards and brave men, traitors and men who are not capable of
being traitors. We learned a lot about all such people [in the Spanish Civil
War]" (*Letters* 480). Such opposite qualities in the extreme belong to the
province of war, and a great writer draws lessons of immense value from
them about the human mind and the human heart, that is to say, the human
condition. These lessons do not lend themselves to sheer reportage. They

can only be expressed through the alchemy of literary invention that draws upon the primal war experience and not its doxa.

Beyond these primary considerations of the relation between war and writing, there is another equally prominent one for Hemingway: justice. As in the case of loving one's enemies as oneself, everything dismayingly appears to conspire against the ideal of justice—equally in peacetime as in wartime. There are those among us whose yearning for justice is as strong as our yearning for love and peace. Perhaps it is even much stronger because we subconsciously ask, if we cannot have love and peace, can we at least have justice? We long for justice, not in the abstract or as a part of ethics that psychoanalysis places in the realm of the superego, but as an abiding principle of life. The fact that it is rarely so does not deter us at all. We may speculate that our longing for justice has its roots in the vicissitudes of the infant-mother relationship, with the infant experiencing anything less than the complete oneness with the mother, no matter how brief, as an unending injustice. The more unjust and *regressive* the society we live in, the more we regress to the infantile and the more acute our desire for justice becomes. It may indeed end up to be our ruling passion, which is tantamount to an obsessional fantasy. In any case, Hemingway believes that the artist of language, the writer, feels injustice more strongly than others and is more vulnerable to it. He, too, clearly connects this sense of injustice with the writer's infancy and childhood. When asked, "What is the best early training for a writer?" he unhesitatingly answers, "An unhappy childhood" (*By-Line* 219). It is no doubt an extraordinary statement which requires the space of a book to explore. When the writer subconsciously has an intimation of childhood as a time of loss of the mother of infancy, and this loss is later experienced as a generalized sense of injustice, writing no doubt expresses a process of unbroken mourning. Correspondingly, Hemingway asserts with conviction that "Dostoevsky was made by being sent to Siberia. Writers are forged in injustice as a sword is forged." In a psychoanalytic sense, it is Mother Russia that unjustly banishes one of her sons to live separately from her. Unlike Stendhal, Flaubert "had not seen war but he had seen a revolution and the Commune and a revolution is much the best if you do not become bigoted because every one speaks the same language." We know, of course, that Flaubert was bigoted and politically reactionary by being against the working classes. One might say; what does that exactly prove? Nothing more than the fact that he profoundly experienced the sense of injustice, but differently as we all do. And, somewhat unkindly, Hemingway fantasizes: "I wondered if it would make a writer of him, give him the necessary shock to cut the over-flow of words and give him a sense of proportion, if they sent Tom Wolfe to Siberia or to the Dry Tortugas" (*Green Hills* 71). Perhaps, because, much like Hemingway himself, Wolfe also had a troubled relationship with his mother.[2]

Finally, I would reiterate that for writers the aggressive-regressive and libidinal aspects of war are repeated every time they attempt to write. As we have seen, the battle is waged on every page against the unyielding nature of language as an all-engulfing and transcendent reality wholly beyond total appropriation. Language presents itself to the writer as the mother of all desires and as an implacable enemy of unlimited conscious and unconscious resources; in other words, an analogue of the mother of infancy. No doubt in this context Hemingway's multi-planar reference to James Joyce as "a great writer of our time," who keeps "quoting from Edgar Quinet, 'Fraîche et rose comme au jour de la bataille,'" makes remarkable sense (*Green Hills* 71). There is at once the sense of beauty, ecstasy, and the strange excitement of the pending bloody battle. Since a total victory against the language by the writer is out of the question, justice—at least in an abstract sense—demands that the writer not be entirely vanquished in this battle. So the most decisive battle, even for the warrior-writer, is with the language itself, which prompts Hemingway to declare, "I want to run as a writer; not as a man who had been to the wars . . ." (*Letters* 712). Or as a disciplined writer, in the manner of a Samurai warrior, he might have added, "My daily routine is now my field of battle" (King 128). No serious writer is likely to challenge this assertion. One may say that writing is a constant struggle against the irreducible resistance of language, a resistance that issues from the alliance of language with the unconscious primary process and demands a conscious secondary process of expression in writing—most often involving a hugely difficult task.

VI. On Life as Means to Knowledge

To sue to live, I find I seek to die;
And, seeking death, find life.
—William Shakespeare, *Measure for Measure* (3. 1. 42–43)

This is the world. Have faith.
—Dylan Thomas, *The Collected Poems of Dylan Thomas* (84)

For a considerably long time, I have been inclined to think that what partakes of the magical in the best of Hemingway's work is its synthesis of the primeval and the modern, the archaic and the contemporary, the simple and the complex. Putting it more technically: the Hemingway brand of stylistic sorcery captures traces of the unconscious primary-process as preconscious intimations and, subsequently, transmutes them into the highly evolved secondary-process of writing that subsumes the archaic and the archetypal. Where this synthesis works well, the paleologic experiences of earth, air,

water, fire, animals, plants, sexuality, birth, and death flow in confluence
with the modalities of their 20th-century lived experiences. To me, this vast
mysterious synthesis, combined with a highly tragic sense of life—which
consistently augments the irreparable sense of loss and its attendant mourning—is the signal trait of the Hemingway style.

In turn, I have also believed that one of the elements that constitutes
the generative matrix of Hemingway's stylistic synthesis and the elegiac dimension in his work is a new epistemology: the general field of experiential
knowledge—with all the energies, intricacies, and ultimate melancholy ambiguities that are inherent in it as its basic constituents. In this new epistemology, among all primal experiences, Hemingway admittedly privileges violent
death. Elaborating on writing about the twin themes of violence and death,
he explains in *Death in the Afternoon:*

> I was trying to learn to write, commencing with the simplest things,
> and one of the simplest things of all and the most fundamental is
> violent death. It has none of the complications of death by disease,
> or so-called natural death, or the death of a friend or some one
> you have loved or have hated, it is death nevertheless, one of the
> subjects that a man may write of. (2)

The two attentively articulated sentences combine the "simplest" with the
"most fundamental." The simplest and the most fundamental, two seemingly contradictory elements, preoccupy Hemingway not only initially but
throughout all his writing life. On the one hand, violent death is one of the
simplest things because it makes manifest the inordinate vulnerability of the
individual human to death, annihilation, and eventual oblivion. The injec-
tion of a bubble of air into the human circulatory system nulls and voids its
integrity as an organic and biological unit—instantly and irreversibly. On the
other hand, violent death intervenes at the juncture where the enormities of
human existence and nonexistence are still proximal as Being is ushered into
Nothingness. So the dialectical opposition between the "simplest" and the
"most fundamental" in violent death has observable if mysterious conjunctive
consequences. It is precisely "one of the subjects that a man may write of."
And it is an essential and perhaps potentially impossible task to attempt.

Furthermore, Hemingway tells us that "The only place where you could
see life and death, *i.e.*, violent death now that the wars were over was in the
bull ring and I wanted very much to go to 'Spain where I could study it"
(*Death* 2). But, after all, why study violent death, anyway? Wouldn't life, in
and of itself, be a large enough subject that a writer may legitimately study
and write of? What is exactly this close connection between life and death
beyond what might be given over to morbid and even sadistic curiosity or

ghoulish fascination? In other words, theoretically, how can we make the life-death problematics in Hemingway's thought comprehensible? As one might easily imagine, psychoanalytic answers to this question abound, some of which I have already briefly discussed. A more instructive answer may come to us from a sub-field of psychoanalysis, existential psychoanalysis, or at any rate that segment of it which believes in the omnipresent reality of the unconscious life. Rollo May, for instance, explains that "Death in any of its aspects is the fact which makes of the present hour something of absolute value" (90). Within the relativity and contingency of human life, all human thought and action of necessity remain relative and contingent. The very concept of time, as *chronos* or "operational time" rather than lived time or *kairos*, with the "hour" as one of its many subcategories, is a human construct and takes up an originary place in theory of relativity. So how are we to understand the "hour" as an absolute value; that is to say, an absolute present at the intersection of *chronos* and *kairos*? Seen from the perspective of our present discussion, and to speak Heidegger's language, the relativity and subjectivity of *this* hour lays claim to the absolute moment that my consciousness as an individual embraces the absolute certainty of my death. Heidegger might have called it the hour of my authenticity. It is in the consciousness of the ever presence and the absolute certainty of *my death* that my thought and action partake of the dimension of the absolute and the immortal. This absolute hour envelops me as I lay claim to the proximity of my death as a supreme integrative moment of my life. My death coincides then with my life and becomes a part of my flesh and blood. Viewed as absolutely proximal, life and death merge and death incontrovertibly vivifies rather than mortifies life. Making my death an inextricable part of my life unites the finite and the infinite in me. In a letter to Charles Scribner, Hemingway reflects that "there is no future in anything. I hope you agree. That is why I like it at a war. Every day and every night there is a strong possibility that you will get killed . . ." (*Letters* 503). At first, there being no future in anything appears to be an unnecessarily dramatic statement in an hour of despair, both, noncommonsensical and counterintuitive. To the contrary, however, in the absolute presence or the proximity of death, it makes a telling point: our certainty of the omnipresence of death confers immortality upon the present and renders it absolute To use the language of an invocation of the Lakota, and perhaps the Northern Plains warriors generally, in a war one may perpetually say: "For those that this day belongs to, it is a good day to die"*(Le ampetu kin t'ab kin wastekte)*.[3] Again, here is Hemingway meditating further on the same subject in a letter:

> I think there is a steady renewal of immortality through storms, attacks, landings on beaches where landing is opposed, flying, when there are problems and many other things which are all awful and

> horrible and hateful to those who are not suited to them. . . . These
> things make a katharsis [sic] which is not a pathological thing,
> nor seeking after thrills, but it is an ennobling thing to those who
> are suited for them and have the luck so that they survive them.
> (Quoted by Meyers 400–401)

If not the tone, certainly the intent of Hemingway's remarks is Hegelian: facing the possibility of death and surviving it signifies a negation of negation; which in turn, elicits a feeling of immortality when what is negated is death. These are lived experiences that concurrently bestow on us mortals feelings of our "unbearable lightness of being," as Milan Kundera might have put it, and its very opposite, a feeling of the unbearable heaviness of immortality, rendering us fleetingly godlike. They generate a transcendental and regenerative passion for Hemingway, generally approximating the sense of Christ's passion, a deliberately and freely chosen mode of being in suffering and self-sacrifice in the name of experiencing a fundamental truth. Such lived experiences at once represent the summation of one's individual life and its conjunction with what incomprehensibly lies forever beyond it. Thus they primarily represent in Hemingway's writings the *principium individutionis* rather than another symptom of masochism. In other registers, one may refer to these experiences as moments of pure sublimation which infuse them with the sublime and the mystical. Such experiences are sublime to the extent that they combine horror and beauty; they are mystical because, as Hemingway reminds us, those who are suited for them risk their lives in searching for them. They do so to have a palpable feeling of the mystery of being at its very point of contact with potential harm or eventual annihilation. Put differently: whoever is ready to lose all is also and at the same time ready to gain immeasurably in transcendental experiences, a notion that gives "Winner Take Nothing" a new dimension. It would seem logical to conclude that for Hemingway the sublime pushes itself beyond Freudian reality and the pleasure principle toward what Lacan calls the "Death Drive," approximating the unbearably ecstatic "*jouissance*" state. Furthermore: the experience of the sublime involves vaguely known and dimly understood masochistic desires augmenting its unconscious side, increasing its affective appeal and its appearance of grandeur. If Hemingway properly considers them as cathartic, it is because they are at once so fearsome and ecstatic as to create a blissful trance, much in the manner of a breakthrough in the analytic situation. Such experiences release all the pent-up masochistic yearnings, making manifest an occult truth of their own without which a crucial part of the existential perspective of human life would be lost. From a dual phenomenological and psychoanalytic viewpoint, Ludwig Binswanger relatedly also observes that life and death are not opposites, that *death too must be lived,* and that *life is "encompassed" by death,* so that both from a biological and a historical point of view the saying holds true that the human being dies in every moment of his existence—this insight was in a certain sense familiar even to Heraclitus. *Indeed, for Heraclitus Hades, the god of the Underworld, and Dionysus, the God of the wildest intoxication of Life, "for whom everyone rages and raves," are the same.* (294 emphasis added)

Returning to tauromaquia, the crucial point to grasp here is Hemingway's insistence in seeing "life and death" in the bull rings of Spain in a new light. For me, it is clearly not cruelty as such that he wants to see. Initially he expects not to like bullfights "because of the poor horses." He relates that "I had just come from the Near East, where the Greeks broke the legs of their baggage and transport animals and drove and shoved them off the quay into the shallow water when they abandoned the city of Smyrna . . . " (*Death* 2). The juxtaposition of images of drowning horses with broken legs in the Near East and their evisceration in the bull ring is evidently not what he seeks. What he does wish to find, to experience, to study, *to learn* from is that dark and mysterious point where the finite and relative open onto the infinite and the absolute; that is, where human life asymptomatically touches the environing mysteries. Hemingway is very emphatic on the necessity of learning, informing Malcolm Cowley:

Every year [I] keep on studying, keep on reading and every year study something new to keep head learning. Learning is a hell of a lot of fun. Don't see why can't keep it up all my life. Certainly plenty to learn. (*Letters* 604)

Bullfights are exciting to Hemingway because while they are going on they represent a way of learning, with "life as means to knowledge"—or, more accurately, in Miguel de Unamuno's words, with the "tragic sense of life" as a medium of access to knowledge. This "tragic" knowledge is highlighted in violent death in war and in the ritual violence of the bullfight. In a confessional tone, he tells us that

So far, about morals, I only know that what is moral is what you feel good after and what is immoral is what you feel bad after and judged by these moral standards, which I do not defend, the bullfight is very moral to me because I feel very fine while it is going on and have a feeling of life and death and mortality and immortality, and after it is over I feel very sad but very fine. (*Death* 4)

Now one may better apprehend how the love of the bullfight lends itself to this admixture of Eros and Thanatos—so bewildering to so many readers and critics—which is the guiding principle of Hemingway's observations on war and violent death.

After what has been said, I hope the preceding sections come into better focus and Hemingway's interest in war and peace in their multiplicity of forms becomes more accessible and understandable. This interest goes far beyond the superficial and excessively simple-minded comments such as Charles Whiting's that Hemingway is only "a writer who glorified action, violence and war" (83). After all due consideration, Hemingway may be said to be more on the side of Raymond Aron, who against all odds argues for "the hope of a gradual, ultimate reconciliation of the human race" (143). Or one may cautiously associate him with William Faulkner's reassuring vision that "man will not merely endure, he will prevail" (8). Faulkner's vision is one of thorough humanism, unaware of the coming of the structuralist anti-humanism and the nostalgia for a return to new modes of 19th century scientism and determinism in the twilight years of our 20th century and its humanist failures.

Epilogue

"There's no one thing that's true. It is all true."
—Ernest Hemingway, *For Whom the Bell Tolls* (467)

As I see it, essentially, Hemingway's vision reveals itself not so much as war against peace; or life against death; or creation against destruction; or self-generation against self-destruction but as a hint of a mystical vision of the interconnectedness of all things harmonious and disharmonious, reconcilable and irreconcilable, and, yes, fraternal and fratricidal in lived human experience. I would say that there is an integrative wholeness in this vision that is much vaster and exceedingly more complex than what one might technically refer to as a "compromise formation." Consciousness of it allows us to make forays into that "undiscover'd country" which, following Freud, we have come to call the unconscious, a country whose borders are closed to intrusions of time and space, as we understand and experience them in our conscious life, and death and oblivion as we imagine them.

I have tried to place Hemingway's views on war and peace in an intertextual, philosophical, psychoanalytic, ethical, aesthetic, and literary context. To push this effort infinitesimally further and to provide an ending, or at least a "sense of an ending," I will simply say that this "undiscover'd," and perhaps undiscoverable, country is no more than a horizon. It stretches ahead of us beyond Faulkner's the "last red dying evening." At this receding twilit horizon, all light is but a mere gradation of the light of a human day which stubbornly refuses to die and the penumbra of the ambient ancient night, unseeing and unhearing. After all, Hegel counseled us that "The owl of Minerva spreads its wings only with the falling dusk" (13). Perhaps in our struggle for preserving what is left of our humanity against the coming of a post-human world, it will not be merely a twilight of the gods that we shall encounter but the predawn of an all-encompassing human consciousness, anticipating the mystic's dark sun, awaiting the awakening of new integrative myths up to now slumbering in our unconscious and as yet unknown to us and our history.

Notes

1. I visited La Finca Vigía several times while attending the First International Hemingway Conference in Havana, Cuba (July 16–23, 1995).

2. For an account of the vicissitudes of Wolfe's early relationship with his mother see John S. Terry's interview with Julia Wolfe in Elizabeth Nowell's *Thomas Wolfe: A Biography* (23).

3. I am grateful to Robert W. Lewis for providing me with this information, quotation, and translation.

Works Cited

Aron, Raymond. *On War.* Trans. Terence Kilmartin. New York: Doubleday Anchor, 1959.

Baker, Carlos. *Ernest Hemingway: A Life Story.* New York: Scribner's, 1969.

Binswanger, Ludwig. "The Existential Analysis School of Thought." In *Existence: A New Dimension in Psychiatry and Psychology.* Eds. Rollo May, Ernest Angel, and Henri F. Ellenberger. New York: Simon & Schuster, 1958.

———. "The Case of Ellen West." In *Existence: A New Dimension in Psychiatry and Psychology.* Eds. Rollo May, Ernest Angel, and Henri F. Ellenberger. New York: Simon & Schuster, 1958.

Clausewitz, Karl von. *On War.* Trans. Anatol Rapoport. London: Penguin, 1982.

Faulkner, William. "Nobel Prize Acceptance Speech." In *Nobel Prize Library.* New York: Helvetica, 1971.

Freud, Sigmund. "Anxiety and Instinctual Life." In *New Introductory Lectures on Psycho-Analysis.* Trans. James Strachey. New York: W. W. Norton, 1989.

———. "A Phobia in a Five-Year-Old Boy." In *Standard Edition of the Complete Works of Sigmund Freud,* vol. 10. Trans. James Strachey. London: Hogarth, 1957.

———. *Civilization and Its Discontents.* Trans. James Strachey. New York: W. W. Norton, 1962.

Gray, J. Glenn. *The Warriors: Reflections on Men in Battle.* 1959. New York: Harper & Row, 1970.

Hegel, G. W. F. *Hegel's Philosophy of Right.* Trans. T. M. Knox. Oxford: Clarendon, 1942.

Heidegger, Martin. "The Origin of the Work of Art." In *Poetry, Language, Thought.* Trans. Albert Hofstadter. New York: Harper & Row, 1971.

Hemingway, Ernest. *Death in the Afternoon.* New York: Scribner's, 1932.

———. *A Farewell to Arms.* 1929: New York: Scribner's, 1949.

———. *For Whom the Bell Tolls.* New York: Scribner's, 1940.

———. *Green Hills of Africa.* New York: Scribner's, 1935.

———. Introduction. *Men at War.* New York: Crown, 1942.

———. Introduction. *Treasury for the Free World.* Ed. Ben Raeburn. New York: Arco, 1946.

———. "Notes on the Next War: A Serious Topical Letter." In *By-Line: Ernest Hemingway.* Ed. William White. New York: Scribner's, 1967. 205–212.

———. *Selected Letters 1917–1961.* Ed. Carlos Baker. New York: Scribner's, 1981.

———. "On the American Dead in Spain." In *Remembering Spain: Hemingway's Civil War Eulogy and the Veterans of the Abraham Lincoln Brigade.* Ed. Cary Nelson. Urbana: University of Illinois Press, 1994.

———. "On the Blue River: A Gulf Stream Letter." In *By-Line: Ernest Hemingway.* Ed. William White. New York: Scribner's, 1967. 237–246.

———. "Monologue to the Maestro: A High Seas Letter." In *By-Line: Ernest Hemingway.* Ed. William White. New York: Scribner's, 1967. 213–220.

James, William. *Varieties of Religious Experience: A Study in Human Nature.* 1902. New York: New American Library, 1958.

Jaspers, Karl. *Philosophy and the World: Philosophical Essays.* New York: Regnery, 1989.

King, Winston L. *Zen and the Way of the Sword.* Oxford: Oxford University Press, 1993.

Lacan, Jacques. *Écrits.* Paris: Seuil, 1966.

Lévi-Strauss, Claude. *Conversations with Claude Lévi-Strauss: Claude Lévi-Strauss and Didier Eribon.* Trans. Paula Wissing. Chicago: University of Chicago Press, 1991.

Marx, Karl, and Friedrich Engels. *The Communist Manifesto.* 1848. New York: International Publishers, 1971.

May, Rollo. "Contributions of Existential Psychiatry." In *Existence: A New Dimension in Psychiatry and Psychology.* Eds. Rollo May, Ernest Angel, and Henri F. Ellenberger. New York: Simon & Schuster, 1958.

Meyers, Jeffrey. *Hemingway: A Biography.* New York: Harper & Row, 1985.

Murdoch, Iris. "Mass, Might, and Myth." In *Existentialists and Mystics: Writings on Philosophy and Literature.* New York: Penguin, 1998.

Nietzsche, Friedrich. *The Gay Science.* Trans. Walter Kaufmann. New York: Vintage, 1974.

———. *The Will to Power.* Trans. Walter Kaufmann and R. J. Hollingdale. New York: Vintage, 1968.

———. *Thus Spoke Zarathustra.* Trans. Marianne Cowan. New York: Gateway, 1957.

Nowell, Elizabeth. *Thomas Wolfe: A Biography.* Garden City: Doubleday, 1960.

Regler, Gustav. *The Great Crusade.* Pref. by Ernest Hemingway. Trans. Whittaker Chambers. New York: Longmans, Green, 1940.

Rochlin, Gregory. *Man's Aggression: The Defense of Self.* Boston: Gambit, 1973.

Schopenhauer, Arthur. *Essays and Aphorisms.* London: Penguin, 1970.

Shakespeare, William. *Measure for Measure.* In *The Complete Works of William Shakespeare.* Ed. David Bevington. Glenview: Scott, Foresman, 1983.

Storr, Anthony. *Human Aggression.* London: Penguin, 1968.

Thomas, Dylan. *The Poems of Dylan Thomas.* New York: New Directions, 1971. 196–197.

Tzu, Sun. *The Art of War.* Trans. Thomas Cleary. Boston: Shambhala, 1998.

Whiting, Charles. *Hemingway Goes to War.* Gloucestershire: Sutton, 1999.

MATTHEW J. BRUCCOLI

Class Ten: A Farewell to Arms

A *Farewell to Arms* is regarded as being close to autobiographical, as a novel based on what happened to Hemingway in World War I and on his unhappy love affair with a nurse in Milan. The evidence shows that *A Farewell to Arms* has very little to do with Hemingway's war experiences apart from the fact that Frederic Henry and Ernest Hemingway were wounded in much the same way—in the legs by shrapnel. But the chronology makes closer identification impossible. *A Farewell to Arms* begins in the summer of 1915. It ends in the spring of 1918, after the Italian retreat from Caparetto late in 1917. Ernest Hemingway did not get to Italy until the summer of 1918. He was wounded in July 1918. The military events of *A Farewell to Arms* were over and done with before Ernest Hemingway ever got to Italy. The war material in the novel is fiction written from books. It's a research job. For those of you who may be interested in seeing how Hemingway researched this novel I recommend to you Michael Reynolds' *Hemingway's First War*, which documents where Hemingway borrowed his information about the Italian front. It also indicates—this is a much more important point—how Hemingway was able to make this second-hand material his own. It is no wonder that people have assumed that *A Farewell to Arms* was autobiography. It doesn't read like something written from reference books, but that is what the war part is. As for the love part, it is well known that

Classes on Ernest Hemingway (Columbia, S.C.: Thomas Cooper Library, University of South Carolina, 2002): pp. 103–141. Copyright © Matthew J. Bruccoli.

Hemingway fell in love with a nurse at the hospital in Milan in 1918. Her name was Agnes Von Kurowsky. She was not British as Catherine Barkley is. Agnes was an American, despite the Von Kurowsky name. Like many of the women in young Hemingway's life, she was older than he was. Hemingway assumed that they were to be married after the war. He returned to the United States to find a job and prepare for their marriage, but he received from her what used to be called a "Dear John." Hemingway's reaction was pain and outrage, which he first put into "A Very Short Story," where we have *A Farewell to Arms* done in three pages or so about an American who falls in love with his nurse in Italy, comes back to the United States, and is jilted. The tone of that little piece is angry or nasty. By the time that Hemingway wrote *A Farewell to Arms* the nastiness had faded, and he was able to invest the experience with an elegiac tone. At the same time, it is possible to detect *A Farewell to Arms* operating as retaliation. Hemingway gets even with Agnes by killing off Catherine at the end of the novel. He also makes the love affair in *A Farewell to Arms* better than it could possibly have been in real life.

From the overture, the two-page opening, we can see Hemingway planting connections and contrasts for future development. The rain/death connection and the fertility/infertility contrast. The mountains and the plains, yes; but that's a problem because it is unclear what Hemingway was doing with this contrast and whether he did intend to develop it consistently through the novel. We'll come back to that. The most obvious connection, of course, is rain and death. But, Hemingway at his best doesn't use these things blatantly. He doesn't erect a billboard announcing Five Miles to the Next Symbol. Where his symbols work best, they work organically: they emerge naturally from the material as part of the material—so naturally that you don't have to see them as symbols.

"In the late summer of that year. . . ." From the history of the war it's got to be 1915. Why doesn't Hemingway say so? I suppose because he's trying to open the novel with a sense of pastness; to say in the late summer of 1915 has a specificity about it which doesn't produce quite the same effect. ". . . .we lived in a house in a village that looked across the river. . . ." We've identified that river and water symbolism—there will be all kinds of water: Frederic Henry will jump into a river to save his life, and later he and Catherine will undertake a journey across a lake which becomes a journey to a new life. It also turns out to be journey to death. ". . . across the river and the plain to the mountains." Here we have, still in the first sentence, that low-land, high-land contrast, which I don't think works consistently. "In the bed of the river there were pebbles and boulders dry and white in the sun." Critics have tried to do something with the pebbles and boulders. I don't think you have to do anything with them. They're just pebbles and boulders. Sometimes a boulder is just a boulder—it doesn't stand for anything. The pebbles and boulders are not symbols of destruction or anything else. "And the water was clear and swiftly moving and blue in the channels. Troops went by the house and down the road and the dust they raised powdered the leaves of the trees." Okay, here we do have something going on: dust standing for everything from infertility to death, as in the funeral service—"Ashes to ashes, dust to dust." The soldiers walking raised the dust, which is appropriate because the soldiers are engaged in death. They will kill and be killed themselves; as they go by, they leave a deposit of dust on the leaves. "The trunks of the trees too were dusty and the leaves fell early that year." All right, we don't have to go into that at any length: early fall and early end of fertility. "And we saw the troops marching along the road and the dust rising and leaves stirred by the breeze falling and the soldiers marching and afterward the bare road white except for the leaves." The leaves have now fallen into the roadbed with the dust. "The plain was rich with crops." This is the first point at which there is going to be trouble about the mountain/plain contrast. Carlos Baker argued that in this novel the mountains, the high-lands stand for cleanliness, peace, health; but that the low-lands stand for death and disaster and destruction. He cites, for example, that Frederic Henry and Catherine Barkley are happiest in the mountains while they are waiting for the termination of her pregnancy; when they come down from the mountains she dies. But take a look at this first chapter where Hemingway is carefully laying out the rules of his novel, and you will see that nothing of the kind obtains. In this first chapter the mountains are associated with death, not goodness, not cleanliness, not peace, not tranquility.

The plain was rich with crops; there were many orchards of fruit trees and beyond the plain the mountains were brown and bare. There was fighting in the mountains and at night we could see the flashes from the artillery. In the dark it was like summer lightning, but the nights were cool and there was not the feeling of a storm coming.

Sometimes in the dark we heard the troops marching under the window and guns going past pulled by motor-tractors. There was much traffic at night [Maybe Hemingway is doing something with night/day; maybe he isn't. Sometimes details are just details.] and many mules on the roads with boxes of ammunition on each side of their pack-saddles and gray motor trucks that carried men, and other trucks with loads covered with canvas that moved slower in the traffic. There were big guns too that passed in the day drawn by tractors, the long barrels of the guns covered with green branches and green leafy branches and vines laid over the tractors. [One of the things Hemingway does in this novel is to point out the way in which war reverses the natural order of things. Here the green leafy branches and vines which normally are associated with growth and nature in its abundance have been perverted to the purposes of war. They have become camouflage for instruments of death.] To the north we could look across a valley and see a forest of chestnut trees and behind it another mountain on this side of the river. There was fighting for that mountain too [Notice again that mountains mean fighting, war, death, destruction.] but it was not successful, and in the fall [here it comes] when the rains came the leaves all fell from the chestnut trees and the branches were bare and the trunks black with rain. The vineyards were thin and bare-branched too and all the country wet and brown and dead with the autumn. [Wet equates with dead.] There were mists over the river and clouds on the mountain and the trucks splashed mud on the road and the troops were muddy and wet in their capes; their rifles were wet and under their capes the two leather cartridge-boxes on the front of the belts, gray leather boxes heavy with the packs of clips of thin long 6.5 mm. cartridges, bulged forward under the capes so that the men, passing on the road, marched as though they were six months gone with child. [That is the most effective symbol in this chapter. The cartridge boxes of the soldiers make them look pregnant, but what they are pregnant with is death. Hemingway is planting the connection between pregnancy and death. The novel repeats that war reverses the natural order of things. War takes the normal expectations of life and turns them into their opposite. Here pregnancy foreshadows not birth, not life. But death. The men are pregnant with 6.5 mm. cartridges.]

At the start of the winter came the permanent rain and with the rain came the cholera. But it was checked [Here's Hemingway with one of his perfect throwaway lines.] and in the end only seven thousand died of it in the army.

I have no evidence whatsoever, but I'm prepared to place a substantial wager that this opening chapter was inserted later. I suspect that Hemingway began writing the novel, and then later on he realized that he needed to introduce certain themes, to plant certain symbols. This chapter gives me the impression of something written later to connect with what has already been done. There is nothing wrong with that, nothing at all. My supposition is not meant to diminish the achievement of that opening chapter. It's superb. I mention my idea to point out something about the way in which novels are written. In most cases writing a novel is a process of discovery. The author finds out what he wants to say, what he has to say, through the process of writing it. Having discovered his symbols, it is quite natural and proper for the author to go back and write the first chapter or the second chapter in which he sets up certain parallels, certain contrasts or connections. Writing has been described as the process of making connections. The connections may not be perfectly clear to the author until he works them out on paper. Hemingway's second wife said that he thought with his fingers. That is an excellent definition of the process of writing: thinking with your fingers. During a newspaper strike one of the columnists was asked what he thought about an event, and he replied, "I don't know what I think until I've written it." There's probably a good deal of that in Hemingway.

What I intend to do now is go through *A Farewell to Arms* with you and point out certain scenes, certain passages, which seem to be the high points of the novel. The first such scene comes in Chapter 15, where Frederic Henry is being examined in the hospital. The Three Stooges have just left—the three doctors who were afraid to operate. One of them can't even read the X-ray; he's looking at the X-ray for the wrong leg. It's a comic scene: they're amateurs. Then comes the pro. In Hemingway's work there are these characters I call the pros. They're not necessarily code heroes because oftentimes we don't know enough about them. They can be minor characters, as Dr. Valentini is here. He's gone in two pages, but the contrast between Dr. Valentini and the Three Stooges who just left is a perfect example of how to tell the good guys from the bad guys in Hemingway's work and in his world:

> Two hours later Dr. Valentini came into the room. He was in a great hurry and the points of his mustache stood straight up. He was a major, his face was tanned and he laughed all the time.
>
> "How did you do it, this rotten thing?" he asked. "Let me see the plates. Yes. Yes. That's it. You look healthy as a goat. Who's the pretty girl? Is she your girl? I thought so. Isn't this a bloody war? How does that feel? You're a fine boy. I'll make you better than new. Does that hurt? You bet it hurts. How they love to hurt you, these doctors. What have they done to you so far? Can't that girl talk Italian? She should learn. What a lovely girl. I could teach her. I will be a patient here myself. No, but I will do all your maternity work free. Does she understand that? She'll make you a fine boy. A fine blonde like she is. That's fine. That's all right. What a lovely girl. Ask her if she eats supper with me. No I won't take her away from you. Thank you. Thank you very much, Miss. That's all."
>
> "That's all I want to know." He patted me on the shoulder. "Leave the dressings off."

"Will you have a drink, Dr. Valetini?"

"A drink? Certainly. I'll have ten drinks. Where are they?" [The Three Stooges didn't drink.]

"In the armoir. Miss Barkley will get the bottle."

"Cheery oh. Cheery oh to you, Miss. What a lovely girl. I will bring you better cognac than that." He wiped his mustache.

"When do you think it can be operated on?"

"To-morrow morning. Not before."

The other guys said they had to wait six months. As we'll find out, Valentini is going to do a good job. Here we have Hemingway's always strong contempt for the amateurs, for the ones who don't know how to do it—whatever it happens to be. We will find Dr. Valentini all over Hemingway's work with different names, and different occupations.

The end of Chapter 19: Catherine says, "I'm afraid of the rain because sometimes I see me dead in it." That's a bit much. Hemingway rather overworks that device. One of the problems with the novel is Catherine's rather stagy talk. She talks like somebody in a novel.

Chapter 21: Catherine has told Frederic Henry that she is pregnant. He is less than overjoyed, and she says, "We mustn't [fight]. Because there's only two of us and in the world there's all the rest of *them*. If anything comes between us, we're gone and then *they* have us." [The *them/they* syndrome.] "*They* won't get us," I said, "because you're too brave. Nothing ever happens to the brave." Apart from *they/them*, something else is going on here, which is Hemingway's fondness for dramatic irony: people making confident statements which will prove to be wrong and which may even function as jinxes. This ties in with that sense of doom. Whenever in Hemingway's work we find a character making sanguine remarks about the future, that's a point to pay attention because the chances are that the result will be just the opposite.

Chapter 23: Catherine and Henry are in that brothel-like hotel room in Milan before he goes back to the front. "After we had eaten we felt fine, and then after, we felt very happy and in a little time the room felt like our own home. My room at the hospital had been our own home and this room was our home too in the same way." Running through this novel is emphasis on Catherine's ability to make wherever she is home-like, despite the fact that these two people never have a home but instead hospital rooms or hotel rooms or rented rooms in somebody else's house.

Chapter 28: One of the most quoted passages in the novel, one of the most quoted passages in all of Hemingway's work. Hemingway on patriotism. An Italian soldier has just made a speech about what has been done this summer cannot have been done in vain and Frederic Henry thinks:

I did not say anything. I was always embarrassed by the words sacred, glorious, and sacrifice and the expression in vain. We had heard them, sometimes standing in the rain [Note the rain.] almost out of earshot, so that only the shouted words came through, and had read them, on proclamations that were slapped up by the billposters over other proclamations, now for a long time, and I had seen nothing sacred, and the things that were glorious had no glory and the sacrifices were like the stockyards at Chicago if nothing was done with the meat except to bury it. There were many words that you could not stand to hear and finally only the names of places had dignity. Certain numbers were the same way and certain dates and these with the names of the places were all you could say and have them mean anything. Abstract words such as glory, honor, courage, or hallow were obscene beside the concrete names of villages, the numbers of roads, the names of rivers, the numbers of regiments and the dates.

This passage calls attention to another popular misreading of Hemingway. Hemingway is thought of as a writer who celebrated heroism in battle as a masculine value. If ever there was an anti-war novel, if ever there was a novel that says that war is senseless slaughter, it's this one. *A Farewell to Arms* is one of the novels written in the Twenties by men who had seen the war and who utterly rejected the values of war and the conduct of war. E. E. Cummings' *The Enormous Room* and John Dos Passos's *Three Soldiers* come to mind; there were more. Until the Spanish Civil War in the late 1930s, Hemingway regularly denounced war.

Chapter 32: This picks up on that passage we just had about the rhetoric of war. Here Frederic Henry thinks:

You had lost your cars and your men as a floorwalker loses the stock of his department in a fire. [Notice the comparison.] There was, however, no insurance. You were out of it now. You had no more obligation. If they shot floorwalkers after a fire in the department store because they spoke with an accent they had always had, then certainly the floorwalkers could not be expected to return when the store opened again for business. They might seek other employment; if there was any other employment and the police did not get them.

Anger was washed away in the river along with any obligation. [A farewell to arms.]

Chapter 34: "I had made a separate peace."

The reunion of Catherine and Frederic Henry in Stresa before they go to Switzerland, another one of Frederick's soliloquies. You may notice that he does an awful lot of pontificating:

> If people bring so much courage to this world the world has to kill them to break them, so of course it kills them. The world breaks every one and afterward many are strong at the broken places. But those that will not break it kills. It kills the very good and the very gentle and the very brave impartially. If you are none of these you can be sure it will kill you too but there will be no special hurry.

This is one of the most admired, one of the most quoted, passages in the novel. Here we have Hemingway's explanation that *They* kill the brave and the good who are not breakable. He is talking about Catherine specifically, but this statement can be generalized into Hemingway's cosmic view. Notice the word *impartially*. "It kills the very good and the very gentle and the very brave impartially." There's no malice. *They* act impartially.

The final chapter is peppered with *They/Them*. Catherine is in the delivery room and is in danger: "So now they got her in the end. You never got away with anything."

More of Catherine's doom-talk, with *They*:

> "I'm not brave anymore, darling. I'm all broken. They've broken me. I know it now."
> "Everybody is that way."
> "But it's awful. They just keep it up till they break you."

More *They*. Frederic Henry has just learned that the baby has strangled on its umbilical cord. Now Catherine will die.

> That was what you did, you died. You did not know what it was about. You never had time to learn. They threw you in and told you the rules, and the first time they caught you off base they killed you. Or they killed you gratuitously like Aymo, or gave you the syphilis like Rinaldi. But they killed you in the end. You could count on that. Stay around and they would kill you.

Hemingway's admirers see this as a statement of a brave man's acceptance of the way things are. Other readers see it as a statement of self-pity. There doesn't seem to be any irony or distance here. Frederic Henry is in rebellion against death. This is followed by a much-quoted metaphysical statement of man's predicament:

Once in camp I put a log on top of the fire and it was a full of ants. As it commenced to burn, the ants swarmed out and went first toward the centre where the fire was; then turned back and ran toward the end. When there were enough on the end, they fell off into the fire. Some got out, their bodies burned and flattened, and went off not knowing where they were going. But most of them went forward toward the fire and then back toward the end and swarmed on the cool end and finally fell off into the fire. I remember thinking at the time that it was the end of the world and a splendid chance to be a messiah and lift the log off of the fire and throw it out where the ants could get off onto the ground. But I did not do anything but throw a tin cup of water onto the log, so that I would have the cup empty to put whiskey in before I added water to it. I think the cup of water on the burning log only steamed the ants.

This is Hemingway's view of what it's like to be God. What seems to be divine intervention, a cup of water, may be just another form of death.

Finally, Catherine's last words: "Don't worry darling," Catherine says, "I'm not a bit afraid. It's just a dirty trick." Death is a dirty trick.

I went through these passages for two reasons. One reason is that I will talk about them some more and I want you to be thinking about them. The other reason is to try to convey an impression of what the impact of this book was like in 1929. It seemed absolutely new. Hemingway was seeing life the way it had never been seen by any major American author except Stephen Crane, author of *The Red Badge of Courage*. Hemingway develops ideas about man's predicament in sentences and paragraphs that read almost like entries in a rule book. How to live with *They/Them*; where to find the courage to survive with the knowledge that inevitably *They/Them* will get you.

Hemingway apparently never knew what he was going to call his novels until after he had written them. Then he would go through the Bible or the *Oxford Book of English Verse* and look for phrases loaded with implication, and pick one that worked for his novel. *A Farewell to Arms* is one of Hemingway's most admired titles. It has everything. It has a nice rhythm to it. It has a meaningful ambiguity: arms meaning war; arms meaning love. It's perfect for this novel. Nonetheless, it is a little disturbing to me that Hemingway found his title by engaging in what might be called a title search. It would seem better for the title to develop in the course of writing, for the author to find his title while he was writing the novel. It's very instructive that we have Hemingway's list of possible titles for *A Farewell to Arms*. I am now working from the book by Bernard Oldsey called *Hemingway's Hidden Craft*. A possible title was from these two lines "Love is an fervent fire / Kindlit without desire." I don't know which of these words he was going to use. "A World to

See." "Patriot's Progress" [ironic title]. "The Grand Tour" [ironic title]. "The Italian Journey" [flat, noncommittal title]. "The World's Room" [not bad]. "Disorder and Early Sorrow" [Thomas Mann used that title]. "An Italian Chronicle" [the same as "The Italian Journey"—not a grabber]. "The Time Exchanged." "Death Once Dead." "They Who Get Shot" [wise-guy title]. "The Italian Experience." "Love in Italy." "Love in War." He's getting to it. He wants a title that's going to hook up love and death, love and war. "Education of the Flesh." "The Carnal Education." "The Sentimental Education of Frederic Henry" [too many words]. "I have Committed Fornication / But that was *In Another Country / And Besides* the wench is dead." Well, Hemingway must have cursed the day he used up that title "In Another Country." "The Sentimental Education" [a title Flaubert had used already]. "Sorrow for Pleasure." "A Farewell to Arms." That comes from a poem by George Peele written in the late sixteenth century. The poem is written as though by a soldier who has served Queen Elizabeth I in war. He's now too old to serve as a soldier and will devote his declining years to praying for his queen. "Late Wisdom." "The Enchantment." "If You Must Love." "World Enough and Time." "In Praise of his Mistress." "Every Night and All." "Of Wounds and Other Causes." "The Retreat from Italy." "As Others Are." "Nights and Forever." "The Hill of Heaven." "A Separate Peace." Hemingway was looking for a title which would convey a sense of loss or detachment. The best of them are faintly bitter.

A Farewell to Arms was serialized in *Scribner's Magazine* in 1929, before book publication. It's a good rule when a novel has been serialized to compare the serial version and the book version. There may be meaningful differences. In the case of *A Farewell to Arms*, in addition to revised passages, including the end of the novel, there is a difference in structure. The novel as you have it is divided into five books, five big sections with chapters within these sections. Therefore it is natural for many people to conclude that the structure of the novel resembles the five-act structure of a play. That works pretty well. But the manuscript is not divided into five books; neither are the magazine installments. The evidence indicates that Hemingway discovered he had a five-part structure sometime between magazine publication and book publication. It may not have been planned that way.

F. Scott Fitzgerald didn't see the typescript of *A Farewell to Arms* until after the novel had started to appear in *Scribner's Magazine*. I'm going to go through Fitzgerald's vetting report in detail because it reveals some of the strengths and weaknesses of the novel. The document was discovered by Charles Mann and published with his commentary as "F. Scott Fitzgerald's Critique of *A Farewell to Arms*," *Fitzgerald/Hemingway Annual 1976*, pp. 140–153. I said when we talked about *The Sun Also Rises* that Fitzgerald was an excellent critic; moreover, his criticism of Hemingway's work was without malice or jealousy. He seems to have been motivated by his honest desire to help Hemingway. The letter is a list of points. Fitzgerald's first point refers to Chapter 19 of the book, the scene in which Frederic Henry meets Mr. and Mrs. Myers and the opera singers in Milan. Fitzgerald wrote that it is "slow + needs cutting—it hasn't the incisiveness of other short portraits in this book or in yr. other books. The characters too numerous + too much nailed down by gags. Please cut! There's absolutely no psychological justification in introducing those singers—it's not even bizarre. If he got stewed with them + in consequence thrown from hospital it would be O.K. At least reduce it to a sharp + self sufficient vignette. It's just rather gassy as it is, I think." Fitzgerald is noting that in Hemingway's novels there are occasional non-functional scenes. They're probably there because they had some meaning for him that doesn't quite come across the paper. Fitzgerald continues: "For example—your Englishman on the fishing trip in T.S.A.R. contributes to the tautness of waiting for Brett. You seem to have written this to try to 'round out the picture of Milan during the war' during a less inspired moment." Fitzgerald is contrasting the way the fishing interlude in *The Sun Also Rises* functions in terms of the rest of the novel and the way this bar scene just hangs there.

> In "Cat in the rain," + the story about "That's all we do isn't it? Go + try new drinks etc." ["Hills Like White Elephants"] you were really listening to women—here you're only listening to yourself, to your own mind beating out facily a sort of sense that isn't really interesting, Ernest, nor really much except a sort of literary exercise—it seems to me that this ought to be *thoroughly* cut, even re-written.
>
> (Our poor old friendship probably won't survive this, but there you are—better me than some nobody in the Literary Review that doesn't care about you + your future.)

Next, in Chapter 20—Catherine and Frederick at the races:

> This is definately *dull*—it's all right to say it was meant all the time + that a novel can't have the finesse of a short story but this has got to go. The scene as it is seems to me a shame.
>
> *Later* I was astonished to find it was only about 750 wds. which only goes to show the pace you set yourself up to that point. Its dull because the war goes further + further out of sight every minute. "That's the way it was" is no answer—this triumphant proof that races were fixed!
>
> — I should put it as 400 word beginning to Chap XXI
>
> Still later Read by itself it has points, but coming on it in the novel I still believe it's dull + slow.

[Important point here:] Seems to me a last echo of the war very faint when Catherine is dying and he's drinking beer in the Café. [We'll come back to that.]

Look over Switzerland stuff for cutting.

Chapter 21 of the book has the scene in which Frederic Henry meets an English officer at the club in Milan and the Brit cheerfully tells him that everything is cooked. Fitzgerald commented:

> This is a comedy scene that really becomes offensive for you've trained everyone to read every word—now you make them read the word cooked (+ fucked would be as bad) *one dozen times*. It has ceased to become amusing by the 5th, for they're too packed, + yet the scene has possibilities. Reduce to five or six *cooked* it might have rhythm like the word wops in one of your early sketches. [You should remember that from *in our time*.] You're a little hypnotized by yourself here. [Fitzgerald is saying that sometimes Hemingway's device of word repetition becomes gimmick. It doesn't work properly when it is over done.]

Chapter 21 includes the scene in which Catherine announces she's pregnant. Fitzgerald wrote: "This could stand a good cutting. Sometimes these conversations with her take on a naïve quality that wouldn't please you in anyone else's work. Have you read Noel Coward? Some of it's wonderful—about brave man 1000 deaths ect. Couldn't you cut a little?" [Fitzgerald will come back to this criticism again. The point of his criticism is that Catherine's speech seems, as I said before, stagey. She seems to be saying things for an audience. She talks portentously: "I sometimes see me dead in it"—referring to rain.]

Chapter 21 again—Fitzgerald still doesn't like Catherine Barkley:

> Remember the brave expectant illegitimate mother is an *old situation* + has been exploited by all sorts of people you won't lower yourself to read—so be sure every line rings *new* + has some claim to being incarnated + inspired truth or you'll have the boys apon you with scorn.
>
> By the way—that buying the pistol is a *wonderful* scene. [Chapter 23.]
>
> Catherine is too glib, talks too much physically. In cutting their conversations cut some of her speeches rather than his. She is too glib—

I mean—you're seeing him in a sophisticated way as now you see yourself then—but you're *still* seeing her as you did in 1917 thru nineteen yr. old eyes. In consequence unless you make her a bit fatuous occasionally the contrast jars—either the writer is a simple fellow or she's Eleanora Duse disguised as a Red Cross nurse. In one moment you expect her to prophecy the 2nd battle of the Marne—as you probably did then. Where's that desperate, half-childish, don't-make-me-think V.A.D. feeling you spoke to me about? It's there—here—but cut *to* it! Don't try to make her make sense—she probably didn't!

"P. 241 is one of the best pages you've ever written, I think." This is the passage in Chapter 34 about people bringing so much courage to this world that the world has to kill them to break them. Fitzgerald wrote in the margin of the typescript: "This is one of the most beautiful pages in all English litera-ture." He's overstating it, but it shows the intensity of his reaction to Heming-way, a reaction that was not unusual at the time. For many of Hemingway's readers his works seemed like scripture.

On pages of your text of *Farewell to Arms* you have dashes. Hemingway had attempted in 1929 to print the word *cocksuckers*, and Fitzgerald warned him that the book would be "suppressed + confiscated within two days of pub-lication." There was no way that word could have been published by Scribners in 1929 or '39 or '49 or even '59. Fitzgerald's next point refers to Chapter 30, the retreat and Frederic Henry's arrest by the battle police.

All this retreat is marveleous the confusion ect.
The scene from 218 on is the best in recent fiction.
I think 293–294 [the opening of Chapter 40] need cutting but perhaps not to be cut altogether.
[Important:] Why not end the book with that wonderful paragraph on p. 241? ["If people bring so much courage to this world.] It is the most eloquent in the book + could end it rather gently + well.

Hemingway tried it. This is worth remembering, because the ending of *A Farewell to Arms* has been greatly admired for its understatement. It gave Hemingway a great deal of trouble, and at one point he followed Fitzgerald's suggestion. He took that passage about "If people bring so much courage to this world…" and tried it out as an ending. Didn't work. Fitzgerald's last note to Hemingway is "A beautiful book it is!"—underneath which Hemingway expressed his appreciation by writing "Kiss my ass, EH". It's always dangerous to help a writer. They don't want helpful criticism. They want praise.

I just told you that Fitzgerald didn't like the opening of Chapter 40. Please turn to the opening of that chapter. I'm about to read you what the manuscript has. It is what Hemingway originally intended to use instead of what you have in print:

We had a fine life; all the things we did were of no importance and the things we said were foolish and seem even more idiotic to write down but we were happy and I suppose wisdom and happiness do not go together, although there is a wisdom in being a fool that we do not know much about and if happiness is an end sought by the wise it is no less an end if it comes without wisdom. [That's pretty bad—Hemingway at his windiest.] It is as well to seize as to seek it because you are liable to wear out the capacity for it in the seeking. To seek it through the kingdom of Heaven is a fine thing but you must give up this life first and if this life is all you have you might have remorse after giving it up and the kingdom of heaven might be a cold place in which to live with remorse. They say the only way to keep a thing is to lose it and this may be true but I do not admire it. The only thing I know is that if you love anything enough they take it away from you. This may all be done in infinite wisdom but whoever does it is not my friend. I am afraid of God at night but I would have admired him more if he would have stopped the war or never let it start. Maybe he did stop it but whoever stopped it did not do it prettily. And if it is the Lord that giveth and the Lord that taketh away I do not admire him for taking Catherine away. He may have given me Catherine but who gave Rinaldi the syphyllis at about the same time. [Those two things are hardly comparable.] The one thing I know is that I don't know anything about it. I see the wisdom of the priest at our mess who has always loved God and so is happy and I am sure that nothing will ever take God away from him. But how much is wisdom and how much is luck to be born that way? What if you are not built that way? What if the things you love are perishable? All you know then is that they will perish. You will perish too and perhaps that is the answer; that those who love things that are immortal and believe in them are immortal themselves and live on with them while those that love things that die and believe in them die and are as dead as the things they love. [Awful.] If that were true it would be a fine gift and would even things up. But it probably is not true. All that we can be sure of is that we are born and that we will die and that everything we love will die too. [Hardly a profound conclusion after all this cosmic marinating.]

The more things with life that we love the more things there are to die. So if we want to buy winning tickets we can go over on the side of immortality; and finally they most of them, do. But if you were born with loving nothing and the warm milk of your mother's breast was never heaven and the first thing you loved was the side of a hill and the last thing was a woman and they took her away and you did not want another but only to have her; and she was gone; then you are not so well placed and it would have been better to have loved God from the start. But you did not love God. And it doesn't do any good to talk about it either. Nor to think about it.

Hemingway at his most pretentious. It's close to self-parody.

I read that cancelled opening of Chapter 40 to show you that it is very instructive to look at a writer's working drafts. One of the gauges of good writing is bad writing. We can assess a writer's style by examining passages in which his style doesn't work. Here there are wordy sentences, fumbling for meaning, attempts to find or to suggest profundities and deep meanings that don't emerge. Hemingway is dealing with the system of divine justice, a subject that gave Milton trouble in *Paradise Lost*. Hemingway at his best is superb. But when his discipline slips, he becomes self-indulgent and pretentious. The prophetic Hemingway is not the great Hemingway. He was thirty when this novel was published. With the advantages of hindsight, it is possible to detect in *A Farewell to Arms* the beginnings of the Papa image, the beginnings of the wise old man. At the age of thirty he began to show signs of being impressed by his own wisdom.

A final point on the Fitzgerald/Hemingway relationship. Hemingway's note at the bottom of Fitzgerald document indicated his displeasure with Fitzgerald's advice. It was not a passing displeasure. For the rest of his life Hemingway remembered this letter with incremental resentment, so that when Charles Poore was editing the *Hemingway Reader*, Hemingway wrote him in 1953, fourteen years after *A Farewell to Arms* was published:

> I did the last of the re-write in Paris I'm pretty sure. Or maybe the proofs there. I rewrote the last chapter over 40 times but I hope it does not read that way. Now I remember; I'm sure the last re-write was done in Paris. Because I had a long letter sent over by F. Scott Fitzgerald in which among other things, he said I must not under any circumstance let Lt. Henry shoot the sergeant [Not in the letter I read to you.] and suggesting that after Catherine dies Frederick Henry should go to the café and pick up a paper and read that the Marines were holding in Chateau-Thierry. [Not in the letter I read to you.] This, Scott said, would make the American

public understand the book better. He also did not like the scene in the old Hotel Cavour in Milano and wanted changes to be made in many other places "to make it more acceptable." Not one suggestion made sense or was useful. He never saw the Mss until it was completed as published.

There are several untruths there. Hemingway did act on certain Fitzgerald suggestions. He cut that opening of Chapter 40, and he tried to move the line about "If you are very brave this world will kill you. . . . " It is not true that Fitzgerald did not see the novel until it was published. He saw it in June, well before the novel was published. There may have been another letter; there's no certainty that Fitzgerald wrote Hemingway just one letter about *A Farewell to Arms*. The thing that seemed to have irked Hemingway the most, because he mentioned it to other people, was his displeasure at Fitzgerald's suggestion that there be a reminder of the war at the end of the novel. If Hemingway can be trusted—and he cannot—Fitzgerald suggested that while Catherine is dying in the hospital, Frederick Henry reads in the paper about the Western Front in France. Hemingway regarded that as an absurd suggestion. Nevertheless, the thematic tension of the novel, as shown in many of the trial titles, is love and war. The plan of the novel, very roughly, is soldier meets nurse; soldier makes separate peace because values of love replace values of war; then nurse dies in way not connected with war. It would not have been absurd for Hemingway at the end of the novel to have reintroduced a suggestion of the war background, reinforcing the irony of Catherine's death despite the circumstance that Catherine and Henry have made a separate peace. Since their love is triggered by war and since they believe they can escape the war, it might have been effective to reintroduce a reminder of the war at the very end.

Maxwell Perkins also advised Hemingway to bring in the war at the end of the novel:

> The first point relates to the combination of the two elements of the book,—Love and War. They combine, to my mind, perfectly up to the point where Catherine and Lieutenant Henry get to Switzerland;—thereafter, the war is almost forgotten by them and by the reader,—though not quite. And psychologically it should be all but forgotten;—it would be by people so profoundly in love, and so I do not think what I at first thought, that you might bring more news of it or remembrances of it into this part. Still, I can't shake off the feeling that War, which has deeply conditioned this love story—and does so still passively—should still do so actively and decisively. It would if Catherine's death might probably not

have occurred except for it, and I etc., might have been largely responsible. If it were, and if the doctor said so during that awful night, in just a casual sentence, the whole story would turn back upon War in the realization of Henry and the reader. [24 May 1929]

Who's just read *A Farewell to Arms* for the first time? All novels are susceptible to time. This book which made such a strong impression on readers in the Thirties and Forties may have become a little old-fashioned.

* * *

I want to go over some of the main concerns in *A Farewell to Arms*. I'll begin with this one. *A Farewell to Arms* is obviously a love story, and it is Hemingway's first extended love story. *The Sun Also Rises* is a love story in which the love cannot be consummated; it is an un-love story. *A Farewell to Arms* is Hemingway's first novel with a heroine. Brett is in no way the heroine of *The Sun Also Rises*. She's the principal female figure, but she's there as a kind of warning example of what a woman should not be. Today I want you to tell me what this novel says about women and about the relationship between men and women which goes under the label of love. Hemingway on women. Hemingway on love. Hemingway on the value of love. The function of love. Who needs it? Why? And what are the roles, what are the responsibilities, what are the duties and obligations of men and women in love? Is it more grief than it's worth? Or does it give life value and meaning and significance? You can talk about women separately. Or you can talk about men separately. Or you can connect them up.

* * *

MJB: Well, she's supposed to be a little screwy in the beginning. She says, "Tell me that you're my own true love, and you'll come back to me." The loss of her fiancé in the war has left her a little unbalanced, and one of the effects of new love with Frederic Henry is to cure that condition. So here you can argue that love is a healing thing. Assuming that Hemingway regards love as a positive thing that makes life meaningful, how does love function in *A Farewell to Arms*?

* * *

MJB: In the world of the novel we see that love is therapeutic and healing. Catherine and Henry are certainly better off being in love than not being in love. She's a little nutty until she falls in love with him; and he has a gap in his life which he fills with alcohol and whores. He describes his leave, about which he says that he was drunk in most of the cities of Italy, and when he woke up in the morning he was never sure who was in bed with him: it sounds like that should've been a good time, but it wasn't. When he and Catherine find each other everything they do together enhances their pleasure. And we have the speech of the priest when he comes to visit Frederic Henry after Henry is wounded but before he goes to Milan where his affair with Catherine really commences. The priest talks about the value of love; he says that love means wanting to do for someone, love means wanting to sacrifice, love means giving up things for the one loved. Does that work? Does Frederic Henry live up to these rules? Giving up and sacrificing?

* * *

MJB: She's his home. It is a one-sided relationship. Catherine worries whether Frederic is happy, whether he's pleased, whether he's bored, whether he's comfortable, whether he's having a good time. What makes love meaningful from the man's point of view—which is the narrator's point of view, which is Frederic's point of view, which is Hemingway's point of view? Remember from whose point of view this story is told. This is Frederic Henry's story told by Frederic Henry. Everything you hear, everything you read is filtered through him. In a way, poor Catherine doesn't exist in the novel except as Frederic Henry tells us about her. What he tells us about her is how devoted she was, how much she loved him, how much she was committed to his happiness, his pleasure. Given this lopsided situation, it is then fair to ask why love is accorded such importance in this novel and other novels by Hemingway. Why does Hemingway insist on the worth, on the necessity of love? What's good about it?

* * *

MJB: What happens when Frederic Henry and Catherine Barkley fall completely in love? That is, after they consummate their relationship. What happens to these two people in terms of the rest of their lives, the rest of the world?

They cut themselves off. Their love leads to self-isolation, and it's isolation compounded. It begins with an American man and a Scottish woman falling in love in Italy. There is in the geographical setting a quality of artificiality, a quality of rootlessness. Then to escape from the things that threaten them in Italy, they flee to another country, Switzerland—which has always been the country of refugees and exiles—where they cut themselves off even further. In Italy they knew people. In Switzerland they know no one. What do they do in Switzerland? Well, they presumably devote a good deal of time to what we might term bedsports, and they play cards. They get a book and learn two-handed card games. You wonder how they pass the time for the months they live in Switzerland. What do they live on? They live on sight drafts. Frederic Henry goes to the bank and cashes drafts on his grandfather in America, which his family then honors. They live comfortably on what is a mild form of larceny. He has no occupation. We're told that before the war he was studying architecture. It might've been anything because there's nothing architectural about him. He never refers to his career ambitions except once to say that Catherine would be very good with his clients-assuming that after this is all over, he will be able to resume school. The point I'm making is the complete artificiality of their existence. They're tourists, and not even tourists touring on their own money. They're touring on the proceeds from the sight drafts that his family in America is honoring, temporarily. Their life together, their love together, has a quality of unreality about it. It is a love that does not have to cope with normal human situations, normal human problems. They live in hotel rooms. There's no permanence. Catherine has none of the responsibilities of a wife. Frederic has none of the responsibilities of a husband. All they do is amuse each other. It sounds damn dull to me. The novel insists on the power, on the necessity of love, but it presents this artificial love that can thrive only in isolation.

Although Hemingway celebrates love, or at least insists on the need for love, there is a streak of misogyny that runs through his work. Hemingway distrusts women. He created what might be called ideal women, such as Catherine Barkley in this novel and Maria in *For Whom the Bell Tolls*—an ideal woman being a woman who knows her place, who knows her duties, who knows her obligations, who is devoted to the well-being of the man. He created these women who have been described as lobotomized; yet he also created some of the grandest bitches in literature: destructive, devouring, man-eating women. These two things operate side-by-side. One is there for the sake of illuminating the other. The bitches help define what a good woman is by contrast. When we talked about the short story "Now I Lay Me," in which young Nick remembers what a bitch his mother was and how she destroyed his father's manhood, I said that this could be seen as Nick's first great wound: the wound of realizing that his father had been unmanned by his strong and ultimately destructive mother. It is not difficult to conclude that Hemingway vowed that it would never happen to him, that no woman would destroy him or unman him. But this misogyny, this distrust of the destructive powers of women does not take the form of doing without them. It takes the form of finding a good woman and then educating her in her womanly duties: which are to tote the barge and lift the bale and always be good-humored and to share his interests and to be concerned above all with his happiness and comfort and pleasure. Frederic and Catherine live in a never-never land with no real duties, no real problems. The only way this kind of love can flourish is in an artificial environment. Hemingway's great love stories are always short in duration and doomed because they carry the seeds of the doom in themselves.

It can't last. Sooner or later, Frederic Henry's going to come home some night and there's no dinner; and Catherine's going to explain that the dishwasher isn't working, and the plumbing isn't working, and the toilet's stopped up, and what've you been doing all day-sitting around drinking with the boys? Real life would get in the way of this idyllic artificial isolated life. Therefore when we come back to reality, it has got to end in the death of one or both partners. Catherine Barkley dies here. The man dies in *For Whom the Bell Tolls,* and the odds are ten to one that Maria will die soon after Robert. The man dies in *Across the River into the Trees.* They are doomed loves because they are not set up in terms of real people with real responsibilities and real problems and real troubles in a real world. They're idyllic. Idyllic means too good to be true, or too good to last. Idyllic means temporary.

* * *

MJB: In the first class I said he was an anti-romantic romantic. He does away with one kind of romanticism and supplies another kind. Look at all of the great love stories in literature and drama and myth and legend. They're all unhappy love stories. They're all tragic. They all end at a peak of ecstasy because they can't go on. Romeo and Juliet die in their teens. Can you envision the old age of Romeo and Juliet? No. So in a sense Hemingway is operating within a romantic tradition of tragic doomed love affairs. In very simplified terms, what Hemingway does is take romantic material and try to make it seem unromantic and real by his technique, by style primarily. But take away the Hemingway style, take away the Hemingway understatement, and take away the Hemingway objectivity-then you have some pretty romantic stuff. The men behave heroically, like knights in days of yore. Notice, for example, that in Hemingway's heroes, there's a streak of knight errantry. The knight by himself, not part of an army, but the knight alone riding out alone to redress wrongs, to rescue maidens in distress, and slay dragons. Frederic Henry is a foreigner. He's in somebody else's army. Same thing in *For Whom the Bell Tolls;* Robert Jordan is a foreigner in somebody else's army, somebody else's country, somebody else's war. In *A Farewell to Arms* the point of view has a good deal to do with this whole matter of love, isolation, women, men. I said this before: remember who's telling the story; and then ask yourself when he is telling it. Frederic Henry's telling the story; therefore it is his story told from within his value system. The *when* is important because the *when* is later. How much later we don't know, but later. The story is not written as a running account or a log of what happened while it was happening. There's a retrospective effect. This is Frederic Henry some years later, two years or five years or ten years. The novel was published in 1929; the action ends in 1918. You could argue that the time of publication was the time of Frederic Henry's telling of the story, so that there is the effect of distance from the actual events. Whatever the novel says about men and women in love, it represents the years of Frederic Henry's assessing and re-assessing of what happened. As I've already said, it's Frederic Henry's book. Catherine comes with the bed.

Now; shift to another topic: If love is doomed what then does the novel say about the meaning of the experience. I'll put it another way, an easier way. One of the things that is said over and over again about fiction, is that the major characters in a work of fiction change, mature, grow, develop. I'm not so sure about that. I've never observed actual people grow, change, mature, or develop much beyond the age of twenty. Whatever development, change, and evolution I've seen occurs early. But let's deal with the literary situation. I grew up hearing in classes that when you read a novel this is what you look for and this is what you write your paper about—growth, change, development, maturation. Does that work in this novel? I'm trying to get from the question of the growth of Frederic Henry to the question of what is the meaning of experience.

* * *

MJB: Instead of portraying the putative changes in characters, skillful writers reveal the truth about their characters. In life we gradually learn about people. They at first seem to be one way, but we discover that they are really something else. Ostensibly truthful people prove to be liars. But they haven't changed. They are what they always were. You have to find that out. I have not discovered significant change in grown-ups outside of fiction. Have you?

Student: Well, I was taught to look for it, too. And I certainly don't see it here. There's supposed to be some kind of metamorphosis, change, and I don't see it here. He's still shallow and empty in the end.

* * *

MJB: It would be an overstatement to say that he doesn't change at all. He undergoes a great loss, a great shock, a great hurt. Inevitably these things have their effects, but there's no massive change in the character. He learns, for example, the value of love. In grossly oversimplified terms, he learns that being in love with and living with Catherine is better than going to the whorehouse, but that's to trivialize the thing. It's more than that. He learns that love can provide a stay against emptiness and loneliness. He'd never been loved before he met Catherine. The experience teaches him certain things. I don't say he doesn't learn anything. I say he doesn't change in any fundamental way. The priest's speeches seem to be written in neon lights: they seem to be signals for the reader. Every time the priest talks about love and sacrifice and unselfishness, you have the feeling that those speeches are planted by the author and you better read them carefully because they're going to apply later on. You're going to have to use them. It seems to me that Frederic Henry does not live up to the various tests that the priest sets up. The priest says that love requires sacrifice, and I don't see Frederic Henry doing any sacrificing at all. You can't even say that he sacrifices his military career. The battle police are getting ready to shoot him. He doesn't give up anything for Catherine. He flees to her from execution. Being in love with her doesn't seem to make him more generous, more caring, more giving. He's a taker, not a giver. Their relationship resembles a horny teen-age boy's daydream of what it would be like to have a mistress and ample money and to do nothing except to engage in pleasures of the flesh.

* * *

MJB: I will deal with what I am capable of dealing with. In terms of literature I think that Hemingway is saying that Frederic Henry starts off not looking for love. He's never known it before. He's not sure that he's capable of it or that he wants it. He begins, as he says, playing a game with Catherine-the love game, the sex game, whatever you want to call it. Then it turns into something else. But it turns into something else under very special circumstances. He's wounded. He arrives at the hospital, and then there she is. It gives their love a kind of momentum. The situation is artificial. How many of us are going to fall in love under circumstances like that? How many of us are going to be wounded in battle and shipped to a hospital where the girl nurses us, loves us, and yields everything to our pleasure, comfort, and happiness? Again, there's an impetus to the Catherine-Frederic relationship to which I apply this word I've been using—"artificial." For "artificial" you could use the word "romantic." The circumstances couldn't be more romantic, which means more unrealistic. Hemingway was writing a kind of love-adventure story. This much I do know about human conduct: setting and timing are very important. If for example, Catherine and Frederic had met before the war—let's say had he been studying architecture in London and he met her at a party or reception or something— what would've happened? Maybe nothing. The circumstances under which they do consummate their love provide the experience with an outside force. Their love is accelerated by, intensified by the circumstances. The whole war mentality: live for the moment; we may all be dead by tomorrow. That is another reason why so many love stories are written against a wartime background, because during war everything happens faster, everything seems to be more valuable because time is more valuable, because time is running out, because death is imminent. Hemingway, like most other writers, was dealing with standard situations. There are very few new plots; there are very few new stories. What the writer does is take old plots, old stories, old characters, and make them seem new and fresh and different. But the material here is as old as the Trojan War.

* * *

Now, let me do some summarizing. Given the doom in Hemingway's work, given the fact that from the first meeting of Frederic Henry and Catherine Barkley, any astute reader knows she's doomed. As soon as she appears in the novel you can see it coming: one way or another she's not going to be alive at the end of this novel. Given this built-in doom, this built-in inevitability of loss, what then remains in the novel to provide a system of the values of living? What makes life worthwhile? How does a Hemingway hero construct a system of values? How does Frederic Henry learn? He does not change, but he learns. What's the learning experience? What's it based on? How does it function?

Student: One of the ways that he learns is from love. Well, for example, in the beginning of the book when he does drink and he does go to the whorehouse, he knows he doesn't like it, but he doesn't know why he doesn't like it. From having the experience of love he gets an idea of why he didn't like doing those things in the first place.

* * *

MJB: Right. The Hemingway hero does all his learning from experience. That isn't as elementary as it sounds, because Hemingway says that there are some people who are capable of experiencing more and better than other people. And there are those on whom experience is wasted. A Hemingway hero has highly developed experiencing capabilities. He notices more and enjoys more than other people. His whole framework of values is based on what he has felt, seen, tasted and on what he has learned from feeling, seeing, tasting. He lives for pleasure. Hemingway says again and again that life is a rotten, disappointing thing; but, my God! you can have pleasure in it. Catherine says that death is a dirty trick. But before *they* get you, you can have a lot of pleasure-in particular, the pleasures of the senses. Hemingway could've made a good living as a restaurant critic. Notice how he describes meals. Characters in other novels walk into restaurants, eat a meal, and that's it. Hemingway tells you what they ordered, tells you how it was cooked, tells you how it was served, tells you whether it was good or not. Same thing with booze. And within the limits of 1929 taste and censorship, the same thing with sex. Hemingway had to do a lot of tippy-toeing around the bedroom scenes here because he couldn't get away with much in 1929. Nonetheless, the same thing holds for the pleasures of sex as holds for the pleasures of the table and the bottle. Having learned through experience what is good, what is better, what is best, the tragedy—if that's what it is—is that it's going to be taken away from you. That leads to the question that I'm not going to deal with today, but I'm going to plant it today because you should be thinking about it: Is tragedy possible in the world of Ernest Hemingway's fiction? Is what happens in *A Farewell to Arms* tragic? Or is it something else? Is it something like tragedy but not the same thing? Did Hemingway write tragedies? Can you have a tragedy when death is a dirty trick? Think about it; it's important. And think about this—I'm just restating the same thing: substitute for "tragic" the words "dignity" or "heroism." Are dignity or heroism possible in this framework? I'll say it another way: Do the pleasures of life, do the values taught from experience ultimately have any meaning? Do they allow for life or death with dignity? One last thought: It has been said that Hemingway's heroes are concerned with survival. Is that true? If so, what threatens them? Why is it necessary to have a system of defense?

MARK CIRINO

"You Don't Know the Italian Language Well Enough": The Bilingual Dialogue of A Farewell To Arms

In a *Farewell to Arms*, Ralph Simmons (aka Enrico DelCredo) is incapable of singing opera like a true Italian, and therefore suffers the indignity of having spectators throw benches at him. When Frederic Henry is captured on the banks of the Tagliamento River, his accent also exposes him as non-Italian, and officers in his own army suspect that he is German and nearly execute him. It is in the interest of both men to speak Italian as natives, but they cannot. Hemingway's representation of the inherent gap between Italian-speakers and English-speakers mirrors the inevitable confusions of war. In addition to the nearly fatal mistaking of Frederic for a German, he is also mistaken for a Frenchman by a doctor; for an Austrian officer by a barber; for an Italian from North or South America by an Italian sergeant; and for a South American by a bartender. In an extension of his decade-old practice in representing the Italian language in his prose, and a precursor of his more acclaimed technique in *For Whom the Bell Tolls*, Hemingway captures this ethnic and linguistic uncertainty by manipulating word choice, tense, grammar, and the translation of phrases.

Before investigating Hemingway's use of Italian in *A Farewell to Arms*, it is important to contextualize his history with the language prior to writing the novel. In March 1918, preparing to depart for Europe, Hemingway announced to his sister, "I now study French and Italian," although

---

The Hemingway Review, Volume 25, Number 1 (Fall 2005): pp. 43–62. Copyright © 2005 The Ernest Hemingway Foundation.

the details and depth of these studies are unclear (Sanford 275). Michael Reynolds believes that Hemingway did not acquire a significant amount of Italian through lessons in Kansas City, but rather through direct immersion while in Italy. Reynolds writes:

> Hemingway spoke no Italian when he arrived in Italy and probably very little more when he returned to Milan wounded six weeks later. During his stay in Milan he picked up enough of the language to make his way on the streets and in the cafés, for he apparently had a quick ear for language and the gift to make himself understood with a limited vocabulary. He was, however, by no means as fluent as Frederic Henry. (179–180)

Hemingway arrived in Italy in early June, and, lack of expertise notwithstanding, began enthusiastic boasts about his Italian not long afterwards. "Gee I have darn near forgot the English language," he wrote in late June to a former Oak Park High School classmate. "If Cannon or old Loftbery could hear me speak Italian all day long they would roll over in their graves" (*SL* 11).

On 8 July, Hemingway was blown up at Fossalta di Piave; one month later he wrote to his older sister Marcelline on American Red Cross stationery, gleefully plunging into novice Italian, joking that she has not written to him because she loves another lieutenant. Hemingway then translated into English what he had attempted to write in Italian, adding, "'Tis thus that the old master learns the Italian language. He can speak it with great fluency and on my return we shall journey to Italian restaurants downtown where I will demonstrate." The letter is filled with other lighthearted boasts—he dubs himself "The Hero of the Peehave," and blusters, "Merely because I am a great man do not stand in awe of me!" (8 August 1918, JFK Library, reprinted with changes in *At the Hemingways* 282–283). The bilingual bombast continues—six weeks later in a letter to two of his sisters, he wrote:

> Now Ivory [Marcelline] I will give you a full list of the old master's titles and other stuff. Tenente Ernesto Hemingway; proposto al medaglia d'argento (valore) proposto per croce d'guerra. Ferito da Prima Linae d'Guerra. Promotzione for Merito D'Guerra. Translated Lieut, cited for the Silver valour medal, cited for the war cross, wounded in the first lines and promoted for merit. Now aint he stuck up? He aint though, I hope. (21 September 1918, JFK Library, reprinted with changes in *At the Hemingways* 287–289)[1]

The letter shows Hemingway as enamored of his knack for writing bilingually (however incorrectly) as with his new military decorations.

In another letter, this one written to his mother in late August, Hemingway claimed:

> Now Mom you may not believe it but I can speak Italian like a born Veronese. You see up in the trenches I had to talk it, there being nothing else spoken, so I learned an awful lot and talked with officers by the hour in Italian. I suppose I'm shy on grammar but I'm long on vocabulary. Lots of times I've acted as interpreter for the hospital. Somebody comes in and they can't understand what they want and the nurse brings 'em to my bed and I straighten it all out . . . I've gotten Italian pretty well . . . I know more French and Italian now than if I had studied 8 years in college . . . (Griffin 85–86)

Hemingway's "long on vocabulary" claim, of course, contradicts Reynolds' assertion of his "limited vocabulary."

Then, in a moving 18 August letter to his family, which he refers to as "the longest letter I've ever written to anybody," Hemingway unveils a narrative technique that he would use to portray Italian speech in short stories and in *A Farewell to Arms*. Hemingway recounts the events surrounding his wounding, and then reproduces a conversation he had with a captain:

> I told him in Italian that I wanted to see my legs, though I was afraid to look at them . . . They couldn't figure out how I had walked 150 yards with a load with both knees shot through and my right shoe punctured two big places. Also over 200 flesh wounds. "Oh," says I, "My Captain, it is of nothing. In America they all do it! It is thought well not to allow the enemy to perceive that they have captured our goats!"
>
> The goat speech required some masterful lingual ability but I got it across . . . (*SL* 14–15, emphasis added)

Here the nineteen-year old Hemingway uses three strategies that are crucial to understanding his representation of the Italian language throughout much of his career. First, he is determined to make sure his readers know the language in which the dialogue occurs. To Hemingway, the language which a character is speaking affects the authenticity of a scene. Second, Hemingway's technique of literal translation debuts in the letter. He includes the translation of an Italian phrase—"of nothing"—to convey the language in which the action occurs. "Of nothing" seems awkward, but matches "*di niente*," a phrase used to minimize something the speaker has done, as if the act was no great effort or inconvenience. Third, notwithstanding his self-deprecating and ironic description of the "masterful" way he translated the American vernacular phrase "get one's goat" into Italian, Hemingway often overestimated his aptitude. His pride in acquiring this new language would surface in his prose, occasionally resulting in errors.

As in *The Sun Also Rises,* the protagonist of *A Farewell to Arms* is an American abroad, where he must interact with the natives. For Jake Barnes, language is not a problem. He is able to speak Spanish or French when he needs to, establishing himself as an insider rather than a tourist. Jake also surrounds himself with a coterie of English speakers. But while Frederic, like Jake, has an English-speaking love interest, his communication in his second language is more crucial; he must command Italian soldiers in their native tongue. In *A Farewell to Arms,* Hemingway needed to balance contradictory challenges, representing members of the Italian Army speaking to each other as authentically as possible—in Italian—while still allowing the novel to be understood by an English-speaking readership. His main strategy in overcoming these obstacles was to produce literal translations of common Italian phrases and words. Hemingway had improbably employed the technique in his 1918 letter home, continued its use in early short stories, and would make it a centerpiece of *For Whom the Bell Tolls,* in which he offered a similar, but far more flamboyant performance with the Spanish language.

This technique has been examined thoroughly with regard to *For Whom the Bell Tolls,* where critics point to strategies similar to those seen in *A Farewell to Arms.* Carole Moses writes that in *For Whom the Bell Tolls* Hemingway "imitates the vocabulary and sentence structure of Spanish, creating a highly stylized prose" (215). Milton M. Azevedo calls the same technique "an admirable stylistic experiment in which Hemingway manipulates English and Spanish syntax and vocabulary to convey the impression that the characters are speaking Spanish" (30). Both observations could also apply to Hemingway's treatment of the Italian dialogue in *A Farewell to Arms.*

In the decade between the 1918 letter and *A Farewell to Arms,* two short stories illustrate Hemingway's developing technique for presenting Italian speech in fiction. In "Out of Season," written in April 1923 (Smith 16), the guide Peduzzi asks the young gentleman if he can have five lire "for a favor" (*CSS* 139). This awkward phrase is not Peduzzi speaking clumsy English; it represents the Italian phrase for "please"—*per favore.* The two Italian words mean "for favor," which Hemingway appropriates for Peduzzi's dialogue. Something quite similar occurs in "Che Ti Dice La Patria?", written in April and May 1927, less than a year before Hemingway began *A Farewell to Arms* (Smith 193). The narrator informs a young Italian man that he will be uncomfortable riding on the outside of the car, to which the Italian responds, "That makes nothing. I must go to Spezia" (*CSS* 223). "That makes nothing" denotes "non fa niente," a common phrase to say that something does not matter. "Fa" is the third-person singular conjugation of the Italian verb "fare," meaning "to make" or "to do." Though strictly English-speaking readers may not understand exactly why the odd "that makes nothing" is used, they still can intuit from the phrasing that there is a mediation between the English on the page and the original language the characters are speaking. Hemingway's narrators supply that mediation.[2]

From the earliest draft of *A Farewell to Arms*, Hemingway used narrative strategies to capture Frederic's impossible task of seamless assimilation into Italian conversation. The original beginning thrusts the reader *in medias res* after the lieutenant (then a third-person protagonist named Emmett Hancock) has been wounded. When an administrator in the hospital tells him "I can't understand Italian," Emmett responds, "I can speak English" (qtd. in Oldsey 94). This exchange matches Hemingway's claim in his letter home that he served as a translator while in the hospital, straightening out everyone else's confusion. He will eventually position it at the beginning of Book Two, where Frederic helps a nurse to understand his Italian stretcher-bearers.

In the first draft's second chapter, Emmett awakens to see a beautiful nurse—a Miss Fairbanks—in his hospital room. When she asks him his rank, he responds "*Tenente,*" which Hemingway then deleted and changed to English—"Lieutenant" (qtd. in Oldsey 96). This change evidences Hemingway's focus on realistic representation. Had the wounded Emmett been communicating with an Italian administrator, "*Tenente*" would be appropriate; to an English-speaking nurse, "Lieutenant" is logical. Not only do such details contribute to the verisimilitude of *A Farewell to Arms*, but as Michael Reynolds notes, they also add an important component to Frederic Henry's character. "The effect of allowing Catherine little or no language ability," Reynolds writes, "is to put Frederic in the dominant position in their relationship" (180).[3] Even in the novel's draft, it is evident that the protagonist does not want to cede linguistic control to his love interest. Frederic says that he did not know what he was getting into and did not care very much. For him, it is "enough" to see and talk with a beautiful girl *who speaks English* and to have some place to go in the evenings beside the brothel for officers (see JFK 64).

Hemingway's experimentation with Italian in *A Farewell to Arms* continues in the first draft. In the original version of the priest's hospital visit to the convalescing Frederic, Hemingway sketches an exchange in which the priest asks Frederic to name the things he loves about life. Frederic's response is a revealing catalogue: "The night. The day. Food. Drink. Girls. Italy. Pictures. Places. Swimming. Portofino. Paris. Spring. Summer. Fall. Winter. Heat. Cold. Smells. Sleep. Newspapers. Reading." Then Frederic confides to the reader: "This all sounds better in Italian" (qtd. in Reynolds 286). Even at this remarkable point where Frederic lists his twenty-one passions in a cathartic secular confession, he explicitly addresses the gap in language, as a reminder that the narrative is only a representation of the action, a translation filtered through his linguistic acumen. The seemingly offhand remark also adds to our knowledge of Frederic. By suggesting that what was said sounds better in Italian than what is being represented in English, the narrator puffs his language skills while simultaneously deprecating his story and its unfortunate but unavoidable linguistic limitations.

As the scene continues in manuscript form, the linguistic gap separating the Italian priest and the American soldier is augmented not only by word choice, but by verb construction. In the draft, the priest says, "I was afraid I shake your faith" and then, "I take your greetings to the mess" (qtd. in Reynolds 286–287), clinging to the present tense in both sentences instead of using the conditional and the future respectively. Hemingway reconsidered this scene; he ultimately eliminated the first comment, and while in the published version the priest still says he will relay Frederic's regards, he uses correct grammar: "I *will take* your greetings to the mess" (73, emphasis added).

The above scene illustrates Hemingway's flirtation with representing a conversation in pidgin Italian, and then deciding against it. Of course, the imperfect language spoken by the priest—which Hemingway discarded—echoes the captain's tortured language in the published novel's early mess hall scene. In that version, the narrator makes explicit mention of the captain's speech patterns: "The captain spoke pidgin Italian for my doubtful benefit, in order that I might understand perfectly, that nothing should be lost."[4] When the captain speaks, readers understand what the narrator means; the captain tells Frederic, "Priest to-day with girls" and "Priest not with girls" and then "Priest every night five against one" (7).

Hemingway's use of pidgin Italian to convey lack of fluency recurs at a moment of tremendous tension. Emilio, the barman in Stresa, warns Frederic that he will be arrested the following day. Frederic asks him, "What time do they come to arrest me?" and then "What do you say to do?" (265), two examples of verbs in the present tense when the future and conditional, respectively, are called for. The Italian is not incorrect because Frederic is too panicked to speak properly; nor is this an example of Frederic not knowing how to speak with fluency. Instead, Frederic chooses to speak in the simplest tense to make certain that he does not commit any errors. Frederic's simplification is an example of Sheldon Norman Grebstein's observation that the dialogue of *A Farewell to Arms*, when represented as Italian, has "a certain formality of expression which hints at the protagonist's . . . concentration in speaking the language correctly" (120). This time, with his life on the line, it is Frederic who speaks pidgin Italian so that "nothing should be lost."[5]

Central to Hemingway's method of conveying foreignness is his literal translation of everyday Italian words and phrases into their English counterparts. Hemingway chooses Italian words whose corresponding words in

English are not typically used in the same contexts, producing the effect of stilted, slightly awkward speech. The result remains understandable to the English-speaking reader, but still slightly unnatural. The effect is not drastic, but noticeable, the equivalent of changing the color of a wall from white to off-white. The English produced through this method is even charming, like an Italian speaking unpolished English, or technically perfect English with an accent.

Throughout Hemingway's history with the technique, he favors the most common Italian words and phrases to translate. When Rocca, an officer in *A Farewell to Arms,* tells the priest a story that Rinaldi rejects as implausible, Rocca responds, "Just as you like" (39). The phrase does not quite fit; it is too proper, even stodgy for an officers' bull session in the mess hall. "Just as you like," however, is meant to conjure the everyday Italian expression *"come vuoi,"* a catchall phrase of deference, meaning, in this case, "think whatever you want." The same phrase recurs when Rinaldi wonders whether his syphilis might require a medical leave. Drunk and frustrated, Rinaldi asks for the priest's opinion, and the priest tells him, "Just as you like" (175); in other words, "Have it your way." The odd, stylized English here paradoxically conveys a very common and ordinary phrase in Italian.

While the English-speaking reader encountering "just as you like" may not associate the phrase specifically with *"come vuoi,"* the allusion should not lead to a misreading of the dialogue. To understand Hemingway's method of representation is to realize that the characters are speaking a foreign language normally, not an unnatural brand of English, and certainly not awkward, formal, or archaic Italian. Hemingway chooses an Italian phrase that, when translated, will produce a comprehensible, yet still foreign-sounding English phrase.

Another of Hemingway's preferred ways of conveying Italian speech is to translate *niente,* the Italian word for "nothing." After Rinaldi gives Frederic coffee beans to chew for clearing up his boozy breath before meeting Catherine Barkley, Frederic thanks him, and Rinaldi's response is, "Nothing, baby. Nothing" (41). "Nothing" seems an odd word choice, but Rinaldi has only used *"niente,"* an informal version of "you're welcome," short for *"non é niente"* or *"di niente."*

"Nothing" happens again later, when the priest visits Frederic in the hospital, and Frederic thanks him for bringing gifts. Like Rinaldi, the priest replies, "Nothing" (73). The more natural rendering of casual speech would be "Don't mention it" or even "It's nothing," but the single word "nothing" is enough to convey the Italianness of the entire dialogue. Hemingway uses a literal translation for *"niente,"* even though its meaning does not transfer into English with perfect fluidity. In fact, he translates *"niente"* precisely *because* it does not transfer with perfect fluidity. Readers intuit that because the presentation is a bit awry, the word "nothing" signifies Italian speech.

The Italian words for "thank you," as well as "you're welcome" are grist for Hemingway's strategy. In *A Farewell to Arms*, the expression "many thanks" occurs four times, unconventional wording for conversational English, but a literal translation of *"tante grazie,"* the commonest of Italian phrases. Frederic himself uses the phrase three times: he thanks the stretcher-bearers who have carried him to the hospital (83); the doctors who evaluate his condition (97); and the silhouette-cutter who gives him a complimentary cutout (135). The fourth occurrence is spoken by the waiter who holds an umbrella over Frederic and Catherine and ushers them into a waiting carriage. After Frederic tips him, the waiter says, "Many thanks. Pleasant journey" (157). These stilted two-word phrases are unremarkable if spoken in Italian: *"Tante grazie. Buon viaggio."* Hemingway translates them directly into English to give readers the sense and rhythm of the language in which the action occurs, rather than the easier-to-read "Thank you very much. Have a nice trip," as a polite American waiter would say.[6] Hemingway's word choice here recalls "Che Ti Dice La Patria?" when *"non capisco"*—Italian for "I don't understand"—is presented both as "Don't understand" and "No understand" (*CSS* 226, 227). In *A Farewell to Arms*, Rinaldi—earlier seen studying a book of English grammar—is confused by a phrase spoken in English and tells Frederic, "No understand" (20). The two-word phrase imparts the rhythm of foreignness, and with it, verisimilitude in the novel.

In "Che Ti Dice La Patria?" the narrator gives an impromptu lecture on the different ways to thank someone in Italian. After he gives a young Italian man a free ride, the narrator observes the new generation's decaying civility by noting that the young man merely says "thanks," and "not 'thank you,' or 'thank you very much,' or 'thank you a thousand times,' all of which you formerly said in Italy to a man when he handed you a time-table or explained about a direction. The young man uttered the lowest form of the word 'thanks'" (*CSS* 225).[7] The narrator refers to the subtle distinctions among *"grazie," "ti ringrazio," "tante grazie,"* and *"grazie mille."* In *A Farewell to Arms*, Frederic never delineates the subtleties of the various gradations of "thank you," but instead four times reproduces *"tante grazie"* as "many thanks."

Just as *A Farewell to Arms* includes designated correspondents for "thank you" and "you're welcome," so it does for "please," recalling Peduzzi's use of "for a favor" in "Out of Season." In *A Farewell to Arms*, *"per piacere"* is translated literally as "for pleasure" when Frederic wants to pay the silhouette-cutter, saying: "'Please.' I brought out some coppers. 'For pleasure'" (135). Here Frederic uses two forms of the Italian word for "please." His first "please" is the equivalent of the standard *"per favore,"* while the second is a literal translation of *"per piacere."*

Although "for pleasure" appears in *A Farewell to Arms*, the novel never features the literal translation "for a favor" to represent the Italian "*per favore*," as in "Out of Season."[8] Frederic does not explicate the difference between the two "pleases" in *A Farewell to Arms* as "thank yous" are explained in "Che Ti Dice La Patria?" Colonel Cantwell, however, later expounds on the nuances of "*per piacere*" in *Across the River and into the Trees*, magnanimously explaining to Renata—who is Italian, it must be noted—the proper way to say "please" in Italian: "*Per piacere*. It means for pleasure. I wish we always talked Italian" (195).

Robert W. Lewis points to another moment in *A Farewell to Arms* where Hemingway's technique of literal translation serves the narrative. Gino, who heads the ambulance unit during Frederic's absence, updates Frederic on the war effort, and reports that there are food shortages because "[t]he dogfish are selling it somewhere else" (184). In English, "dogfish" refers to small sharks, as does its Italian counterpart, "*pescecani*." However, according to the *Bantam New College Italian-English Dictionary*, "*pescecani*" is also Italian slang for war profiteers, the meaning Gino intends. According to Lewis, "Even if readers do not know the Italian reference, 'dogfish' still serves to suggest not only Frederic's fluency but his awareness of the metaphoric basis of language and of the difference between what seems to be and what actually is" (147). Readers will at least recognize 'dogfish' as a putdown for a scoundrel, and not as an actual reference to the animal.[9]

Indeed, to extend Lewis's observation, whenever readers encounter a word or phrase that seems somewhat inappropriate, they can feel confident that this break in fluency is Hemingway's method of representing the Italian language that Frederic encounters on a daily basis. For instance, when Frederic is about to be sent to Milan at the end of Book One, Rinaldi says "Many things" twice (77). This is a literal translation of "*tante cose*," an Italian expression roughly equivalent to "All the best" in English. "*Tante*" means "many" and "*cose*" means "things." Had Hemingway written "all the best," comprehension would have been seamless, but the essence of Rinaldi's Italian speech would have been lost in translation. By literally translating words and phrases, Hemingway places the reader at the crossroads of fluency and foreignness, where Frederic Henry himself is situated.

On other occasions in *A Farewell to Arms*, Hemingway lapses in his careful approach to negotiating the two languages. Before the retreat at Caporetto, Frederic and his fellow soldiers speak in a kind of easy slang that is altogether inconsistent with the dialogue in the rest of the novel. Frederic uses "monkey suit" to refer to a mechanic's outfit; Bonello declares that he wants to use the same bed in which the major "corks off;" Piani refers to the major as "fish-face;" and one of the soldiers uses the putdown "slackers" (190, 192). Although the gist of these phrases can certainly be conveyed by Italian soldiers, the rhythm and diction of Italian speech have been replaced by dialogue that seems distinctly American. Frederic instructs his soldiers with another phrase—"It's time to roll" (192)—that seems even more American now than it did during World War I. By using this untranslatable Americanism, Hemingway departs from his technique of rendering Italian dialogue in English. It would be impossible for Frederic to use this wording and still be understood by his fellow soldiers.[10] Fernanda Pivano's translation of *A Farewell to Arms*—the accepted standard for five decades[11]—uses "*È ora di andare*" (201), or, "It's time to go." Pivano's Frederic Henry speaks differently from Hemingway's Frederic Henry, and in this case the translator had no choice. Hemingway has failed to maintain the slightly formal pitch of Frederic's Italian speech. After the soldiers breakfast in a farmhouse during the retreat, Frederic almost repeats himself, saying this time, "We'll roll" (202). Once more, Pivano's attempt cannot help but be inadequate: "Andiamo" (211), simply, "Let's go." For the second time, the accepted Italian translation renders the particularly American military expression "to roll" as the more mundane "to go."

This ambiguity can be underscored with a quotation from Frederic's fellow driver Bonello, who says "Let's go" (214), which Pivano translates properly as "*Andiamo*" (224). Using "*Andiamo*" for both "Let's go" and "We'll roll," Pivano cannot convey the colloquial or maintain the different shades of formality characterizing Frederic's speech. Therefore, while Hemingway intends Frederic's exhortation to be expressed in the type of military slang common to ambulance drivers and soldiers everywhere, the writer's linguistic decision only leads to confusion, as if Frederic speaks this phrase in English by instinct, or mutters it to himself, rather than giving orders to his troops in Italian. The resulting vagueness could even lead a reader to conclude that Frederic had already taught his fellow soldiers this Americanism—if not, he would never speak in this manner.

Hemingway makes a similar misstep when the bartender in Milan offers Frederic a grappa "on me" (237), slang with no natural correlative in Italian. As with "we'll roll," the use of an American colloquialism like "on me" gives the reader pause, and he or she may double-check to make sure that the Milanese bartender is speaking Italian, and not conversing in English for Frederic's benefit. An Italian would only say that a grappa was "on him" if he was balancing the bottle on his head, or had spilled some on his lap. Predictably, Pivano's translation renders "on me" into Italian without the casual power of the original; in her edition, the bartender says, "*offro io*" (247), which conveys his offer to pay for the drink, but without the colloquial tone Hemingway intends. Had Hemingway adhered to his established technique, the bartender's speech would read, "I offer," replicating the Italian in a manner more consistent with the literal translation found in the rest of the novel.

Towards the end of the novel, when Frederic must escape Italy, he meets Ralph Simmons again. Here, the two English-speakers who have been most maligned for their imperfect Italian can at last speak their native language without fear of reprisal. Their conversation is notable for its relaxed language, even during the most urgent of situations. Frederic visits Simmons at the Porta Magenta in Milan, and appeals for help in the most American of ways: "I'm in a jam, Sim." Simmons empathizes with Frederic: "So am I . . . I'm always in a jam" (241). Idiomatic phrases like "in a jam" clearly demarcate English speech. For this reason, expressions like "on me" and "let's roll"—used when Frederic is presumably speaking Italian—confound the execution of Hemingway's technique.

The most vivid way to understand how the Italian language is represented in the dialogue of *A Farewell to Arms* is to examine it in opposition to the way English is conveyed. When conversations take place in English, they differ noticeably from the dialogues between Frederic and any Italian speaker. In an early scene, Frederic picks up a straggling, struggling soldier, referred to as the "hernia man." Their conversation initially occurs in the Italian we have come to expect from the military scenes, but the soldier, who has spent time in Pittsburgh, recognizes from Frederic's accent that he is not an Italian. The soldier asks him, "You speak English?" and their conversation descends into rough, colloquial English. Frederic protests, "Don't I talk Italian good enough?" The soldier responds, "I knew you was an American all right." He later asks, "Jesus Christ, ain't this a goddam war?" (35). The coarseness of their English is the polar opposite of the correctness of the Italian with which they began their conversation. Not only does the language change, but the tone of the conversation moves from detachment to familiarity. The hernia man first calls Frederic "Tenente" (34) and then "lootenant" (35).

After Frederic is wounded, a British driver assists him, and his brief monologue serves as the Rosetta Stone of Hemingway's technique of presenting the Italian language in *A Farewell to Arms:*

> "We'll be most careful of them," he straightened up. "This chap of yours was very anxious for me to see you." He patted Gordini on the shoulder. Gordini winced and smiled. The Englishman broke into voluble and perfect Italian. "Now everything is arranged. I've seen your Tenente. We will take over the two cars. You won't worry now." He broke off, "I must do something about getting you out of here. I'll see the medical wallahs. We'll take you back with us." (58)

The British driver weaves between English and Italian, both of which are clearly marked in the narrative. Addressing Frederic in English, he uses the British-flavored phrase "most careful"[12] and the word "chap," made famous by Hemingway's most notorious Brit, Brett Ashley from *The Sun Also Rises.* The Englishman then breaks into Italian for four sentences as he speaks to Gordini, and then switches back to English again as he promises to get Frederic "out of here." In Italian, the driver uses the formulation "we will"; in English he twice uses the less formal contraction "we'll." His second speech in English is also distinguished by British slang, this time the Anglo-Indian word "wallah." The writing decisions are small in scope, but Hemingway manipulates such minute details to emphasize the dynamic between languages, just as he will do later in *For Whom the Bell Tolls.*

The dialectic between English and Italian continues in the same scene, as the Englishman carries the wounded Frederic to the ambulance.

"Here is the American Tenente," he said in Italian.

And then later:

"Come, come," he said, "Don't be a bloody hero." Then in Italian: "Lift him very carefully about the legs. His legs are very painful." (58)

The passage indicates which language the driver is speaking, even though word choice makes it self-evident. When the Englishman uses basic, correct speech, he is speaking Italian to Italians. The adjective "bloody," on the other hand, is spoken in English to Frederic. He speaks "perfect" Italian, but his perfection, ironically, conveys foreignness and not fluency. It is through the casual imperfection, as with the soldier with the hernia, that fluency in vernacular speech is represented. As he loads Frederic into the ambulance, the English driver tells him, "I hope you'll be comfy" (61). Here the narrative does not explicitly indicate which language the driver is speaking, but we can be absolutely certain that he is speaking colloquial English—"comfy"—to Frederic.

The Italian officer Ettore Moretti acts as an important contrast to characters who can never completely bridge the linguistic gap. Like Frederic, Ettore was raised in America—"a wop from Frisco" (120)—but unlike Frederic, he speaks flawless Italian, without the accent that gets Ralph Simmons heckled and nearly gets Frederic Henry killed. It is Ettore who relentlessly mocks—or, true to his name, "hectors"[13]—the non-Italian Simmons[14] for his efforts to pass as an Italian opera singer, and it is Ettore who taunts Frederic: "You can't be a captain, because you don't know the Italian language well enough . . . You can talk but you can't read and write well enough" (122). Ettore himself acknowledges that his bilingualism and not his brilliance has put him on the fast track for promotion, while the others are destined by their lack of facility in Italian to be subject to ridicule (in Simmons's case) and danger (in Frederic's case). As Robert W. Lewis observes, "Ettore's power derives directly from his fluency in both languages" (131). Ettore has the same power over Frederic that Frederic has over Catherine. Ettore flaunts his bilingualism, even audaciously venturing a 1920s American catchphrase: "Don't take any bad nickels" (124).

Sheldon Norman Grebstein notes that Hemingway's "most extensive experiment in dialogue . . . is the transliteration of Spanish into English in *For Whom the Bell Tolls*," which Grebstein claims, "is Hemingway's own innovation" and succeeds because the effects "echo the sound of a foreign language" (125). Joseph Warren Beach, also discussing *For Whom the Bell Tolls*, writes that "Nearly all the dialogue is supposed to be talk in Spanish rendered in English . . . to suggest throughout the flavor of the native idiom." To Beach, the effect is "charming, picturesque, and dramatic" (84). The Spanish novelist Arturo Barea offers an opposing view, charging that in attempting to render the speech of Castilian peasants, Hemingway "invents an artificial and pompous English which contains many un-English words and constructions, most of which cannot be admitted as translations of the original Spanish" (209). Gilbert Highet mocks the style of *For Whom the Bell Tolls* in a satirical send-up: "It is a kind of Spanish. It is a bloody kind of unspeakable Spanish . . . We got to turn the whole unspeakable Spanish colloquial speech into a far more unspeakable American language. We got to write pidgin Spanish and pidgin American so the customers will understand every minute it is Spanish" (19).

Other critics have commented on Hemingway's use of the archaic pronouns "thee" and "thou" and "thy" in *For Whom the Bell Tolls*. Carlos Baker describes this as "intentionally heightened language" (248), intended to reproduce the tone of an Elizabethan epic. For Azevedo, the pronouns suggest "an old-fashioned poetic usage or the archaic diction of the King James Bible" (33). Such discussion relates to Hemingway's use of Italian in *A Farewell to Arms*, where this bold technique appears in an inconspicuous, nascent stage. While *For Whom the Bell Tolls* uses "thee" and "thou" and "thy" frequently, in *A Farewell to Arms* "thou" and "thy" are never used, but "thee" appears twice.

In the first instance of "thee," Frederic has just finished a courteous conversation with a silhouette-cutter, who has given Frederic a portrait. The old man refuses the money Frederic offers, and then says, "Until I see thee" (135). Here, the intent is to show the respect of the silhouette-cutter towards Frederic through formal address, which in Italian is the Lei form, the so-called "second person formal"; it is not a random elevation into Biblical gravitas or Elizabethan tragedy. When Frederic says goodbye to Catherine before returning to the front, he refuses the help of a porter, saying, "Thanks. I don't need thee" (157). Although a native Italian would not customarily use formal address to a porter, here "thee" signals that Frederic is addressing the porter with careful politeness.

The two instances of "thee" in *A Farewell to Arms* signify the layers of etiquette built into the Italian language, as outlined so painstakingly by the narrator of "Che Ti Dice La Patria?" In fact, readers are alerted to this concern early in the novel with a subtle gesture. When Frederic calls on Catherine Barkley and the head nurse tells him she is not there, she concludes their brief chat with "*A rivederci,*" the typical way to say "so long." Frederic, on the other hand, says goodbye with a formal flourish, "*A rivederla*" (23), the "*la*" denoting formal address.

No discussion of the Italian in *A Farewell to Arms* should ignore the many, usually minor technical errors Hemingway makes with the language, especially in spelling and capitalization. *A Farewell to Arms* does not stand alone as a Hemingway text with errors. James Hinkle has written on Hemingway's imperfect use of foreign languages in *The Sun Also Rises;* Edward Fenimore discussed Hemingway's Spanish in *For Whom the Bell Tolls,* and Allen Josephs later savaged the use of language in that novel, labeling Hemingway's carelessness with the language as "a kind of chauvinism" (217). In *A Farewell to Arms,* Hemingway's own mistakes mirror Ettore's observation to Frederic; perhaps he can speak Italian, but he does not read or write it well enough. As may be expected when someone learns the language through conversation as opposed to formal study in a classroom, Hemingway's Italian is often phonetically recognizable, but orthographically incorrect. Therefore, while Hemingway may have believed that he properly represented his protagonist's knowledge of Italian, he overestimated his ability to render the language correctly in print.

Hemingway makes himself understood, but is less than fluent, and makes many mistakes that Frederic Henry would not make. Hemingway's technique is not harmed by the gaffes, nor is the novel, yet these mistakes are obviously unintentional, and should be corrected as if they were unintentional misspellings or punctuation errors in English. Hemingway's spelling even in English was erratic; it is inexcusable that no one at Scribner's corrected these simple errors. The appendix at the end of this article suggests a list of errors in Italian to be corrected in future editions. Because elsewhere in *A Farewell to Arms* Hemingway was obsessively accurate in matters of military history, geography, and even meteorology, and was, for the most part, judicious in rendering Italian speech in English, it is a shame to leave these mistakes, as if even his guesses at spelling foreign words were in some way sacrosanct and must never be altered.

The intent in closing with a list of errors in Italian is not to "throw the benches" at Hemingway. The criticism (directed more to Scribner's than to Hemingway himself) is a necessary thread in the overall investigation of

Hemingway's approach to the bilingualism in his Italian fiction. *A Farewell to Arms* marks the extension of Hemingway's previous experimentation with representing Italian speech, the subtle technique of literal translation seen in the short stories "Out of Season" and "Che Ti Dice La Patria?" as well as in its improbable debut, the 1918 letter home from Milan. His use of Italian in *A Farewell to Arms* also foreshadows his later, grander efforts with Spanish in *For Whom the Bell Tolls*. For some, parsing out minuscule linguistic nuances may seem a trivial approach to a novel concerned with life and death, God, catastrophe, and doomed love. But this is precisely the point. Hemingway saw fit to focus intently on the smallest particles of language, even while chronicling the grand sweep of love and death, and to understand his method reveals much to us about both the writer and his great novel.

Notes

1. These two letters are reprinted in full in Marcelline Hemingway Sanford's *At the Hemingways: With Fifty Years of Correspondence Between Marcelline and Ernest Hemingway* (282–283; 287–289). However, because there are editorial changes in the published letters, I have used my own transcriptions from the manuscripts.

2. Robert E. Gajdusek makes a similar point about Hemingway's use of "that makes nothing" to conjure up the German language in the short story "An Alpine Idyll": "the awkward 'that makes nothing' readily suggests the probable '*Mach's nichts*' or '*Das macht nichts*' of the actual exchange" (120).

3. See *The Sun Also Rises*, in which Brett wants to listen to Jake's confession in a Pamplona church, but Jake tells her that "it would be in a language she did not know" (154).

4. In *For Whom the Bell Tolls*, El Sordo's speech is similarly appraised: "Does he talk that way to every one? Robert Jordan thought. Or is that his idea of how to make foreigners understand?" (146); and, "So he does only speak that pidgin Spanish for foreigners, Robert Jordan thought" (147). Likewise, in "A Clean Well-Lighted Place," the narrator refers to "that omission of syntax stupid people employ when talking to drunken people or foreigners" (*CSS* 290).

5. In Hemingway's short story, "In Another Country," the protagonist is exhorted to "Speak grammatically!" and responds with the future tense, "I will go to the States" (*CSS* 209). In that same story the protagonist claims that Italian is an easy language, and the major asks him, "Why, then, do you not take up the use of grammar?" (208).

6. In the manuscript, Hemingway's original rendering of "*buon viaggio*" is not "Pleasant journey" but another intentionally awkward two-word phrase: "Good traveling" (JFK 64).

7. See also Hemingway's short story, "A Natural History of the Dead," in which an Italian doctor says, "Thank you very much . . . Thank you a thousand times" (*CSS* 340).

8. *For Whom the Bell Tolls* features the literal translation of the Spanish "por favor," spoken by the dying Fernando ("Leave me now please, for a favor" [441]), and by the dying Robert Jordan to Maria ("Therefore go for a favor" [463]).

9. The notion of the *pescecani* takes on thematic importance in *Across the River and into the Trees*. Colonel Cantwell and the headwaiter at the Gritti, the *Gran Maestro*, create the Order of the Brusadelli in their shared "true, good hatred of all those who profited by war" (61), or "the Milan profiteers" (46). Cantwell extends the label of *pescecani* to novelists who "write to profit quickly from the war they never fought in" (129). In Hemingway's 1948 introduction to the illustrated version of *A Farewell to Arms*, he writes, "I believe that all the people who stand to profit by a war and who help provoke it should be shot on the first day it starts by accredited representatives of the loyal citizens of their country who will fight it (x). See also Shakespeare's *1 Henry VI*, where Lord Talbot says, "Pucelle or puzzel, dolphin or dogfish" (I.iv.112).

10. In *Across the River and into the Trees*, Colonel Cantwell also orders his chauffeur Jackson with the phrase "Let's roll" (36). However, he is speaking English.

11. In 1945, Jandi Sapi published the first translation of *A Farewell to Arms* into Italian under the title *Un addio alle armi*, translated by Bruno Fonzi. In 1946, Mondadori published an illustrated edition, *Addio alle armi*, with a new translation by Giansiro Ferrata, Puccio Russo, and Dante Isella. For the purposes of this paper, discussion will be limited to Fernanda Pivano's popular 1949 translation.

12. Hemingway underlined "most" in the manuscript, suggesting the way he heard the typically British emphasis on this word (JFK 64).

13. In *Across the River and into the Trees*, a Venetian waiter also named Ettore has a "love of joking and fundamental and abiding disrespect" (85) and "loves to joke" (93).

14. Ettore makes reference to Simmons returning to America to brag of his singing success, and the vice-consul jokes that the American army will need to protect him when he sings in the Scala, but from his speech Simmons seems British. He asks Frederic, "How do you happen to be away from the bloody front?" (241), and then calls Frederic "my dear Henry" (241), and "my dear fellow" six times (242).

Works Cited

Azevedo, Milton M. "Shadows of a Literary Dialect: *For Whom the Bell Tolls* in Five Romance Languages." *The Hemingway Review*. 20.1 (Fall 2000): 30–48.

Baker, Carlos. *Hemingway: The Writer as Artist*. 1972. Princeton: Princeton University Press, 1990.

Barea, Arturo. "Not Spain But Hemingway." In *Hemingway and His Critics*. Ed. Carlos Baker. New York: Hill and Wang, 1961.

Beach, Joseph Warren. "Style in *For Whom the Bell Tolls*." *Ernest Hemingway: Critiques of Four Major Novels*. Ed. Carlos Baker. New York: Scribner's, 1962.

Fenimore, Edward. "English and Spanish in *For Whom the Bell Tolls*." *ELH* 10.1 (March 1943): 73–86.

Gajdusek, Robert E. *Hemingway in His Own Country*. Notre Dame, IN: University of Notre Dame Press, 2002.

Grebstein, Sheldon Norman. *Hemingway's Craft*. Carbondale, IL: Southern Illinois University Press, 1973.

Griffin, Peter. *Along With Youth*. New York: Oxford University Press, 1985.

Hemingway, Ernest. *Across the River and into the Trees*. 1950. New York: Scribner's, 1996.

———. *Un addio alle armi*. Trans. Bruno Fonzi. Milan: Jandi Sapi, 1945.

———. *Addio alle armi.* Trans. Giansiro Ferrata, Puccio Russo, Dante Isella. Milan: Mondadori, 1946.

———. *Addio alle armi.* Trans. Fernanda Pivano. 1949. Milan: Mondadori, 2002.

———. *The Complete Short Stories of Ernest Hemingway.* New York: Scribner's, 2003.

———. *Ernest Hemingway: Selected Letters, 1917–1961.* Ed. Carlos Baker. New York: Scribner's, 1981.

———. Letters to Marcelline Hemingway. 8 August 1918 and 21 September 1918. Hemingway Collection. John F. Kennedy Library, Boston, MA.

———. "Introduction." *A Farewell to Arms.* 1929. New York: Scribner's, 1948.

———. *A Farewell to Arms.* 1929. New York: Scribner, 1995.

———. *For Whom the Bell Tolls.* 1940. New York: Scribner, 1995.

———. Manuscript of *A Farewell to Arms.* Folder #64. Hemingway Collection. John F. Kennedy Library, Boston, MA.

———. *The Sun Also Rises.* 1926. New York: Scribner, 2003.

Hemingway, Marcelline. *At the Hemingways: With Fifty Years of Correspondence Between Ernest and Marcelline Hemingway.* Ed. John Sanford. Moscow, ID: University of Idaho Press, 1999.

Highet, Gilbert. "Thou Tellest Me, Comrade." Studies in *For Whom the Bell Tolls.* Ed. Sheldon Norman Grebstein. Columbus, OH: Charles E. Merrill, 1971.

Hinkle, James. "'Dear Mr. Scribner'—About the Published Text of *The Sun Also Rises.*" *The Hemingway Review* 6.1 (Fall 1986): 43–64.

Josephs, Allen. "Hemingway's Poor Spanish: Chauvinism and Loss of Credibility in *For Whom the Bell Tolls.*" In *Hemingway: A Revaluation.* Ed. Donald R. Noble. Troy, NY: Whitston, 1983 : 205–223.

Lewis, Robert W. *A Farewell to Arms: The War of Words.* New York: Twayne, 1992.

Moses, Carole. "Language as Theme in *For Whom the Bell Tolls.*" *Fitzgerald/Hemingway Annual,* 1978: 215–223.

Oldsey, Bernard. *Hemingway's Hidden Craft: The Writing of A Farewell to Arms.* University Park, PA: Pennsylvania St. University Press, 1979.

Reynolds, Michael. *Hemingway's First War: The Making of A Farewell to Arms.* Princeton, NJ: Princeton University Press, 1976.

Smith, Paul. *A Reader's Guide to the Short Stories of Ernest Hemingway.* Boston: GK Hall, 1989.

APPENDIX OF ERRORS IN ITALIAN AND PROPOSED CORRECTIONS

Page Number	Hemingway's Spelling	Proposed Change
9	soto-tenente (2x)	sottotenente
9	tenentecolonnello	tenente colonnello
9	soto-colonello	sottocolonnello
11 et passim	ciaou (9x)	ciao
33	smistimento	smistamento
36	Emmanuele	Emanuele
38 et passim	capri bianca (8x)	Capri bianco
40	Fillipo (2x)	Filippo
55	mama mia (8x)	mamma mia

55	Dio te salve (2x)	Dio ti salvi
55	porta feriti (2x)	portaferiti
73	Gran Sasso D'Italia	Gran Sasso d'Italia
77	riparto	reparto
87	chianti (4x)	Chianti
112	galleria (7x)	Galleria
112	fresa (2x)	Freisa
112	barbera (4x)	Barbera
120	Edouardo	Edoardo
135	Corriere Della Sera	Corriere della Sera
219	A basso gli ufficiali	Abbasso gli ufficiali

TREVOR DODMAN

"Going All to Pieces":
A Farewell to Arms *as Trauma Narrative*

Bullet wounds do not cause severe bleeding unless they happen to injure some large trunk or smash one of the larger bones. Wounds caused by fragments of shells or bombs tear larger holes in the skin and lacerate the muscles and are, therefore, more often the cause of serious bleeding.
—*Injuries and Diseases of War* (15)

In the final chapter of *A Farewell to Arms,* the narrator and main character, Frederic Henry, describes the protracted labor of his partner, Catherine Barkley. When the attending physician recommends a cesarian section, Frederic anxiously inquires about the dangers associated with the procedure. Assuring him that the risks should not exceed those associated with an "ordinary delivery," the doctor responds to Frederic's question regarding the potential aftereffects of the operation: "There are none. There is only the scar" (321). Although this reply suggests that what remains will be of no lingering concern, *A Farewell to Arms* nonetheless testifies to the persistence of wounds, both visible and invisible. Frederic's particular narration of the events and experiences that mark his wartime years must be understood in such terms, for his entire narrative—no "ordinary delivery"—inscribes a continued struggle with the debilitating aftereffects associated with shell shock. He suffers from the compulsion to remember and retell his traumatic past from

Twentieth Century Literature, Volume 52, Number 3 (Fall 2006): pp. 249–274. Copyright ©
2006 Hofstra University.

185

the standpoint of a survivor both unable and perhaps unwilling to put that very past into words; the novel stands as a record of his narrative collision with the violence of trauma.[1]

Frederic's troubled recollections find expression in apparently embodied and disembodied ways: as pain that registers at the level of the body, breaking apart the perceived unity of the physical self in the presence of terrific bodily suffering; and as trauma that registers at the level of consciousness, breaking down time, language, and the perceived unity of the subjective self in the face of incomprehensible violence. However, in staging an ongoing dialogue between inside and outside, *A Farewell to Arms* also challenges us to reconsider the mind/body dualism that keeps the wounds of the body separate from the wounds of the mind. For Frederic's narration—of his body, his memory, his wounds—destabilizes such distinctions in an effort to hold together a broken past that remains, in the present, a nexus of uncertainty and contestation. In accord with Tim Armstrong's emphasis on the interpenetration of machine and human in the modernist period, and with his identification of the "prosthetic thinking" (3) involved in the repair and augmentation of bodies in the face of radical disruption in warfare, Frederic's narration enacts a kind of prosthetic thinking: he repairs and augments his past as a countermeasure for the pain and trauma that plague him still.[2]

Looking back on events, reconstructing his memories, Frederic reveals a desire for a whole and perfect retelling of the past; his narration functions as a prosthesis meant to stave off a sense of the self as a disarticulated scar. His embodied subjectivity, like the wounds he suffers to represent, calls out for prosthetic completion. But as Elaine Scarry notes, "what is remembered in the body is well remembered" (112), and Frederic's narrative prosthesis cannot hold the wound closed. His traumatic memories bleed into and disrupt his present; his narration operates both as scar and wound, as tissue stitched together and lacerated apart. Though his prosthetic version of events insists on the potential for a "separate peace" (243), Frederic's telling of his past instead goes "all to pieces" (322) in the enduring presence of pain and trauma too "well remembered" to be left behind.

For years, analysts of the novel understood that Hemingway himself was doing the remembering—the author recalling his Great War experiences through his cipher, Frederic Henry.[3] While it seems to me simply impossible to imagine anyone's being wounded in war and not having it affect his or her writing of a novel about war memories and characters who are wounded, I am not principally interested in either the text or the trauma of Hemingway's life but rather in the text of his narrator's trauma. For Frederic's narrative, I contend, unfolds in keeping with the work of prominent trauma theorists such as Dominick LaCapra, who describes trauma as a "disruptive experience that disarticulates the self and creates holes in existence; it has belated effects that are controlled only with difficulty and perhaps never fully mastered" (41).[4] In Frederic's case, the disarticulation of the self occurs in a narrative that shifts unpredictably between past and present, between the time of the action and the time of the telling. To reconstruct the past he must confront the "holes" in his subjective experience of the war, despite the fact that he might not have full mastery over the memories.

Although accounts of the novel often emphasize the centrality of memory in analyzing Frederic's narration, critics have not fully pursued the implications of the fact that the narrative consciousness in charge of these memories is one that has been traumatized.[5] Diane Price Herndl touches on the novel's traumatic terrain, briefly discussing Frederic in the context of shell shock before going on to argue that his "illness" is "masculinity as it was presented to the World War I soldier" (39). While Herndl assesses the silencing of Frederic in terms of sociocultural technologies of the male self, I find in the novel's "enforced silences" the disruptive workings of traumatic memories aggressively imposing themselves on the survivor.[6] Indeed, Frederic's particular narrative "survival" demands extra attention in light of the key critical tendency to focus on the extent to which Frederic changes over the course of the novel. According to James Phelan, Frederic begins the novel as a "naive narrator but also as a character who does not understand the war or the larger destruction of the world" (56); in Michael Reynolds's view, Frederic is a "changed man" ("Doctors" 119) after his wounding. Phelan and Reynolds read in the novel a diminishing ironic gap between the time of the action and the time of the telling, and a corresponding closing of moral distance between Frederic the character and Frederic the narrator. In contrast, I suggest that *A Farewell to Arms* warrants consideration as a trauma narrative that enacts the collapsing of such distinctions.[7] From the very first page of the novel Frederic suffers from shell shock; his voice is always already the voice of a traumatized survivor of grievous wounds and losses. A "changed man" from the outset, his narrative reveals the continued and unchanging hold that his painful past has on his present. My argument, in short, rests on the belief that all of *A Farewell to Arms* must be considered in terms of traumatic aftereffects.

Horrified participant and helpless witness, Frederic, along with his traumatic exposure to dismemberment, killing, and death comes to us via the mediation of his own narration. As Joanna Bourke reminds us,

> there is no "experience" independent of the ordering mechanisms of grammar, plot, and genre, and this is never more the case than when attempting to "speak" the ultimate transgression—killing another human being. (358)

The heuristic imperatives built into "speaking" about trauma add social dimensions to subjective and interior processes. In Kirby Farrell's terms, trauma remains a "psychocultural" matter, an injury that "demands to be interpreted and, if possible, integrated into character" (7). Frederic's narrative task, then, is always double: he must tell the story of his shell-shocked past, integrate it into his "character," while at the same time confronting the shell shock in his present as it transgresses on his capacity to tell. The retrospective organization of his traumatic experiences reflects the simultaneity of his now and then, or as James Young puts matters, the

> survivor's memory includes both experiences of history and of memory, the ways memory has already become part of personal history, the ways misapprehension of events and the silences that come with incomprehension were parts of events as they unfolded then *and* part of memory as it unfolds now. (280)

Frederic's past intrudes on his present, and his interpretation of his injury takes shape in his prosthetic reconstitution of painful and traumatic events and experiences.[8] Bodies bleed in this novel, at times uncontrollably, and Frederic's narrative likewise suffers at times from troubling and uncontrollable outflow. Frederic's prosthetic interventions, his efforts at control, underscore collapsing distinctions between the artificial and the natural, between the mind and the body, and between the past and the present. Prosthetics challenges such distinctions by explicitly drawing our attention to relations of difference. For David Wills, prosthetic relations not only complicate the perceived relation of animate and inanimate but also, at the same time, insist on the measured distance between such domains. The prosthetic emerges in the "articulation of two heterogeneities" (30) but also in the very gap that opens up between a truncated limb and its mechanical extension. As Wills writes:

> no amputation is performed without the forethought of a workable prosthesis; the knife doesn't strike indiscriminately but is guided by the range of prostheses that wait, parasitic, for a suitable host. In this respect the prosthetic possibility determines the shape of the human, the artificial determines the form of the natural. (29)

In the context of *A Farewell to Arms*, Frederic jokes with his doctors about his desire to have his knee cut off, so that he can "wear a hook on it" (97). While Frederic's sarcasm here comments on the incompetence of these particular doctors, his narration itself takes shape as a "workable prosthesis," a hook worn in the place of a lost limb, in spite of—rather than as a result of—the fact that his pain, his wounding, his losses, his trauma do "strike indiscriminately." That is, his narration must confront a traumatic rupturing of the self that cannot be prepared for ahead of time.

In the case of his own wounding, Frederic describes the experience of being hit with shell fragments in a prominent stream-of-consciousness passage:

> I tried to breathe but my breath would not come and I felt myself rush bodily out of myself and out and out and out and all the time bodily in the wind. I went out swiftly, all of myself, and I knew I was dead and that it had all been a mistake to think you just died. Then I floated, and instead of going on I felt myself slide back. I breathed and I was back. (54)

Here Frederic describes a feeling of breaching as he rushes out of himself, his as-yet unnamed, unarticulated wounds producing an exchange across the membrane of the self. His perceptions of his wounding experience emphasize the passivity and helplessness of his situation: he can't control his breathing, he convulses outward and then floats inward at the behest of unknown and unalterable forces; he mistakes the experience as a whole for the certainty of death only to make a gentle return to the uncertainties of life.[9]

Testifying to the profound destabilizations that accompany the passive witnessing of the body's disruption, Frederic registers here a paradoxical and confusing disarticulation of the self into selves: "I felt myself rush bodily out of myself. . . . I felt myself slide back." Bessel A. van der Kolk and Onno van der Hart describe the feeling of uncoupling that Frederic experiences here: "Many trauma survivors report that they automatically are removed from the scene; they look at it from a distance or disappear altogether, leaving other parts of their personality to suffer and store the overwhelming experience" (168). Floating outward, Frederic experiences his wounding at a remove: he rushes out of his wounded body and then glides back into its consolidating confines. Importantly, he also looks at it "from a distance" to the extent that his version of the wounding comes at a considerable temporal remove. His "watching" of the events takes shape in his narration of them, and his return therefore not only describes the recoupling of self and body in the time of the action but also functions as a simultaneous reexperiencing at the time of the telling. Frederic's narration not only describes a past dissociative event but becomes in itself, in its very telling, a terribly present dissociative event.[10] Experienced in the moment of the explosion as a terrifying shuttling back and forth across breached boundaries, his wounding offers, in its recounting, a record of an uncontrollable reexperiencing of the events—a collapsing of distance between past and present. Thus, in the same way that he at once feels both inside of and outside of his "self," he feels himself "slide back" to the moment of his wounding in the moment of his telling.

While the content of such a passage certainly marks his overt efforts to describe in detail the traumatic events suffered, the desperate tone hints at the frustration Frederic feels as he attempts to describe what he cannot forget but cannot manage to put into words. In fact, he quickly resorts to shocking understatement to try to relate events: "I knew that I was hit and leaned over and put my hand on my knee. My knee wasn't there. My hand went in and my knee was down on my shin" (55). The effect is jarring as the vague "out and out and out" crashes into the specific horror of "my knee was down on my shin." Frederic's disembodied sense of floating, his peaceful calm, his relief as he feels himself return to his body—"I was back"—all of these experiences explode apart with the sudden understanding that the perceived integrity of his body has been radically disrupted. The momentary return to wholeness he narrates is important, for it reveals prosthetic thinking that seeks to keep the body together; however, this unity lasts but a short interval before being shattered by the insistence of the body's "well-remembered" wounds.

Reconstructing the scene of his own reconstruction, Frederic again grapples with dissociative aftereffects. Though the medical sergeant who wraps up his damaged legs notes that "there was so much dirt blown into the wound that there had not been much hemorrhage" (57), Frederic's condition still demands immediate intervention in a battlefield dressing station. While the doctor probes for shell fragments in his legs and wraps up Frederic's fractured skull, Frederic lies helpless and in pain on the "hard and slippery" operating table, surrounded by "chemical smells and the sweet smell of blood" (59). Frederic recalls a conversation and operation occurring simultaneously:

> The medical captain, "What hit you?"
> Me, with eyes shut, "A trench mortar shell."
> The captain, doing things that hurt sharply and severing tissue—"Are you sure?"
> Me—trying to lie still and feeling my stomach flutter when the flesh was cut, "I think so."
> Captain doctor—(interested in something he was finding), "Fragments of enemy trench-mortar shell. Now I'll probe for some of this if you like but it's not necessary. I'll paint all of this and—Does that sting? Good, that's nothing to how it will feel later. The pain hasn't started yet." (59)

The simultaneity of probing and talking about it provides an analogue for the dissociative elements governing a recollection that operates as both a retelling and a reliving of a painful reality. Like the doctor who insists that probing the wound is "not necessary" but does so anyway, Frederic's restaging here suggests that his probing of the past simply cannot be avoided, no matter how sharply it hurts. Though he tries to "lie still," tries to establish a protective prosthetic distance between a "Me" who experiences and an "I" who remembers, these self-articulations bleed together in the face of the extremities involved. The pain that arises on the operating table with the probing of a wound brings to Frederic the pain experienced in the moment of his wounding: the "Me" on the table shoots "out and out and out" and back into the "I" of the explosion. Likewise, a dynamic of deferred immediacy marks Frederic's narration of the operation: the "I" looking back at the "Me" on the table brings a chronic condition into contact with its acute origins.

Despite a subsequent series of operations and other treatments, all designed to allow for his return to the front, Frederic's knee does not make a full recovery. Rinaldi runs his finger along the scar and painfully tests the range of motion: "It's a crime to send you back. They ought to get complete articulation" (166). Just as the exigencies of the war call for Frederic's return to duty with a still-damaged knee, so too does his narration compulsively return to the operations involved with a partially articulated sense of the past. Well aware that in many respects the "pain hasn't started yet," his recollection of various procedures consistently reveals the prosthetic thinking at work in their management. At one point, for instance, Frederic's wounded legs must be X-rayed, a process "arranged by holding up the shoulders, that the patient should see personally some of the larger foreign bodies through the machine" (94). Although Frederic himself earlier refers to these items as "old screws and bedsprings and things" (85), the doctor attending to his X-rays has a decidedly more serious opinion of the matter: "He declared that the foreign bodies were ugly, nasty, brutal. The Austrians were sons of bitches" (94).

Frederic confronts here, at a remove and via the "eyes" of a machine, his own disrupted, penetrated body—a body "invaded" by metal Austrians out on maneuver quite literally inside enemy territory. Thus, while he must confront the terrible bodily consequences of modern warfare, he also faces a decidedly modern paradox, as his own experience of bodily integrity—disrupted both by the metal fragments and the X-rays that locate them—depends on continued technological intervention. Frederic's survival depends on seeing the foreign bodies "through the machine," a move that places his felt experience of his wounding's painful reality in a subsidiary relation to that of a machine-produced vision of the causes of the wounds. Full of holes, Frederic's body can only be reconstituted through the mediation of a mechanical device. His experience with the X-rays reveals precisely how modernity, in Armstrong's terms, "brings both a fragmentation and augmentation of the body in relation to technology; it offers the body as lack, at the same time as it offers technological compensation" (3).

The gap that opens up between lack and compensation, between Frederic's disrupted body and his body-made-whole by machine intervention, emerges in the text as Frederic refers to himself in the third person as the "patient" (94). Echoing the earlier dissociation of "Me" and "I," Frederic employs a similar prosthesis as a way for him to imagine and represent not his own, imperfect, nonstandard body but rather the body of another, the body of a perfectly standard patient. His act of divesting himself of the patient that he was also carries with it a corresponding disregard for the patient that he remains. Recourse to such reconstructive surgery, however, while speaking to a desire for prosthetic wholeness, also underscores the notion that desired-for wholeness is as much a construct as any generalized concept of patient.

The disjunction between the wounded Frederic and the "patient," articulated as an uncanny interpenetration of body and machine, reminds us that the human body is, according to Lennard J. Davis, "always already a fragmented body" (62).[11] Frederic establishes here a prosthetic relation to the "patient" as a means of bypassing the awareness of his own body as a fragmented, penetrated disunity: that body seen through the X-ray machine is not "mine" but merely the body of the "patient." He disarticulates himself from his own fragmented body, an act that prefigures later divestments of the body, such as when Frederic insists that his reconstructed knee belongs not to himself but to the doctor who performed the operation: "It was his knee all right. The other knee was mine. Doctors did things to you and then it was not your body any more" (231). In the first instance, Frederic distances himself from his own fragmented status as a patient and reveals a desire for a continued understanding of the self as a whole. In the second, though he foregrounds his fragmentation—*that* knee is *his*—he simultaneously reveals a continued experience of the wounded body as a site of control and order, a place where parts must still be understood as possessions of a whole self that survives: *this* knee is *mine*.

And yet, just as the line between a patient and his prosthesis inevitably blurs, just as the border between past and present dissolves, so too do certainties over bodily possession—over the integrity of the self—come undone in the face of extreme experiences and in the memories of those experiences. If, as Scarry concludes, "the record of war survives in the bodies, both alive and buried, of those who were hurt there" (113), then Frederic's narrative testifies to this. It records the story of his body's hurting and his body's survival, but buried in this record too are the remains of other bodies hurt beyond repair: Aymo, a shot sergeant, a stillborn son, Catherine. His wounding and the wounding of others leave their trace on the narrative in the form of prosthetic measures meant to keep their particular losses at bay. At the same time though, like a local anaesthetic "which froze the tissue and avoided pain until the probe, the scalpel or the forceps got below the frozen portion" (94),

Frederic's prosthesis cannot mitigate the overwhelming losses. He may want to make things whole, but he cannot evade the trauma.

* * *

The principles of the treatment of haemorrhage are well established, and are the same for both civil and military practice, and these principles lay down an essential rule that *bleeding is to be arrested by pressure upon, or ligature of, the bleeding point itself,* and *not* by constriction of the limb above or by tying the artery on the proximal side of the injury.

—*Injuries and Diseases of War* (15)

After his initial operation, Frederic is sent to a field hospital farther behind the lines. On the journey, the man above him, suffering an unstoppable hemorrhage, bleeds onto the immobile Frederic. For a while, he notes, the "stream kept on," but eventually the drops of blood "fell very slowly, as they fall from an icicle after the sun has gone" (61). Soon he feels the man's blood pooling up around his own body: "Where it had run down under my shirt it was warm and sticky." *A Farewell to Arms* sketches a brief history of this man's bleeding to death, but it also stands as a record of that which sticks to Frederic's recounting of his own troubled past. If history, as Cathy Caruth contends, "is precisely the way we are implicated in each other's traumas" (*Unclaimed* 24), then Frederic remains implicated in the trauma of the man above him as he collects the blood that drains out of him and collects it again as he narrates the events in the present. The stream keeps on. At the same time, however, as LaCapra notes,

certain wounds, both personal and historical, cannot simply heal without leaving scars or residues in the present; there may even be a sense in which they have to remain as open wounds even if one strives to counteract their tendency to swallow all of existence and incapacitate one as an agent in the present. (144)

Frederic's prosthetic efforts to "counteract" the memories of passively collecting another man's blood, to arrest the hemorrhaging of his past into his present, stand also as a reckoning with the continued activity of trauma's open wounds. Just as Frederic suspects that wars "weren't won anymore," his narrative expresses anxieties about the uncontrollable persistence of traumatic memories: "Maybe they went on forever" (118).

According to van der Kolk and van der Hart, extreme encounters disrupt the ordinary processing and integrating of experience into narrative memory. Unable to assimilate such disturbing events, the survivor visits the traumatic memories again and again, tends to his or her open wounds, in an involuntary effort to attach meaning to the horrors. Many survivors, they write, "experience long periods of time in which they live, as it were, in two different worlds: the realm of the trauma and the realm of their current, ordinary life"—and it is very often "impossible to bridge these two worlds" (163). Like the prosthetic thinking that governs Frederic's dissociated relations to the "Me" and the "I" of his wounding, to the "patient" he was and continues to be, so too do the novel's many stream-of-consciousness passages operate as instances of efforts to articulate past wounds in a "current, ordinary life" of continued suffering. Early in the novel, Frederic's drunken discussion with the priest puts into circulation a number of elements that his narrative continually returns to: "I tried to tell about the night and the difference between the night and the day and how the night was better unless the day was very clean and cold and I could not tell it; as I cannot tell it now" (13). Although Frederic's narration here precedes the revelation that he suffered a serious wound, it nevertheless disrupts chronology and thereby foregrounds his enduring commitment to an experience that continually defies his efforts to narrate it. Despite his losses, he feels compelled to try again to tell the story, but finds that time has not helped him represent his experience. "I cannot tell it now": the admission speaks to his struggle to articulate a set of wartime experiences that remain resistant to the meaning-making structures of language.

The comment echoes later, when Catherine asks Frederic to explain the retreat from Caporetto. "I'll tell you about it if I ever get it straight in my head," he replies (250). But despite his repeated claims that he cannot tell his trauma, cannot put the story together for others or for himself, he does make revealing efforts to find a language for his experiences. Remembering his reunion with Catherine after his escape from the army, Frederic cycles back to his earlier remarks to the priest, blending past and present:

> We could feel alone when we were together, alone against the others. It has only happened to me like that once. I have been alone while I was with many girls and that is the way you can be most lonely. But we were never lonely and never afraid when we were together. I know the night is not the same as the day: that all things are different, that the things of the night cannot be explained in the day, because they do not then exist, and the night can be a dreadful time for lonely people once their loneliness has started. (249)

Infusing this passage is Frederic's continued awareness that Catherine's permanent absence gives lasting shape to any articulation of the loneliness of the night. On the train to Mestre, her absence shapes his description—

there's a "hard floor for a wife"—and he thinks to himself, "you loved some one else whom now you knew was not even to be pretended there" (232). He now knows that what happened to him "once" is not a singularity closed off in the past but rather a complex of ongoing physiological and psychological disturbances in his present.

Frederic's attempts to articulate the "things of the night" repeatedly involve his hospitalization and link his wound with the loss of Catherine. Considering his always already traumatized state of mind, the following scene—describing a fantasy, before he is wounded, of his first night alone with Catherine—is particularly telling for its complex deployment of prosthetic thinking:

> After supper I would go and see Catherine Barkley. I wish she were here now. I wished I were in Milan with her. I would like to eat at the Cova and then walk down Via Manzoni in the hot evening and cross over and turn off along the canal and go to the hotel with Catherine Barkley. Maybe she would. Maybe she would pretend that I was her boy that was killed and we would go in the front door and the porter would take off his cap and I would stop at the concierge's desk and ask for the key and she would stand by the elevator and then we would get in the elevator and it would go up very slowly clicking at all the floors and then our floor and the boy would open the door and stand there and she would step out and I would step out and we would walk down the hall and I would put the key in the door and open it and go in and then take down the telephone and ask them to send a bottle of capri bianca in a silver bucket full of ice and you would hear the ice against the pail coming down the corridor and the boy would knock and I would say leave it outside the door please. (37–38)

Several revealing moments emerge, not the least of which is the sudden intrusion of the present—"I wish she were here now"—on a recollection that documents his past desires, suggesting Frederic's existence in "two worlds," the ordinary and the traumatic. Departing briefly from the narrative lines along which ordinary memory runs, Frederic's traumatic memory registers itself here, out of time and ahead of itself. His story of this vision in the past simultaneously registers his hopeless desire for Catherine in the present.

Of greater interest, however, is how the rest of the novel gradually reveals the extent to which prosthetic thinking controls this entire passage. For this fantasy is nothing less than an idealized, prosthetically perfect vision of a series of experiences that, as it emerges later, are structured by Frederic's wound. The fantasy amalgamates and sterilizes—cleans out—three future episodes, performing a pastiche of wholeness, a radical effacing of Frederic's disrupted self. For in fact, Frederic and Catherine sleep together for the first time not in a Milan hotel after a romantic dinner but in a Milan hospital before breakfast is served. He does not arrive there with her after a pleasant walk along the canal but travels from the "freight yard" (81) to the hospital in an ambulance. There is no concierge desk, no boy to open the elevator door, and he rides the elevator not with Catherine but with two stretcher-bearers who ignominiously bend his legs to fit into the crowded space. He and Catherine do not walk along the hall together, and there is no key to put in the door; instead, Frederic feels the pain "going in and out of the bone" (83) as they carry him down a long hallway before putting him to bed.

A later episode is likewise prostheticized by the hotel fantasy:

> At the door of the hospital the porter came out to help with the crutches. I paid the driver, and then we rode upstairs in the elevator. Catherine got off at the lower floor where the nurses lived and I went on up and went down the hall on my crutches to my room. (113)

Again, he and Catherine do not walk to a hotel and have the porter bring them up a bottle of wine; instead, they return to the hospital where a porter helps with the crutches, a crucial sign of Frederic's disrupted body. Furthermore, they find themselves separated on entering the hospital—their liaison punctuated at every turn by the realities of hospital life, by her role as a nurse and by the limits of his status as an invalid. Where Frederic once wishes for a silver bucket of ice left outside the door, he finds himself now crutching along the corridors of the hospital after Catherine, a nurse's aide carrying the "basins" (113) of the other patients.

Of course, the couple at last do walk along the canal, share a hotel room in Milan, hear the clicking of the elevator as it goes up to their floor, enjoy a bottle of Capri together. However, the experience is anything but idyllic. In light of his imminent return to the front, they are both despondent. Though the purchase of a new pistol, ironically enough, brightens the mood, they arrive at the hotel only to find it worn and disreputable. "This was the best hotel we could get in," Frederic notes, and the blend of red plush furnishings and satin bedding in their many-mirrored room leave Catherine feeling "like a whore" (152). Though they do manage to enjoy themselves—"After we had eaten we felt fine, and then after, we felt very happy" (153)—they nonetheless spend the remainder of their little time together discussing the logistics of their expected child, and joking apprehensively about the possibility of Frederic being wounded again. Their time together is marked by shame, tension, and uncertainty—hardly the "whole night" that the prosthetic version seamlessly delivers.

Frederic's fantasy thus is governed by a powerful measure of prosthetic thinking meant to stave off the painful awareness not only of his wounding and subsequent hospital treatments but also of other losses. Crucially, like the field service postcard he sends home with everything crossed out except "I am well" (36), Frederic's prosthetic fantasy involves "crossing out" Catherine's loss. Wishing she were here now, wishing he was still "with the British" (37), he disregards not only the fact of Catherine's death at the end of the novel but also that she's been "gone" from its very beginning. Just as in his dream she insists "This doesn't make any difference between us. . . . I'm always here. I come whenever you want me" (198), Frederic disregards distance and death as he reconstitutes Catherine in his present. "Always here," she is essential to his efforts to reconstitute himself in the context of her ongoing absence; narrating his present into wholeness requires that Catherine's broken past emerge here intact and filled once again with potential: "That was how it ought to be" (38). Casting himself in the role of a fiancé blown to bits, Frederic fantasizes about his capacity to compensate for Catherine's loss: "Maybe she would. Maybe she would pretend that I was her boy that was killed" (37). The reiteration emphasizes, however, the capacity of traumatic experiences to break apart any provisional efforts at pretending away the lingering pain. The awkward wording also reflects the inevitability of trauma's return as Catherine once more confronts the loss of "her boy that was killed." That that return should implicate Frederic seems fitting, moreover, given his own continuing trauma. For in fact, though he figures himself here as the embodiment of Catherine's loss, such make-believe—even in the context of a fantasy—cannot prevent the loss of Catherine from continuing to embody him.

* * *

If bleeding has been difficult to stop, a note should always be made on the field medical card, and this should also be marked "Urgent," in large letters.

—*Injuries and Diseases of War* (17)

Just as his wounding breaches his perception of the boundaries of the embodied subject, so too does bearing witness to Catherine's death destabilize the boundaries between Frederic and his partner. "We're the same one" (299), he once tells her, and, like a scar, she stubbornly remains, her losses and wounds incorporated as his own: "The head was mine, and the inside of the belly" (231). Elizabeth Grosz argues that scars become "loci of exchange between the inside and the outside, points of conversion of the outside into the body, and of the inside out of the body" (36). But as points of conversion, as neither inside nor outside, scars and, worse yet, open wounds challenge the limits of both representation and empathetic response. In Frederic's case, Catherine's cesarean section and hemorrhaging death demand his witness, both then and now. Her loss becomes a destabilizing point of conversion between his past and present. Difficult to stop, too "well remembered" to be countered by prosthetic thinking, Catherine's loss, her echoing voice and broken body, takes shape as a trauma narrative relentlessly imposing itself on Frederic's ordinary narrative progression of events.

Paul Fussell described the shocking horrors of mechanized mass slaughter in related terms: "the Great War was perhaps the last to be conceived as taking place within a seamless, purposeful 'history' involving a coherent stream of time running from past through present to future" (21). More recently, Trudi Tate considers veterans and civilians alike struggling to convey a "history one has lived through but not seen, or seen only partially" (1). Thus, in the place of a coherent stream of time, trauma survivors experience what Caruth describes as a future and past united "through a profound discontinuity" (*Unclaimed* 14). In Frederic's narrative, this shattering of his subjective experience of time, this radical discontinuity between his traumatic history and traumatized present, is repeatedly figured by references to the breaking of individuals, epitomized by Catherine's cry "I'm going all to pieces" (322). In elaborating this—"I'm not brave anymore, darling. I'm all broken. They've broken me. I know it now" (323)—Catherine gives voice to a whole set of concerns about the disunity of the embodied subject, confirming what Frederic already knows about himself: that "the legs"—his own legs—resemble "freshly ground hamburger steak" (95).

If we return, then, to their first night at the hotel after he deserts, we find Frederic speaking Catherine's later words: "The world breaks every one and afterward many are strong at the broken places. But those it will not break it kills. It kills the very good and the very gentle and the very brave impartially" (249). Her words, that is, appear as a traumatic intrusion of the past on a retrospective narrative given in the present. Like an echo before the sound, like the "sudden interiors of houses" (6) that appear to Frederic after bouts of shelling, these words register in the text disconcertingly out of place and ahead of their time. Fulfilling what Caruth identifies as the traumatic potential for "the outside [to go] inside without any mediation" (*Unclaimed* 59), they become Frederic's words; he gives them voice—or rather they voice themselves through him, illustrating how "the experience of a trauma repeats itself, exactly and unremittingly, through the unknowing acts of the survivor and against his very will" (2).

Catherine's feeling that she is "going all to pieces" becomes literalized on the operating table, raising the question once more of the relation of a body in pain to a traumatized mind:

> I thought Catherine was dead. She looked dead. Her face was gray, the part of it that I could see. Down below, under the light, the doctor was sewing up the great long, forcep-spread, thick-edged, wound. Another doctor in a mask gave the anaesthetic. Two nurses in masks handed things. It looked like a drawing of the Inquisition. I knew as I watched I could have watched it all, but I was glad I hadn't. I do not think I could have watched them cut, but I watched the wound closed into a high welted ridge with quick skilful-looking stitches like a cobbler's, and was glad. When the wound was closed I went out into the hall and walked up and down again. (325)

Broken apart and sewn back together, Catherine takes center stage in the operating theater. However, as the wound gets closed she seems to get swallowed up by it, disappearing from the scene, becoming, in effect, all wound. Frederic no longer sees Catherine anesthetized on the table but only the wound: great, long, forcep-spread, thick-edged, high-welted, closed. Her reduction to an unspeaking wound would seem to contrast with Frederic's position, both as a witness in the gallery and as the narrator of the scene. At the same time, however, the moment replays Frederic's own wounding and battlefield operation. He thinks she's dead, just as he once "knew" he had died; he looks down from above on Catherine's body, just as he once floated out from his own; he avoids watching the "cutting," just as he does while on the slippery table himself. Catherine's disrupted, broken body thus confronts him with his own shattered frame; her unknowing, passive silence confronts him with the wordless holes in his own experience.

Overwhelmed, Frederic shifts suddenly to relate the parable of the ants. The detail and specificity of the memory—the ants scurrying back and forth on the burning log, his steaming rather than saving them (327)—contrast with the vagueness of its time and place. Does it happen before the war, or after? Before Catherine's death, or in the aftermath? Either way, witnessing Catherine's cesarean section and death, Frederic turns to a time and place where a sense of his own agency, however ambivalent, remains intact. The respite, however, is only momentary, and Frederic returns to the scene of the wounds that won't heal: "So now I sat out in the hall and waited to hear how Catherine was" (328). From Frederic's double perspective at the time of the telling Catherine is, of course, both dead and dying. "So now" he waits in the hall, unable to escape the thought of watching the doctor "sew up." Though his son's death registers with little emotion—"So he's dead" (327)—the loss of the boy and Catherine becomes entangled with his own wounds, sewn together into Frederic's present articulation of their absences.

So active, so *now*, these deaths remain alive for Frederic. They hemorrhage through the narrative—reminders that while many are strong at the broken places, vulnerabilities remain. If, as Caruth observes, trauma emerges as "a kind of double telling, the oscillation between ... the story of the unbearable nature of an event and the story of the unbearable nature of its survival" (*Unclaimed* 7), *A Farewell to Arms* constitutes just this kind of double telling. Driven by the tension between the "patient" and his prosthesis, between the "Me" who cries out on the operating table and the "I" who looks down and sees two broken bodies, Frederic's prosthetic narrative cannot mend his shattered past. In his unbearable present, any former understanding of the self seems hopelessly lost. As he himself notes about his Saint Anthony talisman, "After I was wounded I never found him" (44).

On his way to the battle that will see him wounded, Frederic considers the gift from Catherine: "The Saint Anthony was in a little white metal capsule. I opened the capsule and spilled him out into my hand" (43). He reassembles it, undoes his uniform, and puts the chain around his neck: "I felt him in his metal box against my chest while we drove. Then I forgot about him" (44). Spilled out and put back again, Saint Anthony goes to pieces but returns to wholeness in Frederic's hands, and in his retelling is again spilled out and put back, remembered though still missing. Like Frederic's narrative itself, Saint Anthony is both scar and open wound. And so *A Farewell to Arms*—an "aftereffect," a note marked "Urgent"—manifests a search for what is lost that cannot end.

Notes

1. I use the terms *trauma* and *shell shock* interchangeably, despite the fact that contemporary critics rightly insist on their historical situatedness along a convoluted path marked by stretches of collective forgetting and frenzied attention: from nineteenth-century theories about hysteria and railway spine to First World War conceptions of shell shock, Second World War experiences with combat fatigue, the post-traumatic stress disorder (PTSD) of returning Vietnam veterans and survivors of incest and abuse, and, finally, present-day conceptions of the disorder that increasingly incorporate both neurophysiological and psychological models in research and treatment. Current understandings of trauma have come a long way from Great War–era debates over brain lesions and explosions as the roots of shell shock, but many congruencies remain between our understanding now and then, including a shared emphasis on disruptions to the embodied subject's relation to language, memory, and time. Much as it was during the Great War years, trauma theory today remains a deeply and bitterly contested field marked by controversy and competing theory. Moreover, *shell shock* and *trauma* both point out one thing

that current research confirms and Frederic's narrative illustrates: any attempts to articulate shell shock, to put trauma into words, involves the unavoidable, unpredictable, and perhaps unknowable impress of the past on an embodied subject's present.

For detailed treatments of the histories I have alluded to here, see Allan Young and Ruth Leys. Judith Herman's important and thorough *Trauma and Recovery* provides a feminist accounting of the history of trauma as well as an analysis of modes of treatment in the face of trauma's staying power. Ben Shephard offers a full-length, detailed history focused largely on military psychiatry that criticizes the current direction of trauma studies. Hans Binneveld offers a more concise and less polemical overview.

2. Armstrong explores the human body not only as a "locus of anxiety, even crisis" (4) but also as a site for recovery and regeneration through mechanical and technological intervention. Kirby Farrell extends Armstrong's terms outward from the human body, noting that prosthetic linkages between humans and society develop rapidly in the modernist period. For Farrell, trauma "reflects a disruption of our prosthetic relationships to the world. By exposing the constructed and interdependent nature of our existence, it makes vivid how radically vulnerable and ephemeral we are" (176). *A Farewell to Arms* stages shell shock's radical disrupting of subjectivity throughout a narrative that precisely testifies to the vulnerabilities of a self cut off from the web of prosthetic relations offering security and helping to locate meaning.

3. Hemingway's relations to the Great War and his own wounding are concerns that he returns to again and again in his career. Numerous critical attempts have been made to establish connections between the wartime experiences of the author and his Great War novel, suggesting links between memories that both author and protagonist seem unable to move beyond. For recent detailed treatments of Hemingway's construction of the novel, see Rena Sanderson, Charles Oliver, and Linda Wagner-Martin. Other important treatments of the novel include Michael Reynolds's *Hemingway's First War* and Bernard Stanley Oldsey. Matthew Stewart considers these matters in the wider context of Hemingway's entire career.

4. The early to mid-1990s witnessed an explosion of interdisciplinary interest in trauma. Critics such as Judith Herman, Shoshana Felman and Dori Laub, Cathy Caruth, Kali Tal, and Bessel A. van der Kolk and Onno van der Hart contributed works that address the intersections of history, memory, medicine, psychoanalysis, and literature. Numerous anthologies also appeared, each marked by a particular approach or set of approaches: the psychoanalytically inflected *Trauma: Explorations in Memory* edited by Cathy Caruth, the juridical and scientific studies of *Trauma and Memory* edited by Paul Applebaum et al., the neurobiologically focused *Traumatic Stress* edited by van der Kolk et al., and the discursive identity politics of *Tense Past* edited by Paul Antze and Michael Lambek. Several recent anthologies productively merge trauma studies with other important domains such as comparative genocide studies, geopolitics, and the ethics of witnessing. See in particular *Extremities,* edited by Nancy K. Miller and Jason Tougaw; *Topologies of Trauma,* edited by Linda Belau and Peter Ramadanovic; *Trauma at Home,* edited by Judith Greenberg; and *Witness and Memory,* edited by Ana Douglass and Thomas A. Vogler.

While the works of Caruth and van der Kolk help in particular to focus my argument about *A Farewell to Arms*, it is important to acknowledge that their versions of traumatic operations have detractors. LaCapra, for instance, suggests that in the "affectively charged" (109) writing of Caruth, "trauma may itself be sacralized as a catastrophic revelation or, in more secular terms, be transvalued as the radical other or the sublime" (108). Such transvaluing can foreclose possibilities for working through by reifying trauma as fully and radically unknowable. And van der Kolk, in LaCapra's view, privileges neuroscience over the nuances of psychoanalysis: he relies on "an overly functional specific model of the brain" (109) and conveniently splits off "repression from dissociation and resists any notion of their connection" (108). Chapter-length critiques of Caruth and van der Kolk also appear in Leys, who charges both theorists with manipulative readings and research and disputes their claims about the literal truths of inscribed traumatic memories. However, the recent book by Jenny Edkins offers a direct challenge to Leys's critique of Caruth, charging Leys herself with manipulative misreading:

> It is not the case that "truth" is said to exist in the memory images thought to be implanted by trauma any more than it is to be found in our original perceptions. We do not have access to these images (other than as images) without interpreting or making sense of them. We cannot pass them on unvarnished to others. (39)

As for van der Kolk, Leys's charges notwithstanding, there is much to be found in the work of other trauma theorists—Babette Rothschild, Bruce D. Perry, and Belleruth Naparstek, for example—to support the notion that traumatic experience invokes both mind and body. Perry writes:

> All areas of the brain and body are recruited and orchestrated for optimal survival tasks during the threat. This total neurobiological participation in the threat response is important in understanding how a traumatic experience can impact and alter functioning in such a *pervasive* fashion. Cognitive, emotional, social, behavioral and physiological residues of a trauma may impact an individual for years—even a lifetime. (14)

As it happens, my own critique of Caruth's work may be leveled here. After Freud, who suggests in *Beyond the Pleasure Principle* that wounds or injuries suffered in the context of a frightful surprise tend to work "*against* the development of a neurosis" (12), Caruth contends that "the wound of the mind—the breach in the mind's experience of time, self, and the world—is not, like the wound of the body, a simple and healable event" (*Unclaimed Experience* 4). Her privileging of mind over body, of psychic wounds over physical ones, however, leaves largely out of the picture the upshot of some of the most interesting conclusions about the impact of trauma on the embodied subject. In contrast, Frederic's narrative presciently considers the interpenetration of mind and body in the wake of traumatic experiences and problematizes the notion of wounds of any sort as "simple and healable event[s]."

5. Fine work by Mary Prescott and James Nagel, for instance, gestures toward trauma in the context of Frederic's narrative efforts. Prescott explores the processes by which Frederic reconstructs events "so that he can make sense of them" (43). Along similar lines, Nagel considers Frederic's retrospective efforts at "coming to terms emotionally with the events" (171). But neither essay follows through on the narrative aftereffects in Frederic's version of his past.

6. Margot Norris suggests that *A Farewell to Arms* is "less a novel *about* war than a novel *as* war" (693) and provides a particularly illuminating connection to what trauma theorists document as the aggressive operations of trauma. She convincingly argues that Hemingway's text delivers acts of "narrative aggression" (694) that refigure, in rhetorical terms, "the aggression of combat" (695). Norris reads inconsistencies and ruptures in the novel as coercive efforts to efface responsibility for the violence of war, and I read them as evidence of the suffering of profound traumas. To paraphrase Norris herself, *A Farewell to Arms* is less a novel *about* trauma than a novel *as* trauma.

The works of Lisa Tyler and Richard Badenhausen might also be considered here in the context of Frederic's trauma narrative. In Tyler's article Frederic masters his trauma by "making of it an ordered narrative" (91). While I do agree that Frederic's retelling of his losses should be considered in terms of efforts at resistance and as a measure of healing, to suggest that his narrative "triumphs over trauma" (91) is to overlook the extent to which his past relentlessly continues to intrude on his present in ways that I contend are beyond his control. Badenhausen analyzes Vera Brittain's *Testament of Youth* as a "working through" of the trauma of her wartime losses. Though the redemptive nature of this reading does not help me to account for what I perceive in *A Farewell to Arms* as the continued debilitating effects of trauma that work at denying the satisfactions of closure, Badenhausen's work nonetheless provides compelling analysis of the workings of trauma with respect to narrative.

7. Phelan insists that with "few exceptions, Frederic speaks from his perspective at the time of the action" (68). Reynolds suggests that "the only difference between Frederic in the nurse's garden and in the Milan hospital is his violent wounding. Like a victim of shell shock, he exhibits altered feelings, affection, temper, and habits" ("Doctors" 120). Like Phelan, Reynolds assumes that the novel operates in terms of a pre- and postwounding dynamic, but I suggest that there is no way to untangle Frederic's post-traumatic narration from his present version of the past.

8. Another key source for interpreting his injury remains the *Diagnostic and Statistical Manual of Mental Disorders*. In the manual's terms, PTSD may develop in those who have been exposed to extreme events or stressors

> involving direct personal experience of an event that involves actual or threatened death or serious injury, or other threat to one's physical integrity; or witnessing an event that involves death, injury, or a threat to the physical integrity of another person; or learning about unexpected or violent death, serious harm, or threat of death or injury experienced by a family member or other close associate. (463)

Frederic, an ambulance driver on the Austro-Italian front, remains consistently exposed, both directly and indirectly, to such events. Even a partial list will suggest the extremes involved. Blown up and wounded himself, he attends to Passini: "One leg was gone and the other was held by tendons and part of the trouser and the stump twitched and jerked as though it were not connected" (55). Participating in the massive Italian retreat from Caporetto, Frederic loses one of his men, beloved Aymo: "He was hit low in the back of the neck and the bullet had ranged upward and come out under the right eye. He died while I was stopping up the two holes" (213). Threatened with summary execution for his officer's rank, Frederic evades rifle fire by plunging into the river:

I thought then I would drown because of my boots, but I thrashed and fought through the water, and when I looked up the bank was coming toward me, and I kept thrashing and swimming in a heavy-footed panic until I reached it. (227)

And finally, Frederic loses his son—"cord was caught around his neck or something" (327)—only hours before he loses his partner: "It seems she had one hemorrhage after another. They couldn't stop it. I went into the room and stayed with Catherine until she died. She was unconscious all the time, and it did not take her very long to die" (331).

    9. Babette Rothschild's work in *The Body Remembers: Casebook* suggests that during a traumatic incident the brain's limbic system signals to the sympathetic nervous system (SNS) for preparation to fight or fly; if neither of these options seems appropriate, the parasympathetic nervous system (PNS) initiates the freeze response: "The SNS continues its extreme arousal while the PNS freezes the action of the body" (6). Although freezing "only occurs when the individual's perception is that the threat is extreme and escape impossible" (7), Rothschild speculates that the toll on the "frozen" subject—including intense feelings of shame and humiliation—may be greater afterward because of the lingering belief that more could have been done.

    10. Rothschild notes that PTSD's long-term aftereffects may damage or destroy a survivor's ability to differentiate between external stimuli and to make use of the body's signals to itself regarding threats:

> The ability to orient to safety and danger becomes decreased when many things, or sometimes everything, in the environment are perceived as dangerous. When daily reminders of trauma become extreme, freezing or dissociation can be activated as if the trauma were occurring in the present. It can become a vicious cycle. (*Psychophysiology* 14)

    11. Concerned mostly with the (in)visibility of the disabled body, Davis offers a stirring condemnation of the "reception of disability" that structures the art world's perceptions and attitudes about "the presence of difference" (56) and the "traditional ableist assumptions" (52) that permeate virtually all corridors of Western life. He suggests that any conception of the body as a whole is based on "a repression of the fragmentary nature of the body" (59) as it is experienced early in one's psychic and physiological development and reinforced by a culture deeply invested in this repression.

    I am extremely grateful for Laura Tanner's guidance and efforts at every stage in the writing of this essay. The insights offered by Rosemarie Bodenheimer and James Krasner along the way are also much appreciated. As ever, I extend my deepest thanks to Amy Winchester for her constant support and encouragement.

Works Cited

Antze, Paul, and Michael Lambek, eds. *Tense Past: Cultural Essays in Trauma and Memory.* New York: Routledge, 1996.

Appelbaum, Paul S., Lisa A. Uyehara, and Mark R. Elin, eds. *Trauma and Memory: Clinical and Legal Controversies*. New York: Oxford University Press, 1997.

Armstrong, Tim. *Modernism, Technology, and the Body: A Cultural Study*. Cambridge: Cambridge University Press, 1998.

Badenhausen, Richard. "Mourning through Memoir: Trauma, Testimony, and Community in Vera Brittain's *Testament of Youth*." *Twentieth-Century Literature* 49.4 (Winter 2003): 421–448.

Belau, Linda, and Petar Ramadanovic, eds. *Topologies of Trauma: Essays on the Limit of Knowledge and Memory*. New York: Other, 2002.

Binneveld, Hans. *From Shell Shock to Combat Stress: A Comparative History of Military Psychology*. Trans. John O'Kane. Amsterdam: Amsterdam University Press, 1997.

Bourke, Joanna. *An Intimate History of Killing: Face-to-Face Killing in Twentieth-Century Warfare*. New York: Basic, 1999.

Caruth, Cathy, ed. *Trauma: Explorations in Memory*. Baltimore: Johns Hopkins University Press, 1995.

———. *Unclaimed Experience: Trauma, Narrative, and History*. Baltimore: Johns Hopkins University Press, 1996.

Davis, Lennard J. "Nude Venuses, Medusa's Body, and Phantom Limbs: Disability and Visuality." *The Body and Physical Difference: Discourses of Disability*. Ed. David T. Mitchell and Sharon L. Snyder. Ann Arbor: University of Michigan Press, 1997. 51–70.

Diagnostic and Statistical Manual of Mental Disorders. 4th ed. Washington, D.C.: American Psychiatric Association, 2000.

Douglass, Ana, and Thomas A. Vogler, eds. *Witness and Memory: The Discourse of Trauma*. New York: Routledge, 2003.

Edkins, Jenny. *Trauma and the Memory of Politics*. Cambridge: Cambridge University Press, 2003.

Farrell, Kirby. *Post-Traumatic Culture: Injury and Interpretation in the Nineties*. Baltimore: Johns Hopkins University Press, 1998.

Felman, Shoshana, and Dori Laub. *Testimony: Crises of Witnessing in Literature, Psychoanalysis, and History*. New York: Routledge, 1992.

Freud, Sigmund. *Beyond the Pleasure Principle*. 1920. Trans. James Strachey. *The Standard Edition of the Complete Psychological Works of Sigmund Freud*. Vol. 18. London: Hogarth, 1955. 7–66.

Fussell, Paul. *The Great War and Modern Memory*. London: Oxford University Press, 1975.

Greenberg, Judith, ed. *Trauma at Home: After 9/11*. Lincoln: University of Nebraska Press, 2003.

Grosz, Elizabeth. *Volatile Bodies: Toward a Corporeal Feminism*. Bloomington: Indiana University Press, 1994.

Hemingway, Ernest. *A Farewell to Arms*. New York: Scribner's, 1995.

Herman, Judith Lewis. *Trauma and Recovery*. New York: Basic, 1992.

Herndl, Diane Price. "Invalid Masculinity: Silence, Hospitals, and Anaesthesia in *A Farewell to Arms*." *Hemingway Review* 21.1 (Fall 2001): 38–52.

Injuries and Diseases of War: A Manual Based on Experience of the Present Campaign in France. London: His Majesty's Stationery Office, 1918.

LaCapra, Dominick. *Writing History, Writing Trauma*. Baltimore: Johns Hopkins University Press, 2001.

Leys, Ruth. *Trauma: A Genealogy*. Chicago: University of Chicago Press, 2000.

Miller, Nancy K., and Jason Tougaw, eds. *Extremities: Trauma, Testimony, and Community.* Urbana: University of Chicago Press, 2002.

Nagel, James. "Catherine Barkley and Retrospective Narration in *A Farewell to Arms.*" *Ernest Hemingway: Six Decades of Criticism.* Ed. Linda W. Wagner. East Lansing: Michigan State University Press, 1987. 171–185.

Naparstek, Belleruth. *Invisible Heroes: Survivors of Trauma and How They Heal.* New York: Bantam, 2004.

Norris, Margot. "The Novel as War: Lies and Truth in Hemingway's *A Farewell to Arms.*" *Modern Fiction Studies* 40.4 (1994): 689–710.

Oldsey, Bernard Stanley. *Hemingway's Hidden Craft: The Writing of* A Farewell to Arms. University Park: Pennsylvania State University Press, 1979.

Oliver, Charles, ed. *Ernest Hemingway's* A Farewell to Arms: *A Documentary Volume.* Detroit: Thomson, 2005.

Perry, Bruce D. "The Memories of States: How the Brain Stores and Retrieves Traumatic Experience." *Splintered Reflections: Images of the Body in Trauma.* Ed. Jean Goodwin and Reina Attias. New York: Basic, 1999. 9–38.

Phelan, James. "Distance, Voice, and Temporal Perspective in Frederic Henry's Narration: Successes, Problems, and Paradox." *New Essays on* A Farewell to Arms. Ed. Scott Donaldson. Cambridge: Cambridge University Press, 1990. 53–73.

Prescott, Mary. "*A Farewell to Arms:* Memory and the Perpetual Now." *College Literature* 17.1 (1990): 41–52.

Reynolds, Michael. "*A Farewell to Arms:* Doctors in the House of Love." *The Cambridge Companion to Hemingway.* Ed. Scott Donaldson. Cambridge: Cambridge University Press, 1996. 109–127.

———. *Hemingway's First War: The Making of* A Farewell to Arms. 1976. New York: Blackwell, 1987.

Rothschild, Babette. *The Body Remembers: Casebook.* New York: Norton, 2003.

———. *The Body Remembers: The Psychophysiology of Trauma and Trauma Treatment.* New York: Norton, 2000.

Sanderson, Rena, ed. *Hemingway's Italy: New Perspectives.* Baton Rouge: Louisiana State University Press, 2006.

Scarry, Elaine. *The Body in Pain: The Making and Unmaking of the World.* New York: Oxford University Press, 1985.

Shephard, Ben. *A War of Nerves: Soldiers and Psychiatrists in the Twentieth Century.* Cambridge: Harvard University Press, 2000.

Stewart, Matthew C. "Ernest Hemingway and World War I: Combatting Recent Psychobiographical Reassessments, Restoring the War." *Papers on Language and Literature: A Journal for Scholars and Critics of Language and Literature* 36.2 (Spring 2000): 198–217.

Tal, Kali. *Worlds of Hurt: Reading the Literatures of Trauma.* Cambridge: Cambridge University Press, 1996.

Tate, Trudi. *Modernism, History, and the First World War.* Manchester: Manchester University Press, 1998.

Tyler, Lisa. "Passion and Grief in *A Farewell to Arms:* Ernest Hemingway's Retelling of *Wuthering Heights.*" *Hemingway Review* 14.2 (Spring 1995): 79–96.

van der Kolk, Bessel A., Alexander C. McFarlane, and Lars Weisaeth, eds. *Traumatic Stress: The Effects of Overwhelming Experience on Mind, Body, and Society.* New York: Guilford, 1996.

———— and Onno van der Hart. "The Intrusive Past: The Flexibility of Memory and the Engraving of Trauma." *Trauma: Explorations in Memory.* Ed. Cathy Caruth. Baltimore: Johns Hopkins University Press, 1995. 158–182.

Wagner-Martin, Linda. *Ernest Hemingway's A Farewell to Arms: A Reference Guide.* Westport: Greenwood, 2003.

Wills, David. *Prosthesis.* Stanford: Stanford University Press, 1995.

Young, Allan. *The Harmony of Illusions: Inventing Post-Traumatic Stress Disorder.* Princeton: Princeton University Press, 1995.

Young, James E. "Between History and Memory: The Voice of the Eyewitness." *Witness and Memory: The Discourse of Trauma.* Ed. Ana Douglass and Thomas A. Vogler. New York: Routledge, 2003. 275–283.

ZOE TRODD

Hemingway's Camera Eye:
The Problem of Language
and an Interwar Politics of Form

One finds it in the midst of all this as hard to apply one's words as to endure one's thoughts. The war has used up words; they have weakened, they have deteriorated like motor car tires; they have, like millions of other things, been more over-strained and knocked about and voided than in all the long ages before, and we are now confronted with a depreciation of all our terms, or, otherwise speaking, with a loss of expression through an increase of limpness, that may well make us wonder.

—Henry James, 1915

At some point during the process of writing *A Farewell to Arms* (1929), Ernest Hemingway typed out part of a 1915 *New York Times* interview with Henry James. The quotation, which Hemingway left between the pages of his own manuscript, expresses doubt over language's ongoing capacity for expression; James worries that "the war has used up words" so that "we are now confronted . . . with a loss of expression through an increase of limpness, that may well make us wonder what ghosts will be left to walk" (3–4). Hemingway prefaced this snippet with the phrase: "on the debasement of words by war." Then, echoing James's sentiments about ghostly or limp words and noting their opposite—the "concrete"—Frederic Henry famously observes in *A Farewell to Arms* that "[a]bstract words such as glory, honor,

The Hemingway Review, Volume 26, Number 2 (2007): pp. 7–21. Copyright © 2007 The Ernest Hemingway Foundation.

courage or hallow were obscene beside the concrete names of villages, the numbers of roads, the names of rivers, the numbers of regiments and the dates" (165).[1]

While James questioned "what ghosts will be left to walk," Hemingway chose to offer skeletons instead. As Paul Fussell explains, Second World War writers would eventually express "a general skepticism about the former languages of glory and sacrifice and patriotism." They were "[s]ick of the inflated idiom of official morale-boosting tub-thumping and all the slynesses of wartime publicity and advertising," and "preferred to speak in understatement, glancing less at the center of a topic than at its edges" (xxv). Long before this, however, Hemingway's limited vocabulary, few adjectives, and concrete descriptions of specific objects all countered with minimalism the problem of "used up words."

Yet alongside Hemingway's skeletal sentences was another solution to the "increase of limpness": a camera-eye aesthetic that re-embodied reality and expelled the ghosts. This aesthetic was often multi-focal. Imitating film rather than single-shot still photography, it rejected all apparently coherent and exclusive ways of perceiving the world, and asked readers to "mistrust all frank and simple people, especially when their stories hold together" (*SAR* 12). Against these "stories that hold together," his multi-focal aesthetic asserted the existence of "various angles" (*SAR* 35); after all, the nose of Robert Cohn in *The Sun Also Rises* (1926) could have been flattened in a boxing ring, *or* by a horse, *or* "maybe his mother had been frightened or seen something" (12).

Built upon his "iceberg" theory of omission and taken up as a style by 1930s writers, Hemingway's aesthetic tried to grasp the "many things which it is necessary to know" (238), as he puts it in *For Whom the Bell Tolls* (1940). It was a politics of form that reached for what George Orwell famously termed "*unofficial* history, the kind that is ignored in the text-books and lied about in the newspapers" ("Arthur Koestler" 220). Hemingway noted the "hole in the story" (qtd. in Plimpton 88). Then, with his multi-focal aesthetic, he acknowledged the *whole* story.[2]

I. You'll Lose It If You Talk about It:
Diagnosing and Solving the Problem of Language

Writing in the aftermath of what Bertrand Russell called in 1914 the First World War's "foul literature of 'glory'" (clichéd accounts of heroism and sacrifice, often in the passive voice), Hemingway reiterated James's idea of "used up" words across his own work (qtd. in Dentith 133): Nick Adams believes that "[t]alking about anything was bad. Writing about anything actual was bad. It always killed it" ("On Writing" 237); Krebs of "Soldier's Home" (1925) discovers that stories strip experience of its "cool valuable quality" and that everyone has "heard too many atrocity stories to be thrilled by actualities" (*IOT* 70); and Hemingway observes in *Death in the Afternoon* (1932) that "all our words from loose using have lost their edge" (71). Confirming the communicative failures of language, *The Sun Also Rises* even contains scenes that omit Jake Barnes's responses to questions:

"Don't you think so, Jake?"
"There's a fight to-night," Bill said. "Like to go?" (85).

And:

"Did you get my line, Jake?"
The cab stopped in front of the hotel and we all went in (95).

The war has used up men, like the war-wounded and impotent Jake, and has apparently used up words as well.[3]

Within his form, Hemingway embedded a further commentary upon language's depleted capacity for expression. For example, his paratactic syntax—which juxtaposes clauses and like syntactic units without subordinating conjunctions—creates static, abrupt sentences that seem to stammer or bark; anticipating Arthur Koestler's *Darkness at Noon* (1941), where the leaders of the Revolution have tongues that "stammered and barked" (120). In *For Whom the Bell Tolls*, Robert Jordan intends to "write a book when he got through with this" (238), but knows that "to get a full picture of what is happening you cannot read only the party organ" (236), that he will "have to be a much better writer" than he is now because the "things he had come to know in this war were not so simple" (238). As though confirming the "not so simple" nature of possibly inexpressible things and the problem of how to represent the "full picture" of the war, the novel's dialogue is stilted and foreign. Hemingway uses non-standard but technically grammatical English ("I did not like," "let us go," "we go now," "I am content we are started," "It is a name I can never dominate"), and potentially offensive words are awkwardly replaced with words like "obscenity" or "unprintable." He eventually highlights the deliberate foreignness of his language in this novel, writing: "'Continue thy story,' Massart said to Andres; using the term story as you would say lie, falsehood, or fabrication" (395).[4]

Both Hemingway's paratactic syntax and his use of non-standard English were a politics of form that expressed the damage done to language by abstractions like "glory, honor, courage," as Frederic Henry puts it in *A Farewell to Arms*. After Hemingway, more overtly politicized writers would explore the same problem and propose the solution of a camera-eye aesthetic. For example, James Agee in *Let Us Now Praise Famous Men* (1941) protests what he calls "the breakdown of the identification of word and object" (209) and asserts that "words cannot embody, they can only describe" (210). By way of solution, Agee proposes that the camera is "the central instrument of our time" (9) and explains: "If I could do it, I'd do no writing at all here. It would be photographs" (4). His imagination throughout *Let Us Now Praise Famous Men* is photographic: sunlight is like "a flash bulb" and a child is a "photographic plate" (198). In addition, Agee's focus throughout on the *process* of writing means his words come to light like a developing photograph: Agee wrote, then looked to see what was written. Describing, meditating, and analyzing all at once, as well as noting "you mustn't be puzzled by this, I'm writing in a continuum" (62), he created sentences, paragraphs and a whole book without narrative or chronology. His writing is series of static word-pictures that proceed through long repetitive sentences and mingled tenses, as in the very last sentence of the book: "each of these matters had in that time the extreme clearness which I shall now try to give you; until at length we too fell asleep" (416), he writes, moving from past tense to present to past.[5]

Koestler too attempted to diagnose and solve the problem of language. In *The Invisible Writing* (1954) he remembered that during the 1930s his "feelings toward art, literature, and human relations became reconditioned and ... [his] vocabulary, grammar, syntax gradually changed ... [as he] learnt to avoid any original expression, any individual turn of phrase ... Language, and with it thought, underwent a process of dehydration, and crystallized in the ready-made schematic" (25–26). This problem of language means that in *Darkness at Noon* "inner processes" are spoken of "contemptuously, merely as an abstraction" (125). Koestler's characterization therefore depends upon gesture and physical details rather than words: Rubashov fiddles with his pince-nez (he is nervy, obsessive); Richard has an over-active Adam's apple and inflamed eyes (he is vulnerable and cannot see his fast-approaching fate). The novel often progresses through external observations, as when the prison doctor probes inside Rubashov's mouth and "[s]uddenly Rubashov became pale and had to lean against the wall" (66). Two lines later the reader knows what the character feels ("the pain was throbbing ... "), but initially must judge Rubashov's reaction from a fly-on-the-wall perspective. At moments this perspective is even aligned with the spying eyes of characters in the novel. Koestler writes: "The eye which had been observing him [Rubashov] for several minutes through the spy-hole withdrew" (48) and then ends section ten of the book, forcing the *reader* to withdraw as well.

Rubashov himself eventually realizes the power of external observation (the camera-eye perspective) when he contemplates the removal of a photograph from a wall in the prison, and has "the strange wish, almost a physical impulse, to touch the light patch on the wall [where the photograph of the leaders used to be] with his fingers" (77). A few years later George

Orwell would echo Koestler, again using the theme of photography to connect the physical evidence of people's existence with their humanity. Just as
language fails the characters of Hemingway, Agee, and Koestler, so it fails
Orwell's characters in *Nineteen Eighty-Four* (1949). Their words are "like a
leaden knell" (86) or "some monstrous machine running without oil" (13).
Goldstein's voice becomes a sheep's bleat (16). Mrs. Parsons speaks in half-
sentences throughout, and the gym instructress yaps and barks (29). The tele-
screen gives a "furious deafening roar" (189) and later a "cracked, braying
jeering note, a yellow note" (236). At one point Winston Smith is "deprived
of the power of speech," so that his tongue works "soundlessly" (141), and
Winston and Julia can eventually only echo one another: "You don't feel the
same . . . you don't feel the same . . . we must meet again . . . we must meet
again" (235). Throughout the novel Winston clings wordlessly to concrete
objects: a diary, a paperweight, and a photograph. It thrills him to hold the
photograph, a "fragment of the abolished past" (66), and eventually he all he
wants is "to hold the photograph in his fingers again" (198). Remembering
that image, he is able to tell O'Brien in the Ministry of Love: "'I think I exist
. . . I occupy a particular point in space. No other object can occupy the same
point simultaneously'" (208).[6]

Other writers went further still in their proffered diagnoses of and solu-
tions to the problem of language. In *The Big Money* (1936), John Dos Passos
protests the "monotonous mumble of words" (459), a public made "goofy"
(52) and "groggy with headlines" (193), its "eyes bleared with newspaperreading" (149) and with the journalistic back-formations and blends that
make language a thing of "quick turnover, cheap interchangeable easilyreplaced standardized parts" (50).[7] Like Agee and Koestler, Dos Passos wanted
to "generate the insides . . . of characters by external description" (qtd. in
Diggins 238), as he once explained to Edmund Wilson (who wrote to remind him of this intention in 1939). Dos Passos tried to "see things unusu-
ally vividly, the brilliant winter day, the etched faces of people sitting in the
waitingroom, the colors on the magazines in the newsstand" (*The Big Money*
124). But Dos Passos moved beyond the aesthetic of a one-shot photograph
to reach for a *multi*-focal camera-eye. He explained that he tried to "record
the fleeting world the way the motion picture film recorded it" (qtd. in Pizer
272) and in *The Big Money* offered mini-biographies and "Newsreel" sections
that function as background shots, and "Camera Eye" sections that function
as close-ups.

Dos Passos used this multi-focal aesthetic to assert the existence of multiple, unofficial histories, explaining in a 1964 interview that they offered "another dimension . . . things that were going on at the same time as the actual
narrative" (qtd. in Madden 7). He reiterated in 1968 that his "Newsreel" and
"Camera Eye" sections offered "a different dimension": "I was trying to put

across a complex state of mind, an atmosphere, and I brought in these things partly for contrast and partly for getting a different dimension" (42). In the introduction to *U.S.A.* (1938), he even translated his multi-focal aesthetic into a literary manifesto: "U.S.A. is . . . a publiclibrary full of old newspapers and dogeared historybooks with protests scrawled in the margins in pencil" (7). These layers of communication—public library, newspapers, history books, and margin scrawls—offered "a different dimension" and were a reminder of the existence of unofficial histories during what Dos Passos called in 1939 a "very odd period in human history when it is very difficult to make broad generalizations about events" (27). In his work, the existence of a "different dimension" even means, for example, that while Frank Lloyd Wright in *The Big Money* tries to walk with "long eager steps / towards the untrammeled future" (432), the line-break after "steps" confirms that there are no long eager steps—no untrammeled future. There is only the halting progress of multiple angles upon the same story.

Dos Passos, Orwell, Koestler, and Agee are acknowledged far more often than Hemingway as authors of work containing a clear politics and a clear politics of form. For Orwell, Koestler, and Agee the solution to the problem of a "loss of expression," as James put it in 1915, was photography; apparent as a theme in the work of all three writers, and as a camera-eye aesthetic in the work of Agee and Koestler. For Dos Passos, the solution was a film aesthetic; multi-focal rather than one-shot. But Hemingway's diagnosis of a "loss of expression" led him to a comparable politics of form: across Hemingway's work are the threads of both a one-shot photograph aesthetic and a multi-shot film aesthetic. Together, these camera-eyes answer the problem of abstract language, official history, and the perceived sensation that—in the words of Jake Barnes—"'[y]ou'll lose it if you talk about it'" (*SAR* 249).[8]

II. Just Like the Moving Pictures:
Hemingway's Multi-Focal Camera-Eye

In 1922, Hemingway used a snapshot style to create a montage of juxtapositions. The piece "Paris 1922" begins and re-begins, each listed description containing the phrase "I have seen" in its opening. He revised this device for the first chapter of *A Farewell to Arms*, which also begins and re-begins: "there were pebbles . . . there were many orchards . . . There was fighting . . . There was much traffic . . . There were big guns . . . There was fighting . . . There were mists . . . There were small gray motor cars" (3–4). This process of re-beginning seems to create what Gertrude Stein in "Composition as Explanation" (1926) called a "beginning again and again" and so a "continuous present" (457). Perhaps experiencing such a continuous present, Robert Jordan in *For Whom the Bell Tolls* then feels that a whole lifetime might be crammed into three days. "[I]t is possible to live as full a life in seventy hours as in seventy years," he muses, later thinking: "This is how you live a life in two days" (161, 164).[9]

Both "Paris 1922" and the first chapter of *A Farewell to Arms* represent Hemingway's wider aesthetic on the micro-level. His short sentences and long paratactic ones resist linear progression. Written in a staccato rhythm, without subordination, the sentences achieve stasis through structure. Events pile up and the result is a sense of eyewitness. This commitment to a de-authored, eyewitness style may have been one of the factors driving him to rewrite the ending of *A Farewell to Arms* multiple times. One of the novel's early endings emphasizes its status as text: "I could tell what has happened since then, but that is the end of the story." The published ending just *ends* the story: "After a while I went out and left the hospital and walked back to the hotel in the rain" (294). This rewrite makes the ending less self-conscious, less *authored*, and more photographic. Similarly, Hemingway rewrote the opening of *The Sun Also Rises*, editing out self-conscious passages like the following: "In life people are not conscious of these special moments that novelists build their whole structures on . . . None of the significant things are going to have any literary signs marking them. You have to figure them out by yourself."[10]

But while using this de-authored and potentially static eyewitness style across his work, Hemingway often chose to undercut its effect. Alongside his one-shot photograph aesthetic, with its accompanying stasis, was a multi-focal camera eye. For example, one source for the fishing section in *The Sun Also Rises* is Hemingway's 1922 article for the *Toronto Daily Star*, "Fishing the Rhone Canal." In both the novel and the original article, the narrator catches a trout and then sits under a tree to read. In the novel he reads "something by A. E. W. Mason . . . about a man who had been frozen in the Alps and then fallen into a glacier and disappeared" (124–125), and this "glacier" appears in the article too, along with a warning about perception. The waterfall descending from the glacier looks solid, then appears to be moving—as though shifting between still and motion picture photography:

> It was a hot day, but I could look out across the green, slow valley past the line of trees that marked the course of the Rhone and watch a waterfall coming down the brown face of the mountain. The fall came out of a glacier that reached down toward a little town with four grey houses and three grey churches that was planted on the side of the mountain and looked solid, the waterfall, that is, until you saw it was moving (*BL* 33).

In addition, the sudden presence of "something by A. E. W. Mason" reminds the reader that multiple stories exist—like the various tales of how Cohn's nose was flattened. As an embedded text, it is an alternate story and a reminder of what Hemingway called "various angles" (*SAR* 35), or what Dos Passos called in 1968 "a different dimension" (42).[11]

Hemingway's prose, which he repeatedly described as an iceberg, is also a glacier waterfall, infused with movement by his multi-focal aesthetic. He proceeds with a focus upon "the now and the perception and 'insistence' of sequenced and repetitive, but never identical, nows" (qtd. in Knapp 96), as Stein put it (with reference to her own work). While he does repeat words throughout a paragraph, he often uses the repetition to slowly progress—representing an image or idea from a different angle. A passage toward the end of *The Sun Also Rises* is one example:

> It was hot and bright. Up the street was a little square with trees and grass where there were taxis parked. A taxi came up the street, the waiter hanging out at the side. I tipped him and told the driver where to drive, and got in beside Brett. The driver started up the street. I settled back. Brett moved close to me. We sat close against each other. I put my arm around her and she rested against me comfortably. It was very hot and bright, and the houses looked sharply white (250–251).

The repetition of "hot and bright" is really a *new* impression—the second "hot and bright" prefaced by "very"—and the middle section of the paragraph contains three angle-shots ("Brett moved close to me. We sat close against each other. I put my arm around her and she rested against me comfortably"). The word "close" links the first two sentences of this middle section, and the "against" links the second and third sentences: the effect is of one of slow-motion progression, two steps forward and one step back. As Stein wrote in "Composition as Explanation," "everything being alike everything naturally everything is different simply different naturally simply different" (460).

In *Death in the Afternoon*, Hemingway offers a description that encapsulates this style. He compares the movement of a bullfighter to a "slow motion picture," for the man's movement is "a long glide" that creates "prolong[ed] . . . vision," instead of "a jerk" (14). Elsewhere Hemingway offered a formula for this kind of multi-stage progression, using a billiards metaphor to explain that "it is all done with three-cushion shots" (qtd. in Breit 14). Or, offering yet another formula for his style, he wrote to Edmund Wilson: "Finished the book of 14 stories with a chapter of *In Our Time* between each story—that is the way they were meant to go—to give the picture of the whole between examining it in detail." This was, he explained, like "looking with your eyes at something, say a passing coastline, and then looking at it with 15x binoculars. Or rather maybe, looking at it and then going in and living in it—and then coming out and looking at it again" (*SL* 128). Focusing and refocusing his camera-eye, Hemingway's "picture of the whole" and his examinations "in detail" rendered in prose a series of filmic wide-shots and close-ups.[12]

Further developing his moving-picture aesthetic, Hemingway some-times used a cutting technique, shifting between Jim and Liz in "Up in Mich-igan" (1923) with the speed of celluloid spinning in a theater projector:

> Jim began to feel great . . . He had another drink. The men came
> in to supper feeling hilarious but acting very respectable. Liz sat
> at the table after she put the food on and ate with the family. . . .
> After supper they went into the front room again and Liz cleaned
> off with Mrs Smith . . . Jim and Charley were still in the front
> room. Liz was in the kitchen next to the stove pretending to read
> a book and thinking about Jim (*CSS* 61).[13]

A similarly filmic construction appears during chapters 33–42 of *For Whom the Bell Tolls*, where scenes of preparation for the bridge demolition are spliced with scenes of Andre's attempt to reach the military headquarters. Even within a single scene, Hemingway used the technique of cutting— writing for example in *The Sun Also Rises:*

> "Send him for champagne. He loves to go for champagne."
> Then later: "Do you feel better, darling? Is the head any better?"
> (62).

Amid these elements of Hemingway's filmic aesthetic, it is eventually no surprise to encounter Jake's observation in *The Sun Also Rises* that "all coun-tries look just like the moving pictures" (18).

By drawing upon film to create a multi-focal aesthetic, Hemingway was able to counter what he considered to be photography's "flat" style. Avowedly suspicious of the one-shot photograph aesthetic, he resisted comparisons be-tween his writing and photography, explaining in a 1949 letter to Charles Scribner that photography made reality two-dimensional, and that his novels should be "rounded and not flat like photographs" (*SL* 678). In an interview he expanded upon this theme: "If you describe someone it is flat, as a photo-graph is, and from my standpoint a failure. If you make him up from what you know, there should be all the dimensions" (qtd. in Schnitzer 119).

The multi-focal aesthetic also aligned with Hemingway's "iceberg" the-ory to counter what Koestler referred to as "the novelist's temptations": "The first and strongest temptation which the world outside the window exerts on the writer is to draw the curtains and close the shutters," warned Koestler.

"In temptation No.2 . . . the man behind the desk . . . [leans] right out of the window [and] begins to gesticulate, shout, and declaim." And in temptation number three, "the window is . . . left ajar, and the curtains are drawn in such a way as to expose only a limited section of the world outside while hiding the more painful and menacing sights from the author's eye. He may even push a telescope through a hole in the curtain and thus obtain an image with admirably sharp contours of a small and perhaps not very important fraction of the world" ("The Novelist's Temptations" 27). Resisting temptation number one, Hemingway's "iceberg" theory of omission doesn't "draw the curtains" on omitted things. Instead it leaves—in his own words—"a feeling of those things as strongly as though the writer had stated them" (*DIA* 192). The "iceberg" aesthetic also resists temptation number two: Hemingway's omissions insist upon what he called "the part that doesn't show" (qtd. in Plimpton 88)—the part of his work that doesn't gesticulate, shout, and declaim. But it is his *multi-focal* aesthetic that resists temptation number three: rather than peep through the curtains at "a limited section of the world outside" and push "a telescope through a hole in the curtain," Hemingway telescoped in, out, and around.

Hemingway also asked the reader to assist in this resistance of temptation. His "iceberg" theory of omission demanded that the reader feel the whole story: it was, he explained in *A Moveable Feast,* a "theory that you could omit anything if you knew that you omitted and the omitted part would strengthen the story and make people feel something more than they understood" (75). Hemingway's readers fill the gaps left by his omissions with their feelings and round out his prose to make it three-dimensional, providing the next angle in his multi-shot aesthetic. In so doing they might almost be responding to instructions from the author, embedded in *The Sun Also Rises* and conveyed by the unlikely mouthpiece of Lady Brett. When the count remarks: "'I should like to hear you really talk, my dear. When you talk to me you never finish your sentences at all,'" she leaves the final shot for her audience: "Leave 'em for you to finish. Let any one finish them as they like." (65)

NOTES

1. In his appendix to *Hemingway's Craft* (Carbondale: Southern Illinois University Press, 1973), Sheldon Grebstein recounts his discovery of the typed quotation between the manuscript pages of chapter 34 in *A Farewell to Arms* (206). James's interview is also published in *Henry James On Culture: Collected Essays on Politics and the American Social Scene,* ed. Pierre A. Walker (Lincoln: University of Nebraska Press, 1999), 144–145. For more on Hemingway and James see Neal B. Houston, "Hemingway: The Obsession with Henry James, 1924–1954," *Rocky Mountain Review of Language and Literature,* Vol. 39, No. 1 (1985): 33–46. For more on the problem of war and abstract language, see Christopher Isherwood, *Lions and*

Shadows (1938): war was "never under any circumstances . . . allowed to appear in its own shape, [it] needed a symbol" (47).

2. In 1932 Hemingway observed: "The dignity of the movement of an iceberg is due to only one-eighth of it being above water." He explained: "If a writer of prose knows enough about what he is writing about he may omit things that he knows and the reader, if the writer is writing truly enough, will have a feeling of those things as strongly as though the writer had stated them" (*DIA* 192). Hemingway expanded upon his iceberg theory of writing in a 1958 interview published in George Plimpton (ed.), *Writers at Work: The Paris Review Interviews, Second Series* (New York: Viking, 1960): "I always try to write on the principle of the iceberg. There is seven-eighths of it underwater for every part that shows. Anything you know, you can eliminate and it only strengthens your iceberg. It is the part that doesn't show. If a writer omits something because he does not know it then there is a hole in the story" (88). He continued to explain his iceberg theory in two posthumously published works, "The Art of the Short Story" (composed in 1959) and *A Moveable Feast* (1964). For more on Hemingway's theory of omission see Susan Beegel, *Hemingway's Craft of Omission: Four Manuscript Examples* (Ann Arbor: UMI Research, 1988); Gerry Brenner, *Concealments in Hemingway's Works* (Columbus: Ohio State University Press, 1983); Paul Smith, "Hemingway's Early Manuscripts: The Theory and Practice of Omission," *Journal of Modern Literature* 10.2 (1983): 268–289. For more on what this article calls "the politics of form," see Zoe Trodd, ed., *American Protest Literature* (Cambridge: Harvard University Press, 2006), xxiii–xv, and Ralph Ellison, *Collected Essays:* "from the beginning our novelists have been consciously concerned with the form, technique and content of the novel, not excluding ideas. . . the major ideas of our society were so alive in the minds of every reader that they could be stated implicitly in the contours of the form . . . the form of the great documents of state constitutes a body of assumptions about human possibility which is shared by all Americans, even those who resist violently any attempt to embody them in social action" (708). For examples of politics of form in practice, see for example John Steinbeck's *The Grapes of Wrath* (1939), which has a pre-determining interchapter before each narrative chapter so that the reader experiences the inevitability of the migrants' experience, and James Agee and Walker Evans's *Let Us Now Praise Famous Men* (1941), of which Agee explained that the repetitious prose was designed to make the reader feel the boredom of tenant farmers' work. For more on the politics of modernist form, see Marianne DeKoven, "The Politics of Modernist Form" (1992). DeKoven outlines the politics of "modernist form's disruptions of hierarchical syntax, of consistent, unitary point of view, of realist representation, linear time and plot, and of the bounded, coherent self separated from and in mastery of an objectified outer world, its subjectivist epistemology . . . its formal decenteredness, indeterminacy, multiplicity, and fragmentation" (677).

3. For "[t]alking about anything was bad . . . [etc]" see the excised ending to "Big Two-Hearted River" (1925), published posthumously in *The Nick Adams Stories* (1972) as "On Writing."

4. The year before Hemingway published *For Whom the Bell Tolls*, he wrote a barbed preface to photographer and artist Luis Quintanilla's collection of Spanish war drawings, *All The Brave* (1939), asking: "How many words are there to be? . . . The reader does not need them because the reader can look at the pictures" (n.p.). Hemingway's own aesthetic of juxtaposition (images within paragraphs and clauses

within sentences) is echoed by Quintanilla's images, which subtly juxtapose shapes throughout the collection: a donkey's ears that repeat the shape of a plane's wings; folds in a soldier's trousers that repeat the shape of a dead mule's ribs; wire on a fence that repeats the shape of a dead Moor's braid.

5. Hemingway's paratactic style, which evokes a sense that the same time-zone runs throughout paragraphs and pages, is often compared to the style of Paul Cézanne, who used an eye-level perspective. Hemingway compared himself to Cézanne, commenting to Lillian Ross as they toured the Museum of Modern Art: "I can make a landscape like Mr. Paul Cézanne. I learned how to make a landscape from Mr. Paul Cézanne" (qtd. in Ross 41). He further explained in *A Moveable Feast* (1964) that during the 1920s this learning process involved a search for "dimensions": "I went there [to the Musée du Luxembourg] nearly every day for the Cézannes and to see the Manets and the Monets and the other Impressionists that I had first come to know about in the Art Institute at Chicago. I was learning something from the painting of Cézanne that made writing simple true sentences far from enough to make the stories have the dimensions that I was trying to put in them. I was learning very much from him but I was not articulate enough to explain it to anyone. Besides it was a *secret*" (13). Cézanne's "secret" is perhaps that of omission. Like the hidden seven-eighths of the iceberg, his frequent omissions of color and decisions to sacrifice surface detail to achieve pure lines suggest the existence of a world *beyond* the surface. For more on Hemingway's debt to Cézanne see Ron Berman, "Recurrence in Hemingway and Cézanne," *The Hemingway Review* 23.2 (Spring 2004): 21–36; Theodore L. Gaillard Jr., "Hemingway's Debt to Cézanne: New Perspectives," *Twentieth Century Literature* 45 (Spring 1999): 65–78; Thomas Hermann, "Formal Analogies in the Texts and Paintings of Ernest Hemingway and Paul Cezanne," *Hemingway Repossessed*, ed. Kenneth Rosen (Westport: Praeger, 1994), 29–33; Kenneth Johnston, "Hemingway and Cézanne: Doing the Country," *American Literature* 56 (March 1984): 28–37; and Emily Stipes Watts, *Ernest Hemingway and the Arts* (Chicago: University of Illinois Press, 1971).

6. See also Benji in William Faulkner's *The Sound and the Fury* (1929): Benji, who knows the impossibility of articulating experience through words, remembers the area on a wall where a mirror used to be and tries to touch it. The author would like to thank the anonymous reviewer of "Hemingway's Camera-Eye" for this reference.

7. Dos Passos continued to express the problem of language through his blended word-formations, which embody the "monotonous mumble of words" and the experience of eyes made "groggy with headlines" (see for example "newspaperreading," "easilyreplaced," "waitingroom," "publiclibrary," and "historybooks").

8. For more on Hemingway's politics, see Keneth Kinnamon, "Hemingway and Politics," *The Cambridge Companion to Hemingway*, ed. Scott Donaldson (New York: Cambridge University Press, 1996), 170–197, and Stephen Cooper, *The Politics of Ernest Hemingway* (Ann Arbor: UMI Research, 1987).

9. See Hemingway, "Paris 1922," Item 64 and Story Fragments, Hemingway Collection, JFK Library. For more on Hemingway's montage style, see Amy Vondrak, "The Sequence of Motion and Fact: Cubist Collage and Filmic Montage in *Death in the Afternoon*," *A Companion to Hemingway's Death in the Afternoon*, ed. Miriam B. Mandel (Rochester, NY: Camden House, 2004), 257–282.

10. See Hemingway, *A Farewell to Arms*, Item 64 and Manuscripts and Notebooks for *The Sun Also Rises*, Item 194, The Ernest Hemingway Collection,

John F. Kennedy Library, Boston, MA. Hemingway maintained that he wrote 39 different versions of the ending to *A Farewell to Arms*.

11. In fact, with their disruption of stasis, Hemingway's multi-focal descriptions echo a different aspect of Cézanne's style: his technique of painting a series of planes. For both painter and writer, multiple shots on a scene create an impressionistic reality. In *The Sun Also Rises*, for example, Hemingway writes: "Looking back we saw Burgete . . . Beyond the fields . . . A sandy road led down to the ford and beyond into the woods . . . the road went up a hill . . . the road came out of the forest and went along the shoulder of the ridge of hills . . . Way off we saw the steep bluffs, dark with trees and jutting with gray stone" (121–122). Showing reality from many angles, Hemingway's filmic style echoes Cézanne's *sfumato*—the blurred image or veiled form.

12. Hemingway combines these descriptions of a glacier and of a slow-gliding bullfighter in a different passage of *The Sun Also Rises*, where a slow-moving bullfight crowd is like "a glacier" (168).

13. Hemingway's "Up in Michigan" was first published in *Three Stories and Ten Poems* (Paris: Contact Publishing, 1923).

WORKS CITED

Agee, James and Walker Evans. *Let Us Now Praise Famous Men*. 1941. Boston: Houghton Mifflin, 1960.

Breit, Harvey. "Talk with Mr. Hemingway." *New York Times Book Review*. 17 September 1950: 14.

DeKoven, Marianne. "The Politics of Modernist Form." *New Literary History* 23.3 (Summer 1992): 675–690.

Dentith, Simon. *Epic and Empire in Nineteenth-Century Britain*. Cambridge: Cambridge University Press, 2006.

Diggins, John P. "Visions of Chaos and Visions of Order: Dos Passos as Historian." *American Literature* 46.3 (November 1974): 329–346.

Dos Passos, John. *The Big Money*. New York: Harcourt, Brace, 1936.

———. "The Situation in American Writing: Seven Questions." *Partisan Review* 6 (Summer 1939): 26–27.

———. "John Dos Passos: Interview with Charles F. Madden, Henry T. Moore, and members of Drury College, Jackson State College, Langston University, and Tougaloo College, February 3, 1964." *Talks with Authors*. Ed. Charles Madden. Carbondale: Southern Illinois University Press, 1968. 4–11.

———. "John Dos Passos: Interview with Frank Gado, October 16, 1968." *First Person: Conversations on Writers and Writing with Glenway Wescott, John Dos Passos, Robert Penn Warren, John Updike, John Barth, Robert Coover*. Ed. Frank Gado. Schenectady: Union College Press, 1973. 31–55.

Ellison, Ralph. "Society, Morality and the Novel." 1957. *The Collected Essays*. Ed. John F. Callahan. New York: Modern Library, 2003. 698–729.

Faulkner, William. *The Sound and the Fury*. New York: J. Cape and H. Smith, 1929.

Fussell, Paul. Introduction. *Articles of War: A Collection of American Poetry About World War II*. Ed. Leon Stokesbury. Fayetteville: University of Arkansas Press, 1990. i–xxix.

Hemingway, Ernest. *By-Line: Ernest Hemingway; Selected Articles and Dispatches of Four Decades*. Ed. William White. New York: Scribner's, 1967.

————. *The Complete Short Stories of Ernest Hemingway: The Finca Vigía Edition*. New York: Scribner's, 1987.

————. *Death in the Afternoon*. New York: Scribner's, 1932.

————. *Ernest Hemingway: Selected Letters, 1917–1961*. Ed. Carlos Baker. New York: Scribner's, 1981.

————. *A Farewell to Arms*. 1929. New York: Vintage, 1999.

————. *For Whom the Bell Tolls*. 1940. New York: Penguin, 1955.

————. *In Our Time*. 1925, 1930. New York: Scribner's, 1996.

————. *A Moveable Feast*. 1964. New York: Simon and Schuster, 1996.

————. Preface to Luis Quintanilla, *All The Brave*. New York: Modern Age Books, 1939. n.p.

————. *The Sun Also Rises*. 1926. New York: Scribner's, 1954.

————. "On Writing." *The Nick Adams Stories*. Ed. Philip Young. New York: Scribner's, 1972. 233–241.

Isherwood, Christopher. *Lions and Shadows, an Education in the Twenties*. London: Hogarth Press, 1938.

James, Henry. "Henry James's First Interview." *The New York Times Magazine*. 21 March 1915: 3–5.

Knapp, Bettina L. *Gertrude Stein*. New York: Continuum, 1990.

Koestler, Arthur. "The Novelist's Temptations." *The Yogi and the Commissar*. New York: Macmillan, 1945. 22–29.

————. *The Invisible Writing*. London: Collins with Hamish Hamilton, 1954.

————. *Darkness at Noon*. 1941. Harmondsworth: Penguin, 1990.

Orwell, George. "Arthur Koestler." 1944. *Collected Essays*. London: Secker and Warburg, 1961. 220–232.

————. *Nineteen Eighty-Four*. 1949. Harmondsworth: Penguin, 1977.

Plimpton, George. "The Art of Fiction XXI: Ernest Hemingway." *Paris Review* (Spring 1958): 88.

Ross, Lillian. "How Do You Like It Now, Gentlemen?" *The New Yorker* (13 May 1950): 40–51.

Schnitzer, Deborah. *The Pictorial in Modernist Fiction from Stephen Crane to Ernest Hemingway*. Ann Arbor: UMI Research, 1988.

Stein, Gertrude. "Composition as Explanation." 1926. *Selected Writings of Gertrude Stein*. Ed. Carl Van Vechten. New York: Random House, 1946. 453–461.

Chronology

1899	Hemingway born July 21 in Oak Park, Illinois.
1917	Works as reporter for *Kansas City Star.*
1918	Service in Italy with the American Red Cross; wounded on July 8 near Fossalta di Piave; affair with nurse Agnes von Kurowsky.
1920	Reporter for *Toronto Star.*
1921	Marries Hadley Richardson; moves to Paris.
1922	Reports Greco-Turkish War for *Toronto Star.*
1923	*Three Stories and Ten Poems* published in Paris.
1924	A collection of vignettes, *in our time,* published in Paris by Three Mountains Press.
1925	Attends Fiesta de San Fermin in Pamplona with Harold Loeb, Pat Guthrie, Duff Twysden, and others. *In Our Time,* which adds fourteen short stories to the earlier vignettes, is published in New York by Horace Liveright. It is Hemingway's first American book.
1926	*The Torrents of Spring* and *The Sun Also Rises* published by Charles Scribner's Sons.
1927	*Men without Women* published. Marries Pauline Pfeiffer.

1928	Moves to Key West.
1929	*A Farewell to Arms* published.
1932	*Death in the Afternoon* published.
1933	*Winner Take Nothing* published.
1935	*Green Hills of Africa* published.
1937	*To Have and Have Not* published. Returns to Spain as war correspondent on the Loyalist side.
1938	Writes script for the film *The Spanish Earth*. *The Fifth Column and the First Forty-Nine Stories* published.
1940	Marries Martha Gellhorn. *For Whom the Bell Tolls* published. Buys house in Cuba where he lives throughout most of the 1940s and 1950s.
1942	Edits *Men at War*.
1944	Takes part in Allied liberation of Paris with partisan unit.
1946	Marries Mary Welsh.
1950	*Across the River and into the Trees* published.
1952	*The Old Man and the Sea* published.
1954	Receives Nobel Prize for literature for *The Old Man and the Sea*.
1960	Settles in Ketchum, Idaho.
1961	Commits suicide on July 2, in Ketchum.
1964	*A Moveable Feast* published.
1970	*Islands in the Stream* published.
1986	*The Garden of Eden* published.

Contributors

HAROLD BLOOM is Sterling Professor of the Humanities at Yale University. He is the author of 30 books, including *Shelley's Mythmaking* (1959), *The Visionary Company* (1961), *Blake's Apocalypse* (1963), *Yeats* (1970), *A Map of Misreading* (1975), *Kabbalah and Criticism* (1975), *Agon: Toward a Theory of Revisionism* (1982), *The American Religion* (1992), *The Western Canon* (1994), and *Omens of Millennium: The Gnosis of Angels, Dreams, and Resurrection* (1996). *The Anxiety of Influence* (1973) sets forth Professor Bloom's provocative theory of the literary relationships between the great writers and their predecessors. His most recent books include *Shakespeare: The Invention of the Human* (1998), a 1998 National Book Award finalist; *How to Read and Why* (2000); *Genius: A Mosaic of One Hundred Exemplary Creative Minds* (2002); *Hamlet: Poem Unlimited* (2003); *Where Shall Wisdom Be Found?* (2004); and *Jesus and Yahweh: The Names Divine* (2005). In 1999, Professor Bloom received the prestigious American Academy of Arts and Letters Gold Medal for Criticism. He has also received the International Prize of Catalonia, the Alfonso Reyes Prize of Mexico, and the Hans Christian Andersen Bicentennial Prize of Denmark.

JAMES ASWELL, son of a ten-term U.S. Representative from Louisiana, was a writer who maintained a significant correspondence with Ernest Hemingway, F. Scott Fitzgerald, and Witter Bynner. His papers, including materials related to his novels, *The Midsummer Fires* (1942), *There's One in Every Town* (1951), and *Young and Hungry Hearted* (1955), are at Northwestern University. He died in 1955.

MALCOLM COWLEY, poet, editor, critic, and literary historian was called by the *New York Times* "the most trenchant chronicler of the so-called Lost Generation of post-World War I writers." His many books include *Exile's Return* (1934), *Many Windowed Houses: Collected Essays on Writers and Writing* (1970), and *Second Flowering* (1973). He died in 1989.

T. S. MATTHEWS was former associate editor of *The New Republic* and editor of *Time* magazine. His books include an autobiography, *Name and Address* (1960); *O My America* (1962), *Great Tom: Notes Towards a Definition of T. S. Eliot* (1973) and *Angels Unawares: Twentieth Century Portraits* (1985). He died in 1991.

JOHN DOS PASSOS was regarded, along with Hemingway, as among the most talented young American novelists during the 1920s and 1930s. He and Hemingway were close friends from 1924 until 1937, when they argued bitterly about Communist involvement in the Spanish Civil War. Dos Passos wrote over 40 novels and histories, including *Three Soldiers* (1922). *Manhattan Transfer* (1925), and the *USA* trilogy (collected 1938). He died in 1970.

H. L. MENCKEN, author and journalist, was regarded during the 1920s and 1930s as the most influential literary critic in America. He was editor of the *American Mercury* and co-editor of *The Smart Set*. His many books include *The American Language: A Preliminary Inquiry into the Development of English in the United States* and six volumes of his essays all published as *Prejudices* (1919-1927). He died in 1956.

FORD MADOX FORD is regarded as one of the most important forces in the creation of literary modernism. As editor of the *Transatlantic Review* in Paris during the 1920s, he was personally acquainted with the American expatriates, including Hemingway. The best known of Ford's many novels is *The Good Soldier* (1915). He died in 1939.

ROBERT PENN WARREN was professor of English at Yale University. A distinguished and highly decorated poet, novelist, and critic, he was a forceful voice in American literary criticism after the mid 1930s. The two popular literary textbooks he edited with Cleanth Brooks, *Understanding Poetry* (1938) and *Understanding Fiction* (1943), were pillars of the post-WWII critical movement called New Criticism. The best known of Warren's many novels is *All the King's Men* (1946). He died in 1989.

CARLOS BAKER was Woodrow Wilson Professor of English at Prince ton University. Though his literary interests were broad, he is best known for his work on Ernest Hemingway, including *Hemingway: The Writer as Artist* (1952), *Ernest Hemingway: A Life Story* (1969) and his volume of Hemingway's correspondence, *Ernest Hemingway: Selected Letters, 1917-1961* (1981). He died in 1987.

SHERIDAN BAKER was professor of English at the University of Michigan, Ann Arbor. His many books include *Ernest Hemingway: An Introduction and Interpretation* (1966). With Northrup Frye and George Perkins he edited the influential *Harper Handbook to Literature* (1985). He died in 2000.

MICHAEL S. REYNOLDS was an independent scholar who devoted his career to Ernest Hemingway, writing or editing ten books on him, including the acclaimed five-volume biography *The Young Hemingway* (1987), *Hemingway: The Paris Years* (1989), *Hemingway: The American Homecoming* (1992), *Hemingway: The 1930s* (1997), and *Hemingway: The Final Years* (1999). Reynolds died in 2000.

BERNARD OLDSEY is professor of English, emeritus, at Pennsylvania State University. A specialist on modern British literature, he wrote *Hemingway's Hidden Craft* (1979) and *Ernest Hemingway: The Papers of a Writer* (1981).

MILLICENT BELL is professor of English, emerita, at Boston University. She is the author of *Meaning in Henry James* (1991); she edited *The Cambridge Companion to Edith Wharton* (1998) and *Hawthorne and The Real: Bicentennial Essays* (2005).

ERIK NAKJAVANI is professor of humanities, emeritus, at the University of Pittsburgh. He has published widely in psycho-philosophical literary criticism and specializes in Hemingway studies.

MATTHEW J. BRUCCOLI was Emily Brown Jefferies Professor of English at the University of South Carolina. Perhaps the most productive American literature scholar of his generation, Bruccoli wrote or edited well more than a hundred books, with a particular emphasis on F. Scott Fitzgerald and Ernest Hemingway. His *Scott and Ernest: The Authority of Failure and the Authority of Success* (1978) was revised as *Fitzgerald and Hemingway: A Dangerous Friendship* (1994). Bruccoli was a distinguished bookman who was central to the development of the American literature collection at the University of South Carolina, which includes important archives related to Fitzgerald, Hemingway, and American literature between the World Wars. He was founding editor of the *Dictionary of Literary Biography*. He died in 2008.

MARK CIRINO taught creative writing and American literature at New York University for eight years. He is the author of two novels, *Name the Baby* (1998) and *Arizona Blues* (2000).

TREVOR DODMAN is visiting assistant professor of English at Wake Forest University.

ZOE TRODD teaches in the History and Literature Program at Harvard University. She edited *American Protest Literature* (2006) and *To Plead Our Own Cause: Personal Stories by Today's Slaves* (2008).

Bibliography

Baker, Carlos. *Hemingway: The Writer as Artist.* Princeton: Princeton University Press, 1952.

———, ed. *Hemingway and His Critics: An International Anthology.* New York: Hill & Wang, 1961.

———, ed. *Hemingway: Critiques of Four Major Novels.* New York: Scribner's, 1962.

———, ed. *Ernest Hemingway: Selected Letters, 1917–1961.* New York: Scribner's, 1981.

Baker, Sheridan. *Ernest Hemingway: An Introduction and Interpretation.* New York: Holt, Rinehart, 1967.

Balbert, Peter. "From Hemingway to Lawrence to Mailer: Survival and Sexual Identity in *A Farewell to Arms.*" *Hemingway Review* 3, no. 1 (1983): 30–43.

Benson, Jackson J. *Hemingway: The Writer's Art of Self-Defense.* Minneapolis: University of Minnesota Press, 1969.

Berman, Ronald. *Fitzgerald, Hemingway, and the Twenties.* Tuscaloosa, Ala.: University of Alabama Press, 2001.

———. *Fitzgerald-Wilson-Hemingway: Language and Experience.* Tuscaloosa, Ala.: University of Alabama Press, 2003.

———. *Modernity and Progress: Fitzgerald, Hemingway, Orwell.* Tuscaloosa, Ala.: University of Alabama Press, 2005.

Brenner, Gerry. *Concealments in Hemingway's Works.* Columbus: Ohio State University Press, 1983.

Bruccoli, Matthew J. *Scott and Ernest: The Authority of Failure and the Authority of Success.* New York: Random House, 1978.

229

————. *Classes on Ernest Hemingway.* Columbia, S.C.: Thomas Cooper Library, University of South Carolina, 2002.

Bruccoli, Matthew J.; Scribner, Charles, III; Trogdon, Robert W. *The Only Thing That Counts: The Ernest Hemingway/Maxwell Perkins Correspondence, 1925–1947.* Columbia, S.C.: University of South Carolina Press, 2003.

Bruccoli, Matthew J.; Baughman, Judith S. *The Sons of Maxwell Perkins: Letters of F. Scott Fitzgerald, Ernest Hemingway, Thomas Wolfe, and Their Editor.* Columbia, S.C.: University of South Carolina Press, 2004.

————. *Hemingway and the Mechanism of Fame: Statements, Public Letters, Introductions, Forewords, Prefaces, Blurbs, Reviews, and Endorsements.* Columbia, S.C.: University of South Carolina Press, 2006

Burke, Kenneth. *A Grammar of Motives and A Rhetoric of Motives.* 2 vol. ed. Cleveland: World Publishing, 1962.

Cecil, L. Moffitt. "The Color of *A Farewell to Arms.*" *Research Studies* 36 (June 1968): 168–173.

Cohen, Milton *A Hemingway's Laboratory: The Paris in our time.* Tuscaloosa, Ala.: University of Alabama Press, 2005

Cooperman, Stanley. "Death and Cojones: Hemingway's *A Farewell to Arms.*" *The South Atlantic Quarterly* 63 (1964): 85–92.

Cowley, Malcolm. "Not Yet Demobilized." *New York Review of Books,* 6 October 1929, 6.

————, ed. *Viking Portable Hemingway.* New York: Viking, 1944.

D'Avanzo, Mario L. "The Motif of Corruption in *A Farewell to Arms.*" *Lock Haven Review* 11 (1969): 57–62.

Davis, Robert M. "'If You Did Not Go Forward': Process and Stasis in *A Farewell to Arms.*" *Studies in the Novel* 2 (1970): 305–311.

DeFazio, Albert J., III; Hotchner, A. E. *Dear Papa, Dear Hotch: The Correspondence of Ernest Hemingway and A. E. Hotchner.* Columbia, Mo.: University of Missouri Press, 2005.

Dekker, George, and Joseph Harris. "Supernaturalism and the Vernacular Style in *A Farewell to Arms.*" *PMLA* 94 (1979): 311–318.

Donaldson, Scott. *By Force of Will: The Life and Art of Ernest Hemingway.* New York: Viking, 1977.

Eby, Cecil D. "The Soul of Ernest Hemingway." *Studies in American Fiction* 12 (1984): 223–226.

Engelberg, Edward. "Hemingway's 'True Penelope': Flaubert's *L'Education Sentimentale* and *A Farewell to Arms.*" *Comparative Literature Studies* 16 (1979): 180–216.

Fiedler, Leslie A. *Love and Death in the American Novel.* Rev. ed. New York: Stein & Day, 1975.

Fleming, Robert E. "Hemingway and Peele: Chapter 1 of *A Farewell to Arms*." *Studies in American Fiction* 11 (1983): 95–100.

Gajdusek, Robert E. *Hemingway in His Own Country.* Notre Dame, Ind.: University of Notre Dame Press, 2002.

Ganzel, Dewey. "*A Farewell to Arms:* The Danger of Imagination." *The Sewanee Review* 79 (1971): 576–597.

Gelfant, Blanche. "Language as a Moral Code in *A Farewell to Arms*." *Modern Fiction Studies* 9 (1963): 173–176.

Gellens, Jay, ed. *Twentieth Century Interpretations of* A Farewell to Arms: *A Collection of Critical Essays.* Englewood Cliffs, N.J.: Prentice-Hall, 1970.

Gerstenberger, Donna. "The Waste Land in *A Farewell to Arms*." *MLN* 76 (1961): 24–25.

Glasser, William A. "*A Farewell to Arms*." *The Sewanee Review* 74 (1966): 453–467.

Grebstein, Sheldon. *Hemingway's Craft.* Carbondale: Southern Illinois University Press, 1973.

Griffin, Peter. *Along with Youth: Hemingway, the Early Years.* Oxford: Oxford University Press, 1985.

Grimes, Larry E. *The Religious Design of Hemingway's Early Fiction.* Ann Arbor: UMI Research Press, 1985.

Gurko, Leo. *Ernest Hemingway and the Pursuit of Heroism.* New York: Crowell, 1968. Hackett, Francis. "Hemingway: *A Farewell to Arms*." *Saturday Review of Literature*, 6 August 1949, 32–33.

Hanneman, Audre. *Ernest Hemingway: A Comprehensive Bibliography.* Princeton: Princeton University Press, 1967.

———. *Supplement to Ernest Hemingway: A Comprehensive Bibliography.* Princeton: Princeton University Press, 1975.

Hotchner, A. E. *Papa Hemingway: A Personal Memoir.* Cambridge, Mass.: Da Capo, 2005.

Hovey, Richard B. "*A Farewell to Arms:* Hemingway's Liebstod." *University Review* 33 (Winter 1966, Spring 1967): 93–100, 163–68.

———. *Hemingway: The Inward Terrain.* Seattle: University of Washington Press, 1968.

Keeler, Clinton. "*A Farewell to Arms:* Hemingway and Peele." *MLN* 76 (1961): 622–625.

Kert, Bernice. *The Hemingway Women.* New York: Norton, 1983.

Killinger, John. *Hemingway and the Dead Gods: A Study in Existentialism.* Lexington: University of Kentucky Press, 1961.

Kohler, J. E "Let's Run Catherine Barkley Up the Flag Pole and See Who Salutes." *CEA Critic* 36 (1974): 4–10.

Lee, A. Robert, ed. *Ernest Hemingway: New Critical Essays.* Totowa, N.J.: Barnes & Noble, 1983.

Lewis, Robert W, Jr. *Hemingway On Love.* Austin: University of Texas Press, 1965.

———. "Hemingway in Italy: Making It Up." *Journal of Modern Literature* 9 (1982): 209–236.

Liedloff, Helmut, "Two War Novels: A Critical Comparison." *Revue de Littérature Comparée* 42 (1968): 390–400.

Light, James F. "The Religion of Death in *A Farewell to Arms.*" *Modern Fiction Studies* 7 (1961): 169–173.

McCaffery, John K. M., ed. *Ernest Hemingway: The Man and His Work.* Cleveland: World Publishing, 1950.

McCarthy, Paul. "Chapter Beginnings in *A Farewell to Arms.*" *Ball State University Forum* 10, no. 2 (1969): 21–30.

McIlvaine, Robert M. "A Literary Source for the Caesarean Section in *A Farewell to Arms.*" *American Literature* 43 (1971): 444–447.

McNeely, Trevor. "War Zone Revisited: Hemingway's Aesthetics and *A Farewell to Arms.*" *South Dakota Review* 22, no. 4 (1984): 14–38.

Marcus, Fred H. "*A Farewell to Arms:* The Impact of Irony and the Irrational." *The English Journal* 60 (1962): 527–535.

Mazzaro, Jerome L. "George Peele and *A Farewell to Arms:* A Thematic Tie?" *MLN* 75 (1960): 118–119.

Meyers, Jeffrey. *Hemingway: A Biography.* New York: Harper & Row, 1985.

———, ed. *Hemingway: The Critical Heritage.* London: Routledge & Kegan Paul, 1982.

Nagel, James, ed. *Ernest Hemingway: The Writer in Context.* Madison: University of Wisconsin Press, 1984.

Noble, Donald R., ed. *Hemingway: A Revaluation.* Troy, N.Y.: Whitston Publishing, 1983.

Nolan, Charles J., Jr. "Hemingway's Women's Movement." *Hemingway Review* 3, no. 2 (1984): 14–22.

———. "Shooting the Sergeant: Frederic Henry's Puzzling Action." *College Literature* 11, no. 3 (1984): 2–13.

Oldsey, Bernard. "The Genesis of *A Farewell to Arms.*" *Studies in American Fiction* 5 (Autumn 1977): 175–185.

Oliver, Charles M., ed. *Ernest Hemingway's A Farewell to Arms: A Documentary Volume. Dictionary of Literary Biography*, volume 308. Detroit, Mich.: Gale, 2005.

Reynolds, Michael S. *Hemingway's First War: The Making of* A Farewell to Arms. Princeton: Princeton University Press, 1976.

————. *Hemingway's Reading 1910–1940: An Inventory*. Princeton: Princeton University Press, 1976.

————. *The Young Hemingway*. Oxford: Basil Blackwell, 1986.

Rovit, Earl. *Ernest Hemingway*. New York: Twayne, 1963.

Rovit, Earl; Waldhorn, Arthur. *Hemingway and Faulkner in Their Time*. New York: Continuum, 2005.

Russell, H. K. "The Catharsis in *A Farewell to Arms*." *Modern Fiction Studies* 1 (1955): 25–30.

Sharrock, Roger. "Singles and Couples: Hemingway's *A Farewell to Arms* and Updike's *Couples*." *Ariel* 4, no. 4 (1973): 21–43.

Simpson, Herbert. "The Problem of Structure in *A Farewell to Arms*." *Forum* (Houston) 4, no. 4 (1964): 20–24.

Smith, Paul. "Almost All is Vanity: A Note on Nine Rejected Titles for *A Farewell to Arms*." *Hemingway Review* 2, no. 1 (1982): 74–76.

Steinke, Jim. "Harlotry and Love: A Friendship in *A Farewell to Arms*." *Spectrum* 21, nos. 1–2 (1979): 20–24.

Stephens, Robert O. "Hemingway and Stendhal: The Matrix of *A Farewell to Arms*." *PMLA* 88 (1973): 271–279.

————. *Hemingway's Non-fiction: The Public Voice*. Chapel Hill: University of North Carolina Press, 1968.

Strychacz, Thomas F. *Hemingway's Theaters of Masculinity*. Baton Rouge: Louisiana State University Press, 2003

Stubbs, John. "Love and Role-Playing in *A Farewell to Arms*." *Fitzgerald/Hemingway Annual* (1973): 237–244.

Toole, William B., III. "Religion, Love, and Nature in *A Farewell to Arms:* The Dark Shape of Irony." *CEA Critic* 29 (May 1967): 10–11.

Vernon, Alex. *Soldiers Once and Still: Ernest Hemingway, James Salter, and Tim O'Brien*. Iowa City, Iowa: University of Iowa Press, 2004

Wagner, Linda W. *Ernest Hemingway: Five Decades of Criticism*. East Lansing: Michigan State University Press, 1974.

————. "'Proud and Friendly and Gently': Women in Hemingway's Early Fiction." *College Literature* 7 (1980): 239–247.

Waldhorn, Arthur. *A Reader's Guide to Ernest Hemingway*. New York: Farrar, Straus & Giroux, 1972.

Weeks, Robert P, ed. *Hemingway: A Collection of Critical Essays*. Englewood Cliffs, N.J: Prentice–Hall, 1962.

Wexler, Joyce. "E.R.A. for Hemingway: A Feminist Defense of *A Farewell to Arms*." *The Georgia Review* 35 (1981): 111–123.

White, William. "Hemingway in the Red Cross." *American Red Cross Journal* 42 (March 1966): 28–29.

Whitlow, Roger. *Cassandra's Daughters: The Women in Hemingway.* Westport, Conn.: Greenwood Press, 1984.

Williams, Wirt. *The Tragic Art of Ernest Hemingway.* Baton Rouge: Louisiana State University Press, 1981.

Wilson, Edmund. "Hemingway: Gauge of Morale." In *The Wound and the Bow.* Oxford: Oxford University Press, 1947.

Wylder, Delbert E. *Hemingway's Heroes.* Albuquerque: University of New Mexico Press, 1969.

Young, Philip. *Ernest Hemingway: A Reconsideration.* University Park: Pennsylvania State University Press, 1966.

Young, Philip, and Charles W. Mann, comps. *The Hemingway Manuscripts: An Inventory.* University Park: Pennsylvania State University Press, 1969.

Acknowledgments

James Aswell. "Critic Lavishes Praise on New Hemingway Novel," *Richmond Times-Dispatch* (October 6, 1929): p. 3. Copyright © *Richmond Times-Dispatch*. Reprinted by permission of the publisher.

Malcolm Cowley. "Not Yet Demobilized," *New York Herald Tribune Books*, XII (October 6, 1929): p. 1, 16.

T.S. Matthews. "Nothing Ever Happens to the Brave," *The New Republic*, "Fall Literary Section" (October 9, 1929): pp. 208–210.

John Dos Passos. "Books," *New Masses* (December 1, 1929): p. 16.

H. L. Mencken. "Fiction by Adept Hands," *American Mercury* (January 1930): p. 127.

Ford Madox Ford. "Introduction," *A Farewell to Arms* (New York: Modern Library, 1932): pp. ix, xvii–xx. Copyright © 1932 Random House.

Robert Penn Warren. "The Story Behind the Love Story," "Hemingway," *The Kenyon Review*, Volume 9 (Winter 1947): pp. 2–3, 18–24. Copyright © 1947 *The Kenyon Review*. Reprinted by permission of the publisher.

Carlos Baker. "The Mountain and the Plain," In *Hemingway: The Writer as Artist*. (Princeton: Princeton University Press, 1956): pp. 94–116. Copyright © 1956 Princeton University Press. Reprinted by permission of the publisher.

Sheridan Baker. "Frederic Henry and the Undefeated," In *Ernest Hemingway: An Introduction and Interpretation.* (New York: Holt, Rinehart, and Winston, 1967): pp. 63–73.

Michael S. Reynolds. "Going Back," *Hemingway's First War: The Making of A Farewell to Arms.* (Princeton, Princeton University Press, 1976): pp. 3–19. Copyright © 1976 Princeton University Press. Reprinted by permission of the publisher.

Bernard Oldsey. "The Sense of an Ending," *Hemingway's Hidden Craft.* (University Park, PA: Pennsylvania State University Press, 1979): pp. 70–91. Copyright © 1979 Pennsylvania State University Press. Reprinted by permission of the publisher.

Millicent Bell. "Pseudoautobiography and Personal Metaphor," In *Ernest Hemingway: The Writer in Context.* ed. James Nagel (Madison: University of Wisconsin Press, 1984): pp. 107–128. Copyright © 1984 University of Wisconsin Press. Reprinted by permission of the publisher.

Erik Nakjavani. "Hemingway on War and Peace." *North Dakota Quarterly,* Volume 68, Numbers 2–3 (Spring–Summer 2001): pp. 245–275. Copyright © 2001 *North Dakota Quarterly.* Reprinted by permission of the author and publisher.

Matthew J. Bruccoli. "Class Ten: *A Farewell to Arms,*" *Classes on Ernest Hemingway.* (Columbia: Thomas Cooper Library, University of South Carolina, 2002): pp. 103–141. Copyright © 2002 Matthew J. Bruccoli. Reprinted by permission of the author.

Mark Cirino. "'You Don't Know the Italian Language Well Enough': The Bilingual Dialogue of A Farewell to Arms." *Hemingway Review,* Volume 25, Number 1 (2005 Fall): pp. 43–62. Copyright © 2005 The Ernest Hemingway Foundation. All rights reserved. Reprinted by permission of the publisher.

Trevor Dodman. "'Going All to Pieces': A Farewell to Arms as Trauma Narrative." *Twentieth Century Literature: A Scholarly and Critical Journal,* Volume 52, Number 3 (2006 Fall): pp. 249–274. Copyright © 2006 *Twentieth Century Literature,* Hofstra University. Reprinted with permission from the publisher.

Zoe Trodd. "Hemingway's Camera Eye: The Problem of Language and an Interwar Politics of Form." *Hemingway Review,* Volume 26, Number 2 (Spring 2007): pp. 7–21. Copyright © 2007 The Ernest Hemingway Foundation. All rights reserved. Reprinted by permission of the publisher.

Index